Seeking Security in an Insecure World

Seeking Security in an Insecure World

DAN CALDWELL AND ROBERT E. WILLIAMS JR.

ROWMAN & LITTLEFIELD PUBLISHERS, INC.
Lanham • Boulder • New York • Toronto • Oxford

ROWMAN & LITTLEFIELD PUBLISHERS, INC.

Published in the United States of America
by Rowman & Littlefield Publishers, Inc.
A wholly owned subsidary of The Rowman & Littlefield Publishing Group, Inc.
4501 Forbes Boulevard, Suite 200, Lanham, Maryland 20706
www.rowmanlittlefield.com

P.O. Box 317, Oxford OX2 9RU, UK

British Library Cataloguing in Publication Information Available

Library of Congress Cataloging-in-Publication Data

Caldwell, Dan.
    Seeking security in an insecure world / Dan Caldwell and Robert E. Williams Jr.
        p.   cm.
    Includes bibliographical references and index.
    ISBN 0-7425-3812-5 (Cloth : alk. paper) — ISBN 0-7425-3813-3 (pbk. : alk. paper)
    1. Security, International.   2. National security.   3. Internal security.   4. Economic
security.   5. Security (Psychology)   6. Threat (Psychology)   I. Williams, Robert E., Jr.
1959–   II. Title.
JZ5588 .C35   2006
363.1—dc22
                                                                                    2005016521
Printed in the United States of America

♾™ The paper used in this publication meets the minimum requirements of American
National Standard for Information Sciences—Permanence of Paper for Printed Library
Materials, ANSI/NISO Z39.48-1992.

To Father Greg Boyle, SJ, with respect and appreciation.

D.C.

To my parents, Robert (Bob) and Carolyn Williams, with love.

R.E.W. Jr.

Contents

Preface

We began thinking about and discussing this book several years after the Berlin Wall fell and the Soviet Union disintegrated. Those of us in the field of security studies referred regularly to the "post–Cold War world" but it was not clear immediately what sort of threats this new world posed to individuals, states, or the international system. One especially dramatic threat appeared on September 11, 2001, when terrorists attacked the United States and killed more Americans than in any single day since the Civil War.

To be sure, terrorism is a clear and present danger to the United States and many other countries around the world, but terrorism is not the only threat that has emerged in the post–Cold War world. In the decade between the collapse of Soviet-style communism and the collapse of the World Trade Center, other threats—many of them associated with the shrinking of the world through processes associated with globalization—appeared to ensure the continuing necessity of seeking security in an insecure world.

This book is about security—both the sources of insecurity and the means to greater security—in a time of great change in the world. It offers an introduction to the meaning of security at a time when scholars, reflecting on changes in the world, are debating how we should understand the concept. We have written the book for interested nonspecialists—citizens who would like to gain a better understanding of what contributes to and threatens security in the modern world—as well as for students of international relations, political science, and global studies. Our approach is distinctive, if not unique, in that it presents an overview of security rather than focusing on one particular threat, such as nuclear, chemical, or biological weapons, environmental degradation, infectious disease, and so on.

In writing books, authors incur many debts along the way. Both authors would like to thank Dalton Saunders, who served as a researcher and critic for drafts of many of the chapters. Bob Escudero provided invaluable technical assistance at many different stages in the project.

In addition, the authors would like to thank David Baird and Chris Soper, both of whom are strong supporters of scholarship at Pepperdine University and, in various ways, have assisted this project. At Rowman & Littlefield, we gratefully acknowledge the editorial assistance of Jennifer Knerr, Alden Perkins, and Pelham Boyer. We especially thank Renée Legatt for answering our many questions throughout the process.

Intellectual debts, although no less real, are often more difficult to pinpoint. We have benefited greatly from our association over the years with a group of security studies scholars in the International Studies Association's International Security Studies Section and the American Political Science Association's section on International Security and Arms Control. The opportunity to present papers at conferences organized by these groups and to receive helpful comments on our work from their members has been indispensable. Some measure of what we owe these colleagues can be seen in our citations.

Dan Caldwell would like to thank his former teachers and professors who inspired and encouraged him: Beth McGrath, Cree Kofford, Virginia Pavelko, Carl Degler, and Alexander George.

Robert Williams would like to acknowledge his students, many of whom have read and commented on drafts of various chapters, and all of whom in recent semesters have waited a little longer than usual to get back their exams and papers. He also wishes to thank his sons, Daniel and Stephen, who have stepped up to the plate in many ways: checking facts in the library and online, making photocopies, and taking on extra household responsibilities (including cooking dinner on many occasions). They have also stepped up to the plate literally—offering their father escape from writing to watch them play baseball.

The work for this book was shared equally by the authors, and the placement of their names on the title page is simply alphabetical; both should share equally in any acclaim or criticism of the book.

Robert Williams dedicates the book to his parents, Robert (Bob) and Carolyn Williams, whose love and support have provided security at the most important level. There would be far less insecurity in the world—at all levels—if all parents were like them.

Dan Caldwell dedicates the book to Father Gregory Boyle, SJ, who has worked tirelessly to decrease poverty and violence in East Los Angeles; he is an inspiration to all who know him.

Dan Caldwell
Robert E. Williams Jr.

1

The Meaning of Security Today

We live in an insecure world. The terrorist attacks in New York and Washington on September 11, 2001, dramatically illustrated this fact, but, because insecurity is a state of mind as well as a state of the world, 9/11 also dramatically increased our fear and insecurity. Prior to 9/11, many people in the United States and other parts of the developed world lived in a kind of fool's paradise. The collapse of the Soviet Union a decade earlier had brought to an end the prolonged period of intense insecurity associated with the Cold War and ushered in a brief period in which the principal security concern in the developed world appeared to be whether or not to take responsibility for the protection of people in places such as Bosnia, Somalia, Rwanda, Haiti, East Timor, and Kosovo. Most citizens of the world's industrialized democracies came to take their own security for granted.

The 9/11 attacks on the United States, the coordinated bombings aboard trains in Madrid on March 11, 2004, and the subway and bus bombings in London on July 7, 2005, ended the complacency that developed in the West during the 1990s and refocused attention on security in a way that it had not been since the tensest days of the Soviet-American standoff. Our understanding of security, however, had changed in the interim. No longer is war the only security threat that states face. Nor, for that matter, is war what it once was. Today's security agenda includes the threat posed by environmental degradation, the spread of infectious disease, and failed states and their consequences. It includes global warming and oil shortages. It pits states against ethnic rebellions and transnational criminal organizations and, of course, a global network of terrorist organizations. It contemplates wars in cyberspace and on the ground against elusive individuals and shadowy associations rather than states. Even as the quest for security has become far more salient than it seemed to be during the early days of the post–Cold War period, it has become far more complicated than it was during the Cold War itself.

The new security agenda is based in part on the recognition that most of the world's six and a half billion people are threatened by problems that are unrelated to weapons of mass destruction and terrorist networks. It is also based on the recognition that many of these problems ought to be concerns of those in the developed world who have generally focused only on threats of a military nature. The scope and gravity of the threats on the new security agenda can be shown with a few examples.

- Forty-two million people worldwide are infected with HIV/AIDS. In the absence of a major medical breakthrough, most will die within a decade.
- Each year, over eleven million children under age five die, over half of them due to starvation and malnutrition.
- Between six hundred thousand and four million people are trafficked somewhere in the world each year; most are women and children trafficked for forced prostitution or forced labor.
- Civil conflicts and ethnic violence may be the worst of all. In the Sudan, roughly two million people have been killed in civil war since 1983. Eight hundred thousand people were murdered, primarily with machetes, in a mere hundred days of genocidal rampage in Rwanda in 1994. In the Democratic Republic of the Congo, an estimated 3.8 million people have died as a consequence of civil war since 1998. Sadly, scores of additional examples of intrastate conflict could be cited.

This very brief introduction to some of the sources of insecurity in the world suggests a few questions worth considering as we examine the meaning of security today. Terrorist attacks in the financial district of New York City, at the Pentagon, at a resort in Bali, Indonesia, in suburban Madrid, and in London have demonstrated that no matter where one lives, how much money one has, or how powerful one's country is, there is no such thing as absolute security. Nevertheless, although insecurity clearly transcends socioeconomic and geographic boundaries, the sources of insecurity differ considerably depending on whether one lives in North America or Western Europe, on the one hand, or sub-Saharan Africa or Southeast Asia, on the other. The first question may well be, therefore: Whose security are we talking about?

Following hard on the heels of that question is one that shifts the focus from who to what. While terrorist attacks and civil wars may fit comfortably into our notions of what the study of security is (or should be) all about, where do disease and starvation fit in? If threats posed by famine and HIV/AIDS are the proper subjects of a study of security (and if we have answered the "whose security" question in a way that forces those of us who don't miss many meals to think about those who do), then how is the subject to be limited? Why is the threat posed by disease (or at least a particular pandemic) a fit subject for analysis while the threat posed in some parts of the world by wild animals or monsoons or earthquakes is not? These are certainly fair, and vexing, questions.

Answering these and similar questions requires that we examine the meaning of security with considerable care. Before we undertake that analysis, however, consider what a bit of historical perspective adds to our understanding.

Americans today live in the shadow of 9/11. National debates—about budget priorities, civil liberties, and, of course, electoral politics—are conducted within the context of a shared recognition of the threat that terrorists now pose. For a different generation of Americans, "the Greatest Generation," life (or a part of it) was lived in the shadow of European fascism and Pearl Harbor. That same generation and the baby-boom generation that followed lived in the shadow of the atomic bomb as well. For forty years, most of the world lived in some measure of fear of nuclear war, a fear fed by recurrent crises (over Berlin, Cuba, and the Middle East, for example), diplomatic saber rattling, and even popular culture (including movies like *On the Beach* and *Fail-Safe* in the 1960s and *The Day After* in the 1980s). These different experiences have shaped different understandings of security. This is perhaps the essential point with which to begin a discussion of the meaning of security: Our conception of security changes with the circumstances we face. Each generation and, for that matter, each community determines the meaning of security according to the threats it confronts in its time and place.

WHOSE SECURITY?

The question concerning whose security is at issue is one that could be answered in a number of ways. It is a question that, for students of international relations, raises familiar issues concerning levels of analysis. (Some of these issues will be addressed in the discussion below of the widening of our understanding of security.) It is also, however, a question that, for students of comparative politics, can prompt discussion of the widely divergent security interests of different states. To illustrate the point, Costa Rica, which has no regular military forces and spends 0.4 percent of GDP on defense, operates in a security environment that is dramatically different from that of Israel, which spends 8.7 percent of GDP on defense, or its Middle Eastern neighbor Jordan (20.2 percent).[1]

Our focus in this book is on security as it is conceived in the developed world. We are, in other words, primarily concerned with the meaning of security for people in advanced market democracies, such as the United States, Canada, Japan, Australia, New Zealand, and the European Union. Our focus is, in part, a simple reflection of the fact that we ourselves live, and are writing primarily for an audience that lives, in the developed world. We hope, however, to avoid being overly parochial. The reasons for avoiding narrowness, although perhaps obvious, are worth stating as a means of articulating our principal assumptions about our subject.

First, at the risk of lending support for a strain of Western—and perhaps especially, American—ethnocentrism that we believe is both unwarranted and unwise, we acknowledge that the security of the West is important not only to those who live there but to much of the rest of the world as well. There is no better way to demonstrate this point than to examine, briefly, certain aspects of the American response to the 9/11 attacks. Since the American sense of security was shattered by the terrorist attacks on

9/11, the United States, in response, has waged one war in Afghanistan and another in Iraq, ousting two regimes in the process; imposed significant costs and restrictions on immigration to the United States; looked the other way with respect to revelations concerning Pakistani nuclear technology transfers; imposed on other countries security requirements for airports and harbors as a condition for sending planes and ships to the United States; and underfunded many international aid programs (such as President Bush's pledge to spend fifteen billion dollars on HIV/AIDS in Africa) as resources shifted into the "war on terrorism" and the reconstruction of Afghanistan and Iraq. Additionally, the terrorist attacks in Madrid on March 11, 2004—the deadliest terrorist attack in Spanish history—and in London on July 7, 2005, are widely believed to have been aimed at punishing the Spanish and British governments for their support of the American war in Iraq. The security of the United States and the methods used to defend it have a major impact on the rest of the world. As an old saying familiar to diplomats and businessmen everywhere puts it, "when the United States sneezes, the rest of the world catches a cold."

Against the temptation to adopt an insular focus, however, we must affirm a contrasting set of beliefs about security. First, security is, in many important respects, indivisible. Seeking security in an insecure world for one's state alone is a strategy doomed to failure. This is especially true in light of the increasing interconnectedness of the world's people and their problems, but it has been a fact of life throughout history. Bubonic plague, *Yersinia pestis*, originated in China but killed millions of Europeans in the Black Death of the fourteenth century. World War II, dramatic enough in its impact on Europe and Asia, led to a series of revolutions in Africa that has convulsed that continent now for generations. These are but two of an almost limitless number of examples of security concerns that transcend boundaries.

Those of us in the West—particularly the United States—cannot act in the interest of our own security without having an impact on the security of others. Likewise, we cannot ignore the security of others without endangering our own. There is thus a very powerful consequentialist argument for thinking in terms of international, or global, security rather than of national security alone. To express the point as a paradox, a narrowly self-interested security policy cannot be narrowly self-interested.

Our view of security, however, is not grounded solely in utilitarian considerations. We believe that there are principled reasons for taking a broader view of security. A commitment to human rights—as well as broader humanitarian principles—demands that we give attention to many of the security concerns that are products of injustice in the world. We believe, to take but one example, that those living in the developed world should be exposed to, and should ultimately adopt as a matter of policy, a perspective on security that includes human trafficking as a security issue, because for millions of people worldwide it constitutes a serious threat to basic rights.

Viewed in this way, the question of "whose security" appears to be closely related to the question of what should be included among the things we define as security issues. This is as it should be. To define the boundaries of the contemporary security agenda is to specify what threats to the interests of which subjects ought to be given the priority associated with security issues. This can be a contentious issue.

Over fifty years ago, in the early days of the Cold War, Arnold Wolfers cautioned the realists who had put national security at the center of American foreign policy that "national security," like other commonly discussed terms, might mean different things to different people and, in fact, might have no precise meaning.[2] More recently, John Baylis has observed that the consensus among scholars is that "security is a 'contested concept.'"[3] While the concerns now being expressed about how we define security are both more widespread and more diverse in origin, it is remarkable how little things have changed since the 1950s. Today, as in Wolfers's day at the outset of the Cold War, the concept of security is in search of a definition that can command general assent.

What has changed in our understanding of security over the last half century is this: Security can no longer be defined, if it ever could be, exclusively in terms of the ability of a state to defend its territory and its principal values against military threats. An ability to deal with other threats, including but not limited to transnational drug trafficking, international terrorism, resource scarcities, economic espionage, transboundary pollution, disease pandemics, global climate change, and even computer problems such as viruses or hacking[4] is now thought to be essential to the protection of national security.[5] The security agenda has expanded due both to a growing awareness of the limits of the traditional national security focus and to the combined effect of increased interdependence and complexity in international relations.[6]

While expansion of the concept of security seems to have been unavoidable, given the limits of the traditional understanding and the challenges inherent in rapid globalization, the addition of so many different issues to the security agenda threatens to make the concept of security incoherent while making the study of international security indistinguishable from the broader field of international relations. When one adds to this concern the levels-of-analysis problem, with its implication that security can be seen in individual, state, and international terms (as well as in categories that lie between these), the task of providing a comprehensive account of the quest for security in the modern international system appears challenging, if not overwhelming.

GENERAL CONSIDERATIONS

The word "security" is derived from the Latin *securitas,* which, in turn, comes from *securus,* literally "without a care." Security is a condition or state of being free from the threat of harm. There are both objective and subjective aspects of this condition. Security thus involves both material circumstances and the psychological state produced by those circumstances.

Security and peace have much in common. Psychologically, we often equate security with peace of mind. Politically, the traditional concept of security is commonly equated with an ability either to remain at peace (without having to sacrifice important values to do so) or, failing that, to restore peace quickly. Security and peace, in turn, are closely related to order and stability. The quest for international order is, fundamentally, nothing more than the quest for peace and security.[7]

The unmodified term "security" covers a broad terrain. It can encompass, at one extreme, the individual's perception of well-being when free of threats to his or her welfare and, at the other extreme, that state of order in the international system that is supposed to be the principal pursuit of the United Nations. No book yet written on the subject of security has even surveyed the entire range of meaning. Any book that attempted to do so would no doubt be unsatisfactory to both the psychologist, at one end of the spectrum, and the student of international relations, at the other. In order to make the concept manageable, social scientists have had to circumscribe it so that it conforms to what they perceive to be the primary subjects of their discipline. To the student of international relations, the subjects of security are generally defined in terms of level of analysis. Consequently, it is possible to think in terms of *individual* security, *national* security, and *international* security, as well as security at other, intermediate levels.

THE TRADITIONAL PARADIGM

Because the state was the focus of concern, at least in the dominant realist tradition, most of the attention given the subject of security among scholars of international relations during the Cold War centered on national security. Indeed, during the Cold War the mention of "security studies" suggested to the vast majority of scholars nothing more or less than "*national* security studies." "National security," in turn, was generally limited in common usage to matters relating to the use of military force. In that usage, "national security policy" and "defense policy" were generally regarded as interchangeable terms. While some regimes, particularly authoritarian dictatorships in Latin America, regarded internal threats as within the scope of national security policy,[8] advanced industrial democracies generally avoided the use of military force to promote internal order, preferring civilian police forces for that purpose. Since democracies have also avoided the use of military force in wars of aggression, the use of the term "defense policy" as a close substitute for "national security policy" is understandable in the context of the traditional paradigm.

There are, of course, a variety of purposes for which military force can be used. Within the state, the military may be used to assert the authority of the government over dissident portions of the population. This may include suppressing rebellions, harassing opponents of the regime, or fighting crime. These, as noted, are functions not normally undertaken by the military in most democracies. Looking outward, the military may be used to defend the state against attack, to defend other states (or nonstate actors) against attack, to perform police functions in other states, to punish other states (or nonstate actors) for the violation of international norms, or to attack other states.

The traditional association of national security with the military is due to the nature of the assumptions underlying both the definition of security and the perception of corresponding threats. National security is fundamentally concerned with the preservation of sovereignty against external threats. It encompasses the state's efforts to control what happens to its territory, its citizens, its resources, and its political system. It is, in large measure, concerned with the defense of borders, so that outsiders may play a role within the state only on terms acceptable to the state. Historically, the most significant threat to the integrity of a state's borders and its ability to determine its own course came from the militaries of hostile states. Only armed forces, or so it was thought, could penetrate borders in such a way as to threaten seriously the sovereignty of the state. If the threat to sovereignty came from within, as in the case of insurrection, the military could be the guarantor of security in that instance as well. External threats not susceptible to military solutions were, until recently, virtually unknown.[9]

The traditional assumptions about the link between national security and territorial sovereignty, together with the limited types of threats that states experienced until recently, produced a narrow understanding of the concept of security that is still very much with us even though the landscape has changed significantly. Under the traditional paradigm, the state was considered the primary, if not the sole, subject of security studies. The primary threat to security was the threat of invasion (or, in some circumstances, blockade) by a hostile state and thus was perceived as a military threat. Consequently, preparing for war, either by arming itself or by enlisting allies, was the state's principal means of ensuring its own security.

THE NEW PARADIGM

To the extent that territorial states defended by military force remain central to human affairs, the traditional security paradigm continues to be serviceable. The often-noted decline of the territorial state, however, suggests a need to think about security in new ways.[10]

The concept of security has been stretched in two directions: first, with respect to the issues to be included on the security agenda, and second, with respect to the subject (or what some scholars prefer to call the referent object) of security.[11] Richard Wyn Jones has suggested that the former move be labeled "broadening" and the latter "extending," in order to avoid the ambiguity of the single term—"widening"—often used to refer to both.[12] The effort to open up the concept in both directions began in the 1970s as analysts began to question both the narrow focus within traditional security studies on Cold War defense issues and the problems associated with efforts to think exclusively in terms of *national* security. The interplay of military and economic issues that first attracted the serious attention of analysts in the 1970s, and the rise at about the same time of global environmental awareness contributed significantly to efforts to challenge the traditional paradigm.[13] The end of the Cold War gave added impetus to supporters of a new security paradigm, by diminishing the significance of the issues on the traditional security agenda while raising a host of new questions concerning both the proper subjects of security and the nature of threats to security.

To refer to a new security paradigm in the singular is, of course, an oversimplification, since in reality a variety of contenders for such a designation have emerged since the 1970s. In many instances, the new conceptions of security can be identified by their adjectives. From UN-sponsored discussions of the need to expand the concept of security have come proposals for a shift to *comprehensive* security (emphasizing the need for broadening) or *common* security (emphasizing the need for extending). The collective response to Iraq's invasion of Kuwait in 1990 renewed interest in the Wilsonian concept of *collective* security. In 1993, Australian Foreign Minister Gareth Evans proposed what he called *cooperative* security.[14] Meanwhile, a move to extend the concept of security in the opposite direction (toward the individual rather than the international system as subject) came in 1994 when the United Nations Development Program produced the idea of *human* security.[15]

These and other challenges to the traditional paradigm share a number of characteristics, so that it may be reasonable, at least as a shorthand expression, to speak of a new paradigm. This new paradigm is characterized, first of all, by a willingness to consider a variety of possible subjects of security. Rather than focusing primarily on the state, new conceptions of security consider a wide range of possible subjects, from the individual through the international levels. Second, while under the traditional paradigm security was conceived primarily in terms of defense against military threats (with consideration occasionally being given to economic threats), under the new paradigm security involves defense against many different threats, including environmental problems, the collapse of currencies, human trafficking, and so on. A third difference between the paradigms is that the new conception of security is far more open to the possibility that the principal threat to the lives of citizens and other core values of a state may come from the state itself. In other words, the new paradigm recognizes the tremendous potential of states to generate insecurity both through direct threats against their own citizens and as an indirect consequence of the actions they take in the name of national security.

In general, these and other differences between the old and new paradigms may be reduced to one central point: The new paradigm expands the concept of security by broadening the agenda or extending the subjects. Strong arguments have been advanced for both moves, but important questions concerning the limits of these moves remain. In fact, the difficulties in circumscribing the concept of security under the new paradigm have left it, in the words of R. B. J. Walker, "embarrassingly limp and overextended."[16]

THE QUESTION OF "BROADENING"

How are we to limit the security agenda, given the fact that security, understood as the condition or state of being free from the threat of harm, involves so many different possible threats? Without even considering a range of threats associated specifically with individual security and international security (matters to be considered with respect to the question of "extending"), we can easily recall circumstances in which states have been concerned with threats posed by the military forces of neighboring states, terrorists, indigenous revolutionary movements, the possibility of an accidental nuclear launch, the collapse of national currencies, the collapse of commodity prices, monsoons, earthquakes, the spread of disease, famine, or overpopulation, to mention just a small number of threats on a very long list. Some island states even face the threat of gradual inundation by rising sea levels, as Maumoon Abdul Gayoom, president of the Maldives, noted in his speech at the United Nations Millennium Summit: "Our quest for progress must be sustainable. We have no right to destroy the earth. Ecological damage, including global warming, must be curbed. All low-lying countries must be saved: when the United Nations meets to usher in yet another century, will the Maldives and other low-lying island nations still be represented here?"[17] The inundation of the Maldives by the Indian Ocean tsunami in December 2004 made President Gayoom's question even more urgent than he could have imagined when he spoke in 2000.

Is global warming properly regarded as a threat to the national security of the Maldives and the Federated States of Micronesia, or does it belong in some other category? What about the threat from tsunamis? Are the virus hunters of the Centers for Disease Control and Prevention in Atlanta properly regarded as part of the national security establishment? Was the collapse of the Thai baht or the Mexican peso a national security concern, either for the countries directly involved or for their trading partners? Bangladesh suffers more death and destruction from natural disasters than from the military activities of its neighbors. Does this mean that protecting against the effects of monsoons should be the primary national security priority of the Bangladeshi government? How, to restate the original question, are we to distinguish between threats to security and threats of other types?

Finding an answer to this question that is at once both direct and generally acceptable has proved impossible thus far. The best we can do is clarify the issues involved and offer some general principles as possible means of delimiting the field of security studies. The first step in doing this may well be to consider how we understand threats.

Under both the old paradigm and the new, the concept of security can be understood only in relation to threats. Indeed, the concept of threat is a necessary part of any intelligible definition of security and insecurity. Threats have traditionally been understood as the products of some combination of capabilities and intentions. A threat exists where a potential adversary has both the capability to do harm and malign intent. In the realist account, the potential adversaries are, of course, states, and their capability to do harm comes in the form of military power. The understanding that a threat must combine capability and intention conforms very well to what we see in the world. The United States perceives little or no threat from states with negligible capabilities, regardless of their level of hostility. Likewise, the existence of certain well-armed states in Western Europe, for example, poses little or no threat because the intent is benign. The value of this simple definition of threat is further demonstrated by the fact that it has been the foundation, at least implicitly, of two important concepts related to security: the security dilemma (in which threats are exacerbated because malign intent is assumed)[18] and the security community (in which threats are diminished because efforts have been made to provide assurances of benign intent).[19]

Consider the relationship of this formula to the security dilemma. Because military capabilities are, to some degree, out there for all to see while intentions are both largely unknowable and subject to rapid change, the prudent assessor of foreign threats must take what is known about the potential adversary's capabilities and combine this information with a worst-case reading of intentions. As a result of this better-safe-than-sorry approach, threats are inflated, measures are taken to counter the inflated threats, and the prudent assessor of threats on the other side is given evidence that seems to require a similar response. This, more or less, is the problem of security and insecurity as seen by the realists. The point here, however, is not to deconstruct realism or even the notion of the security dilemma. It is, instead, to consider whether, under the new paradigm, we can still work with the understanding that threats involve a combination of capabilities and intentions.

First, we should acknowledge that the term "capabilities," when used in this context, may conjure up thoughts of troops, tanks, ships, bombers, and perhaps even weapons of mass destruction, for those of us who remember security studies back in the good old days when life may have been "nasty, brutish, and short" but at least we knew who the enemy was. Simply to avoid privileging the military view of security, we can substitute the phrase "potential to cause harm" for "capabilities" in the threat equation. But what are we to do with intentions?

The new paradigm in security studies appears to regard intentions as an unnecessary element of threat. Consider the addition of environmental threats or the rise of drug-resistant diseases to the list of security threats under the new paradigm. Except in cases of environmental warfare or biological warfare where the associated threats are wielded by human agents, what role can intentions play in assessments of these new security threats? It appears that the answer is none whatsoever. This might suggest, for those intent on defending the traditional paradigm against the broadening that has inevitably made security studies a much less focused discipline, that human agency might be the ticket to a return to coherence. This view would suggest that we should only consider as threats to security those possibilities that combine the potential to cause harm with an intent—that is, a human desire—to cause harm. Such an understanding would allow for the inclusion on the security agenda of some nontraditional threats, such as terrorism, the deliberate creation of refugee flows (as in Kosovo), and attacks on computer networks, while maintaining a familiar look to the field.

However tempting it may be to fight off the wideners on the grounds of intent, it is simply not possible without stipulating some counterintuitive limits. If a security threat, properly defined, can only exist where human intent is present, then President Gayoom of the Maldives, concerned about the possible inundation of his island state due to a rise in sea level produced by global warming, has a problem but not a security threat. If scientists determine that one of the thousands of asteroids in near-Earth orbits is destined to plow into our planet three revolutions around the Sun from now, we have a problem but not a security threat.[20] This, some will no doubt argue, is too restrictive.

There are serious problems with the alternative of simply arguing that threat equals capability (or potential to cause harm). Most notably, the list of threats would quickly become unmanageable even for advocates of widening the security agenda. Such a formulation, left unmodified, also fails to discriminate between imminent and remote threats. Some of the problems, however, can be addressed by allowing for the operation of deterministic phenomena as a substitute for human intent. Threat, using the revised formula, becomes a product of potential to cause harm and *either* intent or deterministic natural processes.

It is important to note that it may not always be possible to draw a hard-and-fast dividing line between human and natural threats. The interaction of humans with the environment means that threats to human well-being from such things as global warming, the spread of disease, population growth, and famine will generally have some combination of human and natural causes. However, the difficulty of drawing a line between human and natural agency in some cases does not negate the potential significance of such a distinction for our efforts to limit the scope of the security agenda.

Another distinction that needs to be examined in trying to delimit the proper concern of security policy is the distinction between threats that arise as a result of intentional behaviors and those that result from unintentional behaviors. Once again, the distinction is not absolute, as a number of examples will illustrate, but in assessing the proper concerns of security policy it nonetheless appears fitting that we should consider the extent to which threats emanate from deliberate actions. The more deliberate a threatening action appears to be, the more conclusively it merits consideration as a security issue. To illustrate, compare two threats to Western Europe emanating from the Soviet Union during the 1970s and 1980s, respectively. In 1977, the Soviet Union began deploying in Eastern Europe a new intermediate-range ballistic missile known as the SS-20. The deployment of SS-20s, aimed at targets in Western Europe, provoked antinuclear demonstrations and a counterdeployment by NATO of Pershing II missiles and ground-launched cruise missiles beginning in 1979. In 1986, an explosion at the nuclear power plant at Chernobyl resulted in the dispersal of radioactive material all over Europe. Although the effects of the Chernobyl blast on the well-being of the citizens of Western European states were more direct, more immediate, and more tangible than the effects of the earlier SS-20 deployment, the missile deployment was characterized as a security concern while the reactor accident was not. It is the absence of intentionality that accounts for this difference. Had the Soviet Union deliberately released radioactive material in order to cause panic in Western Europe, defense ministries would have been called upon to respond along with public health officials.

Some threats produced by human actions have a quasi-intentional character. The mismanagement both of agricultural policies and of foreign assistance has been a factor in some of Africa's more devastating famines. It is unclear, however, that the production of famine was intentional in most of these cases. More troubling from the standpoint of our efforts to distinguish threats to national security from more "natural" threats is that category of activities involving deliberate actions with unintended consequences. On the one hand, there are action-reaction processes (arms races, for example) in which the behavior of one party is in some measure determined by the behavior of the other party. On the other hand, there are situations, such as the collapse of financial markets, in which the cumulative effect of rational individual decisions is unintended and sometimes dire.

One possible response to this distinction is to suggest that threats reflecting no underlying human intent ordinarily should not be the subjects of security policy. This has the effect of excluding all natural disasters (or "acts of God," in the parlance of theologians and insurance underwriters) from consideration. It also has the effect of excluding accidents and cases of mass hysteria from our list of security concerns. But is this as it should be? What about the classification of military accidents (e.g., accidental nuclear launches) as security issues? Nuclear accidents have been considered an important concern in U.S. national security policy since the late 1950s.[21]

It may seem that a definition of security that excludes threats that are "natural" or "unintentional" is simply a rationalization of the view that security policy cannot concern itself with threats against which no defense is possible. But there are defenses against currency crises, environmental degradation, and even some natural disasters. This suggests that the effort to distinguish between threats to national security and other types of threats (that is, nonsecurity threats) must somehow focus on human agency and intentionality.

THE QUESTION OF "EXTENDING"

Recognition that the national security of any given state cannot be meaningfully assessed in isolation from the national security of other states—that one state's quest for security may actually promote insecurity in other states—has led to calls for greater attention to *international* security or *global* security. Even in the quest for national security, such international measures as the establishment of international organizations, the progressive development of international law, and the negotiation of multilateral arms control agreements have long been regarded as indispensable.

As Barry Buzan has noted, the nature of states and the nature of the international system are so closely intertwined that it is impossible to address national security without considering international security, and vice versa. He writes,

> The political connection between states and system is so intimate that one is at risk of introducing serious misperception even by speaking of states *and* the international system as if they were distinct entities. Although they are distinguishable for some analytical purposes, states and the international system represent opposite ends of a continuous

political phenomenon. The international political system is an anarchy, which is to say that its principal defining characteristic is the absence of overarching government. The principal defining feature of states is their sovereignty, or their refusal to acknowledge any political authority higher than themselves. The essential character of states thus defines the nature of the international political system, and the essential character of the political system reflects the nature of states. If units are sovereign, their system of association must be anarchy, and if the system is anarchic, its members must reject overarching government.[22]

Moving in the other direction, the recognition that the state, which is the subject of *national security*, is—or ought to be—merely an instrument for the promotion of the well-being of individuals has suggested a need to emphasize *individual* security or *human* security. The deference shown to states and the harm to the lives of individuals that resulted is widely regarded to have been one of the great evils of the twentieth century. One need only reflect on the terrible human rights abuses perpetrated in the Soviet Union by the KGB—the Committee for State Security—or the shameful U.S. record of nuclear tests involving military personnel to realize that national security has often threatened the security of people. As Richard Wyn Jones puts it, "In much of the world, states, far from fostering an atmosphere within which stability can be attained and prosperity created, are one of the major sources of insecurity for their citizens."[23]

It is also the case that, just as national security and international security are intimately linked, national security and individual security are strongly connected. This is true even for those who reject the realist assumption that the security of the state guarantees the security of the individual. Robert Kaplan's concerns about the impact of international peace on domestic crime rates suggest one form that this interaction may take. A reduction in the size of the standing army, together with its gradual transformation into a better-educated and more elite force, means that large numbers of young males—a notoriously impulsive and violence-prone segment of any nation's population—will be released into society. This, Kaplan argues, portends "an increase in gang activity and other forms of violent behavior."[24] Of course, one need not range into controversial sociological conjectures to find circumstances in which national and individual security concerns merge. The reverse of Kaplan's example, namely, the conscription of young men into the army rather than their release from it, provides an obvious example.

From a liberal perspective, there are strong arguments for making the individual the primary subject of security. The state, according to this view, is valuable primarily as a means to the end of the well-being of the citizens who constitute the state. To concede primacy to the state is to risk making people instrumental agents in the service of the state rather than the reverse. The difference between a liberal state and an authoritarian state often turns on this distinction. Instead of providing security for their citizens, authoritarian regimes are often guilty of threatening the security of the individual in the name of national security. To state the difference bluntly, in democracies the state exists to protect the rights of individuals; in authoritarian states, individuals exist to serve the state. The suppression of political dissent by Latin American dictators operating under the so-called national security doctrine provides an example of this. As a result, there appears to be a strong case, at least from a liberal perspective, for bypassing the state in favor of the individual as the primary subject of security. On the other hand, human rights law, which is now well established in the international system, may offer a better means of protecting individuals by working with and through states.

What conclusions concerning efforts to broaden and extend the concept of security does this analysis suggest? The narrowness of the Cold War focus on security as a military matter could not help but provoke a reaction toward broadening the security agenda. Unless limits are established, however, broadening can create more problems than it solves, including, at the extreme, undermining the coherence of the discipline. Assessing whether threats merit inclusion on the security agenda on the basis of the extent to which they result from human agency rather than natural processes and on the degree of intentionality they exhibit offers a partial solution to the problem.

Extending the concept of security to include individuals may be useful as a corrective to the excessive focus on the state and its needs that characterized the Cold War period. It is important, however, to ensure that notions of individual security are fully compatible (as the concept of human security is) with the well-established system of international human rights. Moving in the other direction to make groups of states (or the international system itself) the subjects of security appears unavoidable, given the reciprocal effects of states and the international system on each other. In fact, significant moves toward the concept of international security were part of the traditional security paradigm long before serious efforts to widen the scope of security studies began.

As an academic discipline, security studies can exist, and even thrive, indefinitely without achieving consensus on the limits of the concept of security. It is, arguably, very beneficial for a discipline to be populated with at least a vocal minority of scholars willing to push the boundaries of their field and question central assumptions.[25] Doing so can assist in the essential task of attempting to envision security threats that lie beyond the horizon.

SEEING BEYOND THE HORIZON

As warfare has evolved from an activity in which the battlefield is small and killing occurs at the point of a sword to one in which the battlefield can embrace an entire continent or ocean and killing commonly occurs at long range, combatants have been forced to extend their range of vision in an effort to see threats as they develop at greater and greater distances. In the nineteenth century, observers were sometimes sent aloft in hot-air balloons to see what enemy forces were doing beyond the ridgeline. The range of aerial reconnaissance was dramatically extended in the twentieth century as first airplanes and then satellites gave military commanders the ability quite literally to see beyond the horizon. Since at least the time of Sun Tzu, it has been understood that the defender who knows what is coming is far more likely to succeed than the one who fails to anticipate an attack. The analysis of American intelligence failures prior to 9/11 and with regard to Iraqi weapons of mass destruction was widely reported in terms of its significance for the 2004 presidential campaign, but its more fundamental significance was related to the need to address a problem that left the United States inadequately equipped to defend itself in a dynamic threat environment.

Thinking tactically about security requires seeing over the horizon. Thinking strategically about security, on the other hand, requires seeing over the *years*. Technology cannot help us as much with strategic threat assessment as it does with tactical threat assessment. In order to plan for threats over the long term—that is, to see beyond the time horizon in the same way that soldiers now see beyond the terrestrial horizon—requires qualities that remain uniquely human and, consequently, imperfect. Strategic thinking about security requires all the knowledge we can assemble—of human nature, of history, of politics, of technology, and much more—but it also requires a great deal of imagination.

The effort to define security in a way that expands our ability to perceive the threats that are truly worth worrying about while avoiding the self-defeating temptation to worry about everything has occupied the time and talents of many scholars and policy makers. The outcome of that effort remains contested. It is not an idle intellectual exercise, however; decisions that are made on the basis of some definition of security about, for example, whether to devote more resources to disease prevention and control rather than ballistic-missile defense (or vice versa) are decisions that may determine someday well beyond the time horizon whether people live or die. This, in the final analysis, is what the study of security is all about: who lives, who dies, why, and how.

We do not contend that our definition of security is the only one possible. It offers, we believe, a necessary correction of the Cold War's myopic focus on states and weapons without lapsing into inability to discriminate between common threats, on the one hand, and significant (and thus security-worthy) threats, on the other.

We also do not intend to suggest that our method of organizing the subject in the pages that follow is the only possible method. Our starting point is the assumption that the quest for security must begin with a thorough understanding of the sources of insecurity; solutions must always be grounded in an understanding of the problems. We focus, as a result, on threats. Some assessments of threat (especially those informed by the traditional paradigm) have focused almost exclusively on the potential to cause harm, suggesting that it is enough to know how many weapons of a certain type exist and what their capabilities are. The crucial matter of intentions has often been left, understandably, to foreign-policy or comparative-politics analyses.

As we have noted, the traditional understanding of threats as the product of capabilities and intentions is somewhat too simplistic for the new, widened security agenda. In order to impose some order on our effort to describe a broad range of security threats, we have divided the book into three parts. Part I focuses on traditional threats—conventional weapons and war, weapons of mass destruction, and proliferation issues. It is, in large measure, a survey of technologies—the weapons that, combined with malign intent, threaten lives—that advocates of the traditional paradigm should find completely comprehensible. Part II addresses new sources of insecurity. To be more precise, two of the three issues addressed—disease and trafficking—are not new, but their inclusion in studies of international security is new. Part III moves away from instruments of insecurity toward the conditions that engender threats. We examine the state (the traditional focus of security studies) but also the role that ethnic conflict, economic conditions, environmental degradation, and the rise of new forms of terrorism play in generating insecurity. The division is imperfect, but by the end of the book, we hope, the underlying rationale for this approach will appear compelling.

RECOMMENDED READING

Printed Sources

Brown, Michael E., ed. *Grave New World: Security Challenges in the Twenty-first Century*. Washington, D.C.: Georgetown University Press, 2003.

Buzan, Barry, Ole Waever, and Jaap de Wilde. *Security: A New Framework for Analysis*. Boulder, Colo.: Lynne Rienner, 1998.

Kolodziej, Edward A. "Renaissance in Security Studies? Caveat Lector!" *International Studies Quarterly* 36 (December 1992): 421–38.

———. *Security and International Relations*. Cambridge: Cambridge University Press, 2005.

Krause, Keith, and Michael C. Williams, eds. *Critical Security Studies: Concepts and Cases*. Minneapolis: University of Minnesota Press, 1997.

Mathews, Jessica Tuchman. "Redefining Security." *Foreign Affairs* 68 (Spring 1989): 162–77.

Ullman, Richard H. "Redefining Security." *International Security* 8 (Summer 1983): 129–53.

Websites

Center for Contemporary Conflict (Naval Postgraduate School): www.ccc.nps.navy.mil/

Foreign Military Studies Office (Fort Leavenworth): fmso.leavenworth.army.mil/

Global Security: www.globalsecurity.org/index.html

International Crisis Group: www.crisisgroup.org/home/index.cfm.

I

Traditional Sources of Insecurity

2

Conventional Weapons and War:
Traditional Threats in New Forms

Since the bombing of Hiroshima and Nagasaki in 1945, weapons of mass destruction (WMD) have received an enormous amount of attention. Efforts to restrict access to and prevent the use of nuclear, biological, and chemical weapons have been at the top of the agenda for states, intergovernmental organizations, and many nongovernmental organizations. Given the devastating potential of WMD, the concern exhibited is entirely reasonable. Nevertheless, what we call "conventional weapons" annually kill over twice as many people as died in Hiroshima and Nagasaki combined. Long before the first nuclear bomb was tested in the New Mexico desert, long before the British and the Germans used chemical weapons against each other in World War I, conventional weapons were making warfare a nasty business.

They continue to do so. The deadliest wars of the post–Cold War era, most of them intrastate conflicts, have generally been fought with small and technologically unsophisticated weapons. And yet such weapons have been extraordinarily destructive. Consider what has been done with conventional weapons (assisted in many instances by war-related starvation and disease) in modern conflicts:

- A study by the International Rescue Committee published near the end of 2004 reported that the war in the Democratic Republic of the Congo has resulted in 3.8 million deaths since August 1998, making it the deadliest conflict since World War II.[1]
- Over 3.7 million Vietnamese were killed in Indochina's wars between 1954 and the fall of Saigon in 1975.[2] While the number of Americans who died in Vietnam (58,209)[3] pales in comparison, the Vietnam War nonetheless ranks as one of the most traumatic events in American history.
- During the Korean War (1950–53), between two and three million were killed, including over five hundred thousand South Koreans, over one million

North Koreans, approximately five hundred thousand Chinese, and almost thirty-seven thousand Americans.

- In the course of almost a quarter century of conflict in Sudan, close to two million people have been killed by fighting and famine.

It is important to remember that in each of these cases (and in many others), weapons of mass destruction were unnecessary to achieve what amounted to mass destruction. In fact, less than 1 percent of the fifteen million deaths in World War I and the fifty million deaths in World War II were caused by WMD. In contrast, a significant number of the eight hundred thousand people killed during the Rwandan genocide of 1994 were hacked to death with machetes. These realities bring to mind an observation made by Thomas C. Schelling in an influential book on strategy published in 1966. Acknowledging that "it is a grisly thing to talk about," Schelling wrote: "Against defenseless people there is not much that nuclear weapons can do that cannot be done with an ice pick."[4] So, however reasonable it might be for security experts to worry about the possibility of a nuclear device being detonated in a major city, we should remember that conventional weapons produce casualty totals year in and year out that are comparable to those in our nuclear nightmares.

During the Cold War, security analysts tended to focus on issues related to nuclear weapons, including deterrence theory, proliferation, and arms control. In the post-9/11 world, many have focused on terrorism and forms of warfare involving nonstate actors. Both of these emphases reflect the common impulse to worry most about threats that are new and unfamiliar. But they also reflect an emphasis on the kinds of problems that seem most likely to affect the security of those of us living in the developed world. More and more, war seems to be a phenomenon confined largely to the developing world. Even when the world's advanced industrialized states go to war, they project their military power into the developing world and, typically, suffer far fewer casualties than the forces they fight against.

Although war in the twenty-first century, as in the last half of the twentieth century, affects the world's poor far more than it affects the rich, conventional war remains a vitally important concern of the developed world, for a number of reasons. First, the militaries of the developed world are often involved in conventional wars in the developing world. Indeed, rich states are often responsible, whether directly or indirectly, for those conflicts. Even where they bear no responsibility, their interests are often affected as a consequence of refugee flows, threats to nationals, or resource supply interruptions. And then (although this should by no means be treated as an afterthought), there are humanitarian considerations. We cannot—or at least should not—be indifferent to the suffering and the deaths of millions of people, a majority of whom are innocents, in warfare, no matter where in the world it occurs.

It would be impossible to cover thoroughly in a single book, much less in one chapter of a book, conventional war and conventional weapons. Our intent in this chapter is simply to provide some sense of the big, seemingly intractable, issues associated with war and weapons, along with a brief look at a few of the problems, such as those associated with the use of private militaries and child soldiers, that are especially significant at present. As always, our emphasis will be on threats to security and what can be done about them.

WAR AS COERCIVE VIOLENCE

A useful place to begin our consideration of conventional war and weapons is with a set of fundamental points concerning the objectives served by the use of force. In *Arms and Influence,* Thomas Schelling began by noting that force can be used to take what a country wants or to keep what it has. "Forcibly a country can repel and expel, penetrate and occupy, seize, exterminate, disarm and disable, confine, deny access, and directly frustrate intrusion or attack." But there is something else that force can accomplish: "Force can be used to hurt. In addition to taking and protecting things of value it can destroy value. In addition to weakening an enemy militarily it can cause an enemy plain suffering."[5]

With this insight Schelling proceeded to explain the evolution of modern warfare from a point at which the ability to inflict punishment on an enemy depended on the ability to defeat that enemy in war to a point at which punishment could be inflicted *prior to* the military defeat of the enemy. Under the former circumstances, the conquest of a city or an entire state would enable the conqueror to seize economic assets and to enslave or kill the enemy's civilian population. The latter situation, in contrast, is one in which the destruction of noncombatants and property occurs in the course of the war. The aerial bombardment of cities in World War II offers the classic example.

The understanding that military force can be used to punish as well as to seize or defend leads to Schelling's most important observation: when punishment can be meted out before the military defeat of the enemy is achieved, it can be deliberately employed as a means of coercion. With weapons of mass destruction, the mere threat of such punishment can be used to coerce an adversary.[6]

Much of modern warfare has as its object seizing territory, overthrowing governments, or merely fending off the attacks of others. Superior military force is necessary to accomplish these ends. There is also, however, a great deal of fighting that occurs when one side has no hope of prevailing by brute force. Such warfare, far from being irrational, is based on the idea that one's objectives can often be accomplished merely by inflicting sufficient pain to make the adversary yield. It is this—the logic of coercive violence—that explains suicide bombers and videotaped beheadings in Iraq. It also explains the difficulty of defeating insurgencies in Algeria, Vietnam, Afghanistan, Chechnya, and Iraq. When a military contest becomes a matter of inflicting pain rather than demonstrating the superiority of one's weapons, matching the enemy's ability to endure pain is more important than matching the enemy's military power.

This understanding of coercive violence illuminates many important features of modern military strategy—from the desire of a growing number of states to acquire weapons of mass destruction (and the desire of others to prevent them from doing so) to the widespread use of terrorism and guerrilla warfare tactics. It also helps to explain why, in spite of a level of military dominance some believe to be unmatched in the history of the world, the United States does not enjoy a commensurate level of security at home or a commensurate ability to control events abroad. Paradoxically, the vulnerability of the United States and other developed countries may be a consequence of their military dominance. To see why this is the case, we need to examine the concept of asymmetric warfare and its relationship to the "revolution in military affairs" (RMA).

ASYMMETRIC WARFARE

During much of the modern period, war has been fought symmetrically—that is, contending armies have battled each other with comparable weapons, tactics, and organizational modes. The army that has prevailed has generally been the one with some measure of superiority, whether quantitative or qualitative, in these areas. Technological innovations have been decisive, but only for as long as it has taken other states to adopt the new weapons. Steam-powered ships defeated sailing ships on the high seas, armor defeated cavalry on land, and so on, but the advantages were fleeting.

On the whole, states have fought wars, if not exactly on equal terms, at least in ways that were similar. Japan provides a dramatic example of the pressure to conform. Japan's arrival as a world power, signaled by its victory over Russia in the Russo-Japanese War of 1904–1905, came at the point at which a military culture dominated by the ideal of the *samurai* warrior was supplanted by Western ways of waging war. But what happens when states are unable to win on terms dictated by their adversaries?

World War II illustrates the tendency of states to move to asymmetric modes of waging war when they are unable to prevail in a symmetric war. Beginning with the attack on Poland in September 1939, Nazi Germany was able to sweep across Europe in large measure due to its blitzkrieg tactics. To fight on at all, conquered states were required to adopt guerrilla warfare tactics. The French Resistance, in other words, was engaged in asymmetric warfare. But the British and the Americans, while certainly not conquered, were also obliged to engage in asymmetric warfare initially. With most of Western Europe occupied by the Germans and no means available to mount a direct assault on German forces, the United Kingdom decided in 1940 to initiate a bombing campaign that targeted German cities. The United States joined beginning in 1942 and eventually extended the counter-city bombing strategy to Japan.[7] Michael Walzer, who accepts the necessity of the decision to bomb cities, nonetheless labels the bombing "Allied terrorism" and notes that over half a million civilians were killed by Allied bombs in Germany and Japan.[8] When the stakes are high enough, the prospect of defeat often compels the adoption of asymmetrical tactics.

Today, the United States military is so dominant that, with very few exceptions, any state (or nonstate actor) that finds itself at war with the United States must wage asymmetric warfare. This is true in part simply because the United States has retained a large military force since the end of World War II, but it also has much to do with what is called the revolution in military affairs.

The revolution in military affairs is the effect generated by the marriage of advanced communications and information-processing systems with state-of-the-art weapons-delivery systems. When information (including visual imagery) is collected from hundreds of sources, including satellites over the theater of operations, transmitted instantaneously to decision makers at all levels, from the head of state to individual tank drivers on the battlefield, and immediately processed by computers into a readily usable form, the effect on the ability to wage war is indeed revolutionary. The RMA is, in essence, a means of overcoming the confusion and uncertainty—what the Prussian military thinker Carl von Clausewitz called "the fog of war"—that has been a constant feature of battle throughout history. The location of enemy forces, the speed and direction of mobile targets, the success or failure of weapons in hitting their targets, and even the content of the enemy's communications can be monitored in real time by battlefield commanders, thanks to the existence of digital cameras (and other information sensors) and the ability to collect the information they provide from locations all over the theater of operations. To know and to be able to control what one's own forces are doing in the confusion of combat is a tremendous advantage; the advantage of knowing as well what enemy forces are doing is almost invariably decisive.

The effect of the RMA has been most apparent in the two wars fought by the United States in Iraq since 1991. In the first of those conflicts (the Persian Gulf War, as it is generally known in the United States), the United States and its allies began by "blinding" the Iraqi military. Radar and communications facilities (pinpointed by prewar satellite surveillance) were destroyed with precision-guided munitions, including "smart bombs" dropped from airplanes and cruise missiles launched from destroyers and submarines located hundreds of miles from their targets. The success of the initial strike gave coalition forces the advantage throughout the war of owning the skies over Iraq. American generals were able to see virtually everything the Iraqis were doing, while the Iraqis themselves were, electronically speaking, operating in the dark.

The U.S. military's advantage was also apparent in the way distance factored in. During the war, the Pentagon frequently released cockpit-camera videos from American combat aircraft. Such videos invariably showed pinpoint strikes on targets from great distances. Rather than trying to defeat the Iraqi army, which in 1991 was the fourth largest in the world and battle hardened from a long war with Iran, on the ground using conventional tactics, the United States was able to use air superiority, information dominance, and precision-guided weapons to deliver devastating blows from positions in the air, at sea, and on the ground that the Iraqis simply could not reach in retaliation.

One of the most significant effects of these changes in warfare is the dramatic reduction in casualties for military forces fighting at a distance and enjoying information dominance. In the Persian Gulf War, only 147 Americans were killed in combat.[9] A similar number (139) were killed in Operation Iraqi Freedom up to the end of major combat operations in 2003.[10] Perhaps even more remarkably, during a two-and-a-half-month period in 1999, NATO pilots flew over thirty-eight thousand sorties in Kosovo and Serbia suffering no fatalities.[11] For better or for worse, low casualty rates make it easier for leaders in a democracy to contemplate a decision to go to war.

The RMA has opened up a tremendous gap between the military capabilities of those states able to benefit from satellite guidance systems, precision weapons, real-time battlefield imaging, and more, and states (and nonstate actors) unable to afford high-tech military systems. And yet, there are some respects in which even the poorest and least sophisticated military forces are able to use new information capabilities for military purposes. By now the extent to which Al Qaeda was able to plan and coordinate a global campaign of terror via the Internet is well known. The March 11, 2004, terrorist bombings in Madrid linked cheap information technology to old-fashioned explosives with devastating effect. There cell phones were wired to explosives, as they still are in the roadside bombs in Iraq known to American troops as "improvised explosive devices" (IEDs), in such a way that an incoming call could trigger the bomb. However primitive such devices may seem in comparison to laser-guided bombs, the principle is the same: using information technology to make it possible to launch devastating attacks from a distance.

Military dominance of the sort the United States has achieved is not without certain problems. There is, first, the enormous cost of high-tech weaponry and the C4I (command, control, communications, computers, and intelligence) that backs it up. (The cost of modern weapons and war will be examined in the next section.) Second, by dramatically reducing the casualties that the United States can expect when going to war, there is a danger that decision makers may come to regard war as something other than a last resort. The RMA is widely credited with helping the United States to overcome the "Vietnam syndrome" (that is, reluctance to use military force due to public unwillingness to endure large numbers of U.S. casualties in a conflict not thought to be related to a vital interest), but not everyone regards this development as a good thing.

The most vexing problem associated with American military dominance is that it forces most states or nonstate actors that might become involved in military conflicts with the United States to fight using unconventional means only. Twice in Iraq and once in Afghanistan, the futility of fighting the United States in a conventional war has been demonstrated, and yet the United States has been hurt by Al Qaeda and by insurgents in Iraq fighting asymmetrically. As Sun Tzu stated 2,500 years ago in *The Art of War,* "In war, the way is to avoid what is strong and to strike at what is weak."[12] It is a lesson that is becoming increasingly familiar to America's adversaries. To put the point directly, the wider the gap in military capabilities between the strong and the weak, the more incentive there may be for the weak who feel compelled to attack the strong to resort to terrorism and guerrilla warfare.

The situation in the Iraq war before and after the end of major combat operations announced by President Bush on May 1, 2003, is instructive in this regard. As noted earlier, the initial phase was a conventional war dominated by coalition forces. There were relatively few coalition casualties. Between May 1, 2003, and June 25, 2005, however, there were 1,529 U.S. military personnel killed.[13] In the insurgency, coalition forces have been attacked by individuals without uniforms who drive ordinary cars (sometimes laden with explosives) and who are capable of blending in with the civilian population. Attacks often come in the form of bombs planted on the roadside that are triggered remotely when coalition convoys pass. Targets on which American precision-guided munitions could be used have simply faded into the Iraqi society, and efforts to locate them risk alienating the population. The RMA, in short, offers few resources suitable for fighting the insurgency.

THE QUESTION OF COST

The military dominance made possible by the RMA comes at an enormous economic cost. But then, it isn't cheap to fight a low-tech war either.

In 2003, the world's states spent close to a trillion dollars for defense. At $417.4 billion dollars (not including special appropriations for the war in Iraq), the United States accounted for 47 percent of the world's military spending.[14] The enormity of this figure can best be seen by comparing it to other global expenditures. For example, the budget for United Nations peacekeeping operations for the period from July 2001 to June 2002 was $2.77 billion. For its other operations (the peacekeeping budget is separate from the normal operating budget of the UN), the United Nations spent $1.149 billion in 2002.[15]

Defense spending must be considered in terms of opportunity costs. What is spent on the military is unavailable to be spent for other social needs. President Eisenhower stated the point eloquently in a speech to the American Society of Newspaper Editors in 1953:

> Every gun that is made, every warship launched, every rocket fired, signifies, in the final sense, a theft from those who hunger and are not fed, those who are cold and are not clothed. This world in arms is not spending money alone. It is spending the sweat of its laborers, the genius of its scientists, the hopes of its children. . . . We pay for a single fighter plane with a half million bushels of wheat. We pay for a single destroyer with new homes that could have housed more than 8,000 people.[16]

The issue associated with opportunity costs has become even more challenging since Eisenhower's day. With the new F/A-22 Raptor projected to cost $258 million per plane[17] and wheat at roughly three dollars per bushel, a single fighter plane now costs the equivalent of eighty-six million bushels of wheat.

Defense expenditures are even more vexing when one considers that money spent on weapons does not generally enhance productivity in other areas the way money spent for health care, education, transportation, or many other purposes does. Two-thirds of the money spent on research and development (R&D) in the United States promotes military purposes. In contrast, only 35 percent of the total R&D budget in the United Kingdom goes toward the military rather than the civilian sector. To make the point differently, the United States spends 0.4 percent of its gross domestic product on military R&D, while Japan's military R&D budget consumes a mere 0.03 of GDP.[18]

The economic drain associated with defense spending is especially apparent in the developing world, where all too often corrupt governments ignore pressing social needs in order to spend limited state revenue on military forces. In Eritrea, for example, a staggering 23.5 percent of GDP was spent on defense from 2000 to 2002, while only 4.8 percent was spent on education and 2.8 percent on health.[19]

Of course, the cost of preparing for war might be regarded as well worth whatever price is paid if military preparations were certain to prevent war, which has its own enormous costs, or at least to prevent defeat in war. But one can never be certain how much "security" is obtained for each dollar spent. Nor, for that matter, can one be certain in all circumstances that defense spending produces more good than harm.

In fact, the precise relationship between weapons and war has long been a matter of debate. Weapons are necessary to wage war, but they are also considered essential in order to promote peace and security. As a presidential candidate in 1960, John F. Kennedy said, "It is an unfortunate fact that we can only secure peace by preparing for war."[20] Kennedy's observation, of course, was not new. The Romans were fond of the expression, "If you want peace, prepare for war." The opposite perspective was perhaps stated most cogently by Sir John Frederick Maurice in 1883: "I went into the British Army believing that if you want peace you must prepare for war. I now believe that if you prepare thoroughly for war you will get it."[21]

CONVENTIONAL WEAPONS AND WAR: HUMAN SECURITY CONCERNS

The traditional perspective on security pushes us to consider the impact of conventional weapons on national security and to ask questions such as those we have already noted: Are such weapons necessary to preserve the peace, or does their accumulation push states toward war? Are the costs of armaments justifiable, or does defense spending (at least beyond a certain point) jeopardize the state's ability to fulfill other important responsibilities? From a human security perspective, however, we must consider the ways that conventional weapons affect the well-being of individual human beings.

The welfare of individuals is, of course, commonly tied to the health of the states they inhabit. A country under the domination of another or constantly at war is unlikely to be in a position to promote human rights or human development to the fullest. Human security and national security are not alternatives. Instead, a focus on human security helps to protect against an extreme emphasis on national security in which the state and its defense are held, implicitly at least, to justify an indifference toward individuals. All too often, states have sacrificed human security for national security.

Here we wish to consider three of the issues related to human security that are presented by conventional weapons and war. Each is commonly ignored in studies focused solely on national security, and yet each is an issue attracting increasing attention from nongovernmental organizations (NGOs), international organizations, and a few states that perceive themselves to be "humanitarian great powers." The issues are small arms and light weapons (SALW), explosive remnants of war (ERW), and child soldiers.

Small Arms and Light Weapons

Small arms are believed to be responsible for over half a million deaths—homicides, suicides, and war-related fatalities—each year.[22] In a speech before the UN Security Council Ministerial on Small Arms on September 24, 1999, former Canadian foreign minister Lloyd Axworthy called them "small arms of mass destruction."[23] The impacts of small arms and light weapons are not new, but the end of the Cold War prompted an increased awareness of those impacts even as it exacerbated the problem in significant ways.

Small arms and light weapons have been the primary instruments of the many intrastate conflicts that have plagued the globe since the end of the Cold War. They are inexpensive and widely available, which makes it easy for aggrieved groups to take up arms against governments or other nonstate actors. These same characteristics facilitate illicit trade and make regulation more difficult to enforce. Their ease of use and small size make small arms ideal for untrained combatants and even child soldiers. Making the problem even worse, the end of the Cold War was accompanied by both a loss of superpower control over the SALW trade and the creation of a tremendous surplus of weapons. Furthermore, the existence of transnational criminal organizations trafficking in drugs and persons provided a ready-made network of dealers for the illicit weapons trade. (On this point, see chapter 8.) In short, a broad convergence of factors brought the issue of small arms and light weapons to the fore during the 1990s.[24]

The issue of small arms and light weapons was added to the agenda of the United Nations through a resolution adopted by the General Assembly in 1991.[25] Little progress occurred, however, until the 1997 Ottawa Convention banning antipersonnel land mines was adopted. In an address to the UN General Assembly, Lloyd Axworthy pressed for UN action on small arms and light weapons just days after the text of the Ottawa Convention had been finalized at a conference in Oslo. Noting the spread of intrastate conflicts, Axworthy said, "As this type of war increasingly accounts for the great majority of all conflicts, the distinctions that once informed the work of international diplomacy—between military security concerns and humanitarian or civil concerns—break down." Consequently, Axworthy suggested, the concept of human security "takes on a growing relevance" and requires "addressing issues that cut across traditional boundaries between areas of concern." The issue of small arms, like the land-mine issue, was, according to Axworthy, one such cross-cutting issue.[26]

NGOs and a few states constituting the Human Security Network pushed the small arms issue at the United Nations, and in July 2001 the UN Conference on the Illicit Trade in Small Arms and Light Weapons in All Its Aspects was held. In his speech on behalf of the United States on the opening day of the conference, Under Secretary of State John Bolton listed five broad areas of disagreement with the draft Program of Action being discussed at the session. Each point, from opposition to measures that would regulate arms manufacture and trade to opposition to any international threat to "the Constitutional right to bear arms," was significant.[27] The effect was to place the United States in a position of intransigence on the SALW issue rather than the more neutral position on the sidelines it had taken during the negotiations leading to the Ottawa Convention. U.S. opposition combined with a variety of structural and political obstacles (including the enormous profitability of the global trade in SALW) meant that no significant progress was made on the issue in 2001, nor has any significant movement taken place since then.

Explosive Remnants of War

An often overlooked aspect of armaments that must be thrown into the equation when considering the security implications of conventional weapons is their persistence. Many weapons are destroyed or expended in war, but not all of them. Some weapons are removed from service—and even destroyed—as a consequence of disarmament (most commonly when the victor forcibly disarms the vanquished). In many instances, however, weapons continue to be a factor in security (or insecurity) long after the conflict for which they were created and deployed has been resolved. This can be due to the circulation and reuse of weapons, as was noted in the discussion of SALW, but it can also be a consequence of the deadly residue that modern warfare often leaves behind.

Consider, as an example, the problem of land mines. An estimated hundred million land mines have been left over from recent conflicts. In Angola, roughly 40 percent of the population has experienced amputations due to land-mine accidents.[28] In Cambodia, where a decade-long civil war following the overthrow of the genocidal Khmer Rouge regime was concluded in 1991, land mines continue to kill and maim people almost every day. A World Bank report noted that, in 2001, 173 people were killed and 640 people were wounded by mines or other forms of unexploded ordnance (UXO) in spite of the fact that 313,586 antipersonnel land mines had been removed from the country between 1992 and 2001. As the report notes, "Mine and UXO contamination restricts access to homes, agricultural land, pastures, water sources, forests, schools, dams, canals, markets, business activities, health centers, pagodas, bridges, and neighboring villages. Thus the threat of UXO and mines impedes mobility, security, economic activity, and development."[29]

As noted above, land mines were the subjects of a 1997 treaty, the Ottawa Convention, that bans their use and mandates their removal where they have been deployed. The treaty was the product of a remarkable coalition of states and NGOs determined to arouse global public interest in the problems posed by explosive remnants of war. In fact, American activist Jody Williams and the International Campaign to Ban Landmines (ICBL) shared the 1997 Nobel Peace Prize for their efforts to promote the land-mine ban. While over a hundred states have ratified the Ottawa Convention and have made significant progress in demining conflict zones, the United States has thus far refused to ratify the agreement, because of its interest in continuing to use land mines for the defense of South Korea.

Even weapons from wars far removed in time sometimes pose threats. In February 2004, thirty thousand people were evacuated in Sevastopol, a Ukrainian port city, when a World War II–era mine weighing over a ton was dredged from the Black Sea. The mine was transported through a portion of the city (thus the need for evacuations) to an unpopulated location where it could be destroyed.[30]

At present, a movement is under way to address problems associated with other explosive remnants of war, including antivehicle mines, grenades, artillery shells, mortars, and rockets. Cluster bombs, described by William Arkin as "a greater hazard to civilians than virtually any other weapon that is legal,"[31] are at the top of the list of weapons ripe for arms control initiatives related to explosive remnants of war.

Cluster bombs disperse "bomblets," or "submunitions," over a broad area when dropped from a plane or fired by rockets on the ground. The bomblets (202 per device in the cluster bomb used most commonly by the United States in the Afghan campaign) are designed to explode on impact, spraying the area with deadly shrapnel and, in some cases, incendiary material. For a variety of reasons, including submunitions units malfunctioning or landing on soft surfaces, anywhere from 5 percent to 20 percent of the bomblets fail to explode as intended. Bomb canisters can then remain on the ground for years before being accidentally detonated, with tragic consequences. The use of cluster bombs in Afghanistan during the first several months of the war was particularly problematic, due to the fact that unexploded bomblets were yellow, the same color as the packaged meals dropped by the United States to sustain Afghan civilians on the ground.

The war in Afghanistan is not the first time that cluster bombs have been used extensively by the United States and created a significant postconflict problem with unexploded ordnance. In fact, cluster bombs have been in use for over fifty years. NATO reported in 2000 that 1,392 cluster bombs had been dropped during the Kosovo campaign, with a failure rate of 8 to 12 percent. Within a year of the end of the conflict, forty-seven people (over half of them children) had been killed and 101 people had been injured by unexploded canisters. It is estimated that in the aftermath of the Persian Gulf War (1991), as many as two million unexploded cluster bomblets remained in Iraq and Kuwait.[32] These weapons are believed to have killed over 2,500

Iraqi civilians since the end of the war, far more civilians than were reported to have been killed during the war itself.[33]

Child Soldiers

Children are often the victims of explosive remnants of war, but land mines and cluster bombs are not the only war-related problems affecting children. Indeed, the impact of modern warfare on children is staggering. During the 1990s, as a consequence of war, approximately two million children were killed, over four million were disabled, over ten million were psychologically traumatized, over one million were orphaned, approximately twenty million were displaced, and three hundred thousand children were forced to serve in armies as soldiers, spies, sex slaves, and other roles.[34]

Although it is not a new problem, the international community has become increasingly sensitive over the past decade to the problem of children in combat. In 1996, Graça Machel, Mozambique's minister of education, prepared a report at the request of UN secretary general Boutros Boutros-Ghali entitled *Impact of Armed Conflict on Children*. Much of what we know about the problem comes from this study and from subsequent surveys conducted by NGOs in the years since 1996.[35]

In its most recent international survey, the London-based Coalition to Stop the Use of Child Soldiers found that in half of the armed conflicts occurring between April 2001 and March 2004 for which information was available, governments were using children in combat. Burundi, the Democratic Republic of the Congo (DRC), Côte d'Ivoire, Guinea, Liberia, Myanmar, Rwanda, Sudan, Uganda, and the United States were among the governments found to be using persons under eighteen in combat.[36] Not only governments are culpable. Children are also forced to fight in a variety of paramilitary organizations and rebel groups around the world.

Children serve a variety of functions in armies; not all are, strictly speaking, soldiers. Some carry weapons and engage in combat, but others serve as (aside from the capacities mentioned above) couriers, minelayers, cooks, and domestic servants. In the DRC, almost all of the girls questioned by surveyors reported having been raped in the army. The Lord's Resistance Army, a rebel organization in northern Uganda that has abducted an estimated twenty thousand children, has forced girls both to fight and to serve commanders as sex slaves.[37]

Although some children are taken out of schools and orphanages by soldiers, not all of those who end up in armies are abducted. Many enlist voluntarily, often to escape poverty or because the lack of educational or employment opportunities leaves few alternatives. Some see entry into an army or rebel force as deliverance from the violence and fear inflicted on civilian populations by those same groups. In some instances, governments encourage enlistment by requiring military training programs in schools and camps.[38]

The proliferation of small arms and light weapons, in addition to fueling intrastate conflict, has made it easier for children to participate in combat. Weapons are so common and inexpensive that armed forces need not worry about whether putting a gun in the hands of a child will be a waste of resources. As Machel reported, in Uganda in 1996 an AK-47 could be purchased for about the cost of a chicken. More important, however, is the fact that small arms are so light and simple to operate that ten-year-olds have no difficulty using them. The global trade in small arms and light weapons, which the international community has thus far been unable to address effectively, must be regarded as a contributing factor in the tragedy of child soldiers.

On May 25, 2000, the General Assembly of the United Nations adopted the Optional Protocol to the Convention on the Rights of the Child on the Involvement of Children in Armed Conflict, to outlaw military recruitment and the use in combat of those under eighteen. The Optional Protocol entered into force on February 12, 2002. Although not a party to the Convention on the Rights of the Child, the United States is a signatory to that treaty and thus is eligible to be a party to the Optional Protocol. The United States ratified the Optional Protocol on January 23, 2003.

PRIVATIZED MILITARY FIRMS

We turn now to an issue that holds the possibility of transforming how wars are waged in the twenty-first century: the rise of privatized military firms (PMFs). Over the course of the past two decades, states—both rich and poor—have increasingly turned to private companies to provide services that were previously considered the responsibility of governments alone.

On March 30, 2004, four employees of Blackwater USA, a private security firm hired to protect the employees of one of the Defense Department's many suppliers in Iraq, were ambushed as they drove through the city of Fallujah. They were shot, and their bodies were dragged from their vehicle, mutilated, and burned. Two were suspended grotesquely from a bridge. Photographs of the grisly scene were published or broadcast in less discreet media outlets around the world.

The incident in Fallujah drew attention to an issue that had, up to that point, attracted relatively little attention. From the very beginning of the war, privatized military firms were employed in Iraq to perform services traditionally considered the responsibility of uniformed military forces. In Iraq at the time of the Fallujah killings, at least twenty thousand private military contractors were employed to protect diplomats (including the head of the Coalition Provisional Authority, Paul Bremer), American and Iraqi businessmen, aid workers, and many others.[39]

While the large number of private security contractors in Iraq may be surprising, the role of privatized military firms has been even more important in a number of other conflicts. During the 1990s, the government of Sierra Leone halted a bloody civil war and recaptured the country's diamond mines from rebel forces by hiring Executive Outcomes, a PMF based in South Africa. Executive Outcomes used airpower, armored vehicles, and a small but highly trained force to accomplish what the government had been unable to do in years of fighting.[40]

Privatized military firms are employed by governments for a variety of reasons, some that appear legitimate and some that may not be. First, PMFs allow the military to contract-out jobs that are temporary, that involve skills that are in short supply among the armed forces, or that can be performed more efficiently by contractors. Second, when private contractors sustain casualties, those casualties are not typically reported in the media and do not affect public opinion in democracies the way military casualties do. (The Pentagon does not include contractor casualties on its casualty lists in the Iraq war.) The use of PMFs, in other words, may serve to conceal the true human costs of military operations, but it may also permit defense establishments to keep fewer troops under arms, since shortfalls can be handled by calling in the private sector.

The rise of privatized military firms also means, however, that defense establishments may find themselves competing for the services of military professionals. In February 2005, the Department of Defense approved a plan to offer financial incentives (up to $150,000 for a six-year reenlistment) to stem the flow of experienced Special Operations Forces personnel to private security companies. The bonuses were devised to deal with a situation in which Army Green Berets or Navy SEALs with twenty years' experience and making fifty thousand dollars in base pay could leave the military and go to work for a private security firm at salaries close to two hundred thousand dollars a year.[41]

Perhaps more troublesome for the international system is the fact that an industry has emerged that gives those who can pay, whether governments or corporations—or even rebel organizations and drug traffickers (PMFs are reported to have trained drug dealers in Mexico and UNITA rebels in Angola in military tactics and the use of advanced weapons)—access to military force. In spite of certain advantages associated with contracting-out warfare, a tremendous potential for abuse exists as well.

In the realm of conventional weapons and war, security can be bought. Private contractors are available to supplement military forces and thereby reduce the need for large armies. High-tech weapons also play a role in reducing the number of troops needed for many missions; they have the added advantage of reducing casualties for the military that is able to attack from a distance while enjoying information dominance. But the security that is available for purchase is not absolute. Resourceful enemies are always able to find and exploit weaknesses. If those weaknesses are not to be found on the conventional battlefield, determined adversaries may decide to attack nonmilitary targets.

War, as we noted at the outset of this chapter, is a form of coercive violence. Militarily powerful states, such as the United States, have an incentive to contain the use of coercive violence with rules that protect noncombatants, exclude children from participation, and limit the kinds of weapons that can be used. All of these are laudable rules, but if, in combination with the distribution of power in the system, these rules preordain the outcome of most conflicts, we should not be surprised if some actors in the system decide to ignore the rules. This should not be construed as a justification for terrorism, the use of weapons of mass destruction, or any other form of unlawful warfare. It is, instead, a caution for those who would consider the possession of overwhelming military power a panacea for a pluralistic world.

RECOMMENDED READING

Printed Sources

Berkowitz, Bruce. *The New Face of War: How War Will Be Fought in the 21st Century.* New York: Free Press, 2003.

Cohen, Eliot A. "A Revolution in Warfare?" *Foreign Affairs* 75 (March/April 1996): 37–54.

Kagan, Donald. *On the Origins of War and the Preservation of Peace.* New York: Doubleday, 1995.

Keegan, John. *A History of Warfare.* New York: Alfred A. Knopf, 1993.

Knox, MacGregor, and Williamson Murray, eds. *The Dynamics of Military Revolution, 1300–2050.* Cambridge: Cambridge University Press, 2001.

Schelling, Thomas C. *Arms and Influence.* New Haven, Conn.: Yale University Press, 1966.

Singer, P. W. *Corporate Warriors: The Rise of the Privatized Military Industry.* Ithaca, N.Y.: Cornell University Press, 2003.

Websites

Coalition to Stop the Use of Child Soldiers: www.child-soldiers.org/

International Action Network on Small Arms: www.iansa.org/

National Defense University: www.ndu.edu/

Stockholm International Peace Research Institute: www.sipri.org/

United States Department of Defense: www.defenselink.mil/

U.S. Army Chief of Staff's Professional Reading List: www.army.mil/cmh-pg/reference/CSAList/CSAList.htm.

3

Nuclear Weapons: Living in the Shadow of the Mushroom Cloud

At 2:45 AM on August 6, 1945, a lone American B-29 bomber named the *Enola Gay*, after the pilot's mother, took off from the Pacific island of Tinian, flew 1,600 miles in five and a half hours to Hiroshima, Japan, and dropped the most destructive weapon ever used in warfare to that time—a nuclear bomb ten feet long, twenty-eight inches in diameter, and weighing nine thousand pounds. Forty-three seconds after it left the *Enola Gay*, the bomb, code-named "Little Boy," exploded 1,900 feet above ground with a destructive yield equivalent to 12,500 tons of TNT.[1] The explosion lasted about one second; the temperature at ground zero, the point directly below the detonation, rose to three to four thousand degrees centigrade, a temperature several times that of the surface of the sun. The temperature was so hot and intense that birds ignited in midair.

The effects on the residents of Hiroshima were horrific; one eyewitness later reported, "Men whose whole bodies were covered with blood, and women whose skin hung from them like a kimono, plunged shrieking into the river. All these become corpses and their bodies are carried by the current toward the sea."[2] The official estimate of the number of people killed was seventy thousand, although more recent estimates indicate that by the end of 1945, 140,000 had died.

When he felt the concussion of the bomb hit his plane and saw the mushroom cloud rising over the city, the copilot of the bomber, Capt. Robert Lewis, asked, "My God, what have we done? If I live a hundred years, I'll never quite get these few minutes out of my mind."[3]

Even after the bombing of Hiroshima, the Japanese government did not surrender; the government was torn between the civilian leaders who wanted to sue for peace and the military leaders who preferred death to the disgrace of surrender. Three days after the bombing of Hiroshima, at 3:47 AM, a B-29 named *Bock's Car* (after the last name of the pilot) took off from Tinian with another nuclear weapon—code-named "Fat Man"—and flew to Nagasaki. The bomb exploded 1,650 feet above the city at 11:02 AM with a destructive force estimated to be equivalent to twenty-two thousand tons of TNT. Unlike Hiroshima, Nagasaki was surrounded by hills, and these provided some limited protection from the blast of the explosion. Still, forty thousand people died immediately, seventy thousand by the end of 1945, and 140,000 altogether. The day after the bombing of Nagasaki, Emperor Hirohito, despite the continuing opposition of Japanese military leaders, surrendered unconditionally, and the most costly war in human history ended. But if the development and first use of nuclear weapons ended the war, they raised profound questions, questions that have remained to this day like shadows of the mushroom clouds that rose ominously over Hiroshima and Nagasaki.

Nuclear weapons are the most powerful, destructive weapons devised, built, and used by human beings. Although it would have been possible to kill as many Japanese with nonnuclear bombs, guns, or even knives and clubs, nuclear weapons made it dramatically easier—both technically and morally—to do so. More people were killed in the March 1945 firebombing raids on Tokyo or the February 1945 bombing raids on Dresden than were killed in either Hiroshima or Nagasaki, but those earlier attacks had involved hundreds of planes dropping thousands of bombs.

In the first issue of *Time* magazine published after the bombings, writer James Agee noted:

> The greatest and most terrible of wars ended, this week, in the echoes of an enormous event—an event so much more enormous that, relative to it, the war itself shrank to minor significance. The knowledge of victory was as charged with sorrow and doubt as with joy and gratitude. More fearful responsibilities, more crucial liabilities rested on the victor even than on the vanquished. With the controlled splitting of the atom, humanity, already profoundly perplexed and disunified, was brought inescapably into a new age in which all thoughts and things were split—and far from controlled.[4]

Others, like Agee, noted the revolutionary character of nuclear weapons. The day after the bombing of Hiroshima, a brilliant, young political science professor at Yale, Bernard Brodie, picked up a copy of the *New York Times* and read the headline: "First Atomic Bomb Dropped on Japan; Missile Is Equal to 20,000 Tons of TNT; Truman Warns Foe of a 'Rain of Ruin.'" Brodie had written extensively on naval and military strategy. After reading the lead article concerning the bombing of Hiroshima, Brodie told his wife, "Everything that I have written is obsolete."[5]

Soon after World War II ended, Bernard Brodie assembled a small group of civilian strategists to think about the implications of nuclear weapons for international politics and security. The group published in 1946 a remarkably prescient collection of essays, in which one of the contributors asserted, "To speak of it [the nuclear weapon] as just another weapon was highly misleading. It was a revolutionary development which altered the basic structure of war itself."[6] Brodie pointed to the revolutionary implications of nuclear weapons. Ever since the time of Carl von Clausewitz, military strategists had believed that an attacker should have a superiority of three to one in order to ensure success.[7] Brodie turned this equation on its head: "If 2,000 bombs in the hands of either party is enough to destroy entirely the economy of the other, the fact that one side has 6,000 and the other 2,000 will be of relatively small significance."[8] Nuclear weapons, according to Brodie, negated the teachings of the greatest military strategists.

Other policy makers and strategists thought of nuclear weapons as significantly more powerful than previous weapons but not radically different. Herman Kahn was the strategist who best represented this position.[9] In the decades following the development and use of nuclear weapons by the United States, these two positions, broadly speaking, have characterized the ways of thinking about nuclear weapons.[10] In specific terms, six different approaches to dealing with nuclear weapons have been developed since 1945: (1) pacifists (or "nuclear pacifists") argue that the use of nuclear weapons is never justified; (2) some Americans argued that the only way to reassure the Soviets after World War II was to give nuclear weapons to them; (3) Soviet and American postwar leaders presented several plans for the international control of nuclear weapons; (4) when these proposals came to naught, strategists argued that nuclear weapons should be used to deter other states' use of nuclear weapons or conventional weapons; (5) some contended that nuclear weapons should be subject to quantitative and qualitative limitations; and (6) some contend, following those who believe nuclear weapons are not fundamentally different from previous weapons, that they can and should be used to fight and win wars. In this chapter, these six views will be described.

Before turning to these six approaches, however, it is important to note the growth in the number of nuclear weapons from the two that existed in August 1945 to the tens of thousands that existed during the Cold War. Table 3.1 presents a snapshot of the number of nuclear weapons that the United States and the Soviet Union/Russia possessed from 1964 through 2003.

Table 3.1. Strategic Nuclear Warheads: United States, USSR/Russian Federation

| Year | USSR/Russian Federation | | | | United States | | | |
	ICBM	SLBM	Bombers	Total	ICBM	SLBM	Bombers	Total
1964	201	74	548	821	952	605	6,471	8,028
1974	1,666	722	596	2,985	2,041	6,569	6,788	15,398
1984	7,135	2,140	756	10,032	2,231	5,611	6,118	13,960
1994	4,530	2,436	1,468	8,434	2,215	3,021	3,565	8,801
2003	2,922	1,732	632	5,286	1,600	2,880	1,660	5,340

Sources: Table 6.1 in George Perkovich, Joseph Cirincione, Rose Gottemoeller, Jon B. Wolfsthal, and Jessica T. Mathews, *Universal Compliance: A Strategy for Nuclear Security* (Washington, D.C.: Carnegie Endowment for International Peace, June 2004), 67. Based on data from Natural Resources Defense Council, "Table of USSR/Russian Nuclear Warheads," November 2002, available at www.nrdc.org; "U.S. Nuclear Forces, 2003," *Bulletin of the Atomic Scientists* 59, no. 3 (May/June 2003): 73–76.

THE PACIFIST AND "NUCLEAR PACIFIST" POSITION: NUCLEAR WEAPONS SHOULD NEVER BE USED

Some people, absolute pacifists, contend that no weapons should ever be used; this is the position of such religious groups as the Quakers and the Mennonites. Others do not reject the use of all military force but argue that nuclear weapons are so destructive and indiscriminate that they should never be used. This "nuclear pacifist" position was that of the eminent diplomat and scholar George Kennan, who argued:

> We would have to begin by accepting the validity of two very fundamental appreciations. The first is that there is no issue at stake in our political relations with the Soviet Union— no hope, no fear, nothing to which we aspire, nothing we would like to avoid—which could conceivably be worth a nuclear war. And the second is that there is no way in which nuclear weapons could conceivably be employed in combat that would not involve the possibility—and indeed the prohibitively high probability—of escalation to a general nuclear disaster.[11]

Kennan subscribed to this position at least by 1950 and held to it throughout the Cold War.[12]

SHARE NUCLEAR WEAPONS: GIVE THEM TO THE SOVIETS

In August 1939, the Soviet Union and Nazi Germany signed a nonaggression pact that protected Germany's eastern flank. The following month Germany attacked and occupied Poland, the event that launched World War II. Many people believed that the Nazi-Soviet Pact had enabled Hitler to begin his conquests and therefore blamed the Soviet Union for cooperating with Hitler. After Poland, Germany attacked and occupied most of Western Europe. In June 1941, Germany attacked the Soviet Union. The United Kingdom was now faced with a dilemma: Should it cooperate with the dictatorial state that had enabled Germany to attack Western Europe, or should it go its own way? Winston Churchill provided a characteristically forceful, unambiguous answer: "I have only one purpose, the destruction of Hitler, and my life is much simplified thereby. If Hitler invaded Hell I would make at least a favourable reference to the Devil in the House of Commons."[13] The reference to Stalin as the devil was not lost on anyone, least of all Stalin himself, and throughout the war the relationship among the "Big Three"—Roosevelt, Churchill, and Stalin—was tense.

From 1942 on, Stalin repeatedly demanded that the United States and Britain open a second front so that Germany would have to move some of its two hundred divisions on the eastern front to the western front, where it had twenty divisions. Roosevelt first promised Stalin to open a second front in the western part of Europe in 1942, but this was not done until June 6, 1944. This delay was caused by a number of factors, including a shortage of landing craft, but irrespective of the reasons, the delay caused deep resentment on the part of the Soviets. By the end of the war, distrust and suspicion characterized the relationship between the United States and Great Britain, on the one hand, and the Soviet Union, on the other.

When the United Sates bombed Hiroshima and Nagasaki, the military superiority of the United States was unquestioned, even though Stalin tried to dismiss nuclear weapons as simply "long-range artillery." What could the United States do to reassure the Soviets that nuclear weapons would not be used against them?

On September 11, 1945, one month after the bombings of Hiroshima and Nagasaki, Secretary of War Henry L. Stimson wrote a memo to President Truman:

> Dr. [sic] Mr. President,
>
>   In handing you today my memorandum about our relations with Russia in respect to the atomic bomb, I am not unmindful of the fact that when in Potsdam I talked with you about the question whether we could be safe in sharing the atomic bomb with Russia while she was still a police state. I still recognize the difficulty and am still convinced of the ultimate importance of a change in Russian attitude toward individual liberty but I have come to the conclusion that it would not be possible to use our possession of the atomic bomb as a direct lever to produce the change. I have become more convinced that any demand by us for an internal change in Russia as a condition of sharing the atomic weapon would be so resented that it would make the objective we have in view less probable.[14]

Stimson went on to argue that "unless the Soviets are voluntarily invited into the partnership on a basis of co-operation and trust, we are going to maintain the Anglo-Saxon bloc over against the Soviet [and that would result in] a secret armament race of a rather desperate character."[15]

McGeorge Bundy, who as a young man assisted Stimson in writing his memoirs, contends that Stimson was in favor of a three-power agreement with the United States, the Soviet Union, and the United Kingdom "to control and limit the use of the atomic bomb as an instrument of war."[16] He dismisses Stimson's idea of sharing nuclear weapons with the Soviet Union as something only casually and briefly mentioned to President Truman. Whether or not Stimson presented this idea seriously, it nevertheless stands as an alternative for dealing with nuclear weapons.

Curiously, the proposal to share nuclear weapons with the Soviet Union was revisited in modified form three decades later. In March 1983, President Ronald Reagan called for the development of a "Strategic Defense Initiative," which journalists, focusing on its space-based components, quickly dubbed "Star Wars." Reagan's idea was to develop a defensive system that would protect the United States and its population from a missile attack from the USSR or other countries. Such a system would require some of the most advanced technology that the United States possessed; one expert described the technical problems associated with missile defense as akin to "hitting a bullet with a bullet." Despite the level of technological sophistication, President

Reagan proposed to give the technology to the Soviets:

> If a defensive system could be found and developed that would reduce the utility of these [offensive missiles] or maybe even make them obsolete, then whenever that time came, a President of the United States would be able to say, "Now we have both the deterrent, the missiles—as we have had in the past, but now this other thing that has altered this—" And he could follow any one of a number of courses. He could offer to give that same defensive weapon to them to prove to them that there was no longer any need for keeping these missiles. Or with that defense, he could then say to them, "I am willing to do away with all my missiles. You do away with all of yours."[17]

The United States did not deploy missile-defense technologies until the early twenty-first century, almost twenty years after they were first proposed by President Reagan. By that time, there was no further talk of providing this technology to the state that succeeded the Soviet Union, Russia.

NUCLEAR WEAPONS SHOULD BE PLACED UNDER INTERNATIONAL CONTROL: THE BARUCH AND GROMYKO PLANS

In December 1945, a committee chaired by Under Secretary of State Dean Acheson was appointed to study policies related to nuclear energy, and the following month a group of consultants headed by David Lilienthal, then head of the Tennessee Valley Authority, was formed. After three months of work, the Acheson-Lilienthal Report was released; it called for the creation of an international authority to exercise control over all nuclear research and development. The proposed International Atomic Development Authority would also be granted the power to manage, license, and inspect all nuclear facilities. The proposal furthermore called for an agreement banning nuclear weapons and for the suspension of U.S. nuclear weapons production and development until the international authority was established.

In June 1946, the U.S. representative to the newly established United Nations Atomic Energy Commission, Bernard Baruch, presented a plan that incorporated the provisions of the Acheson-Lilienthal Report and called for the cessation of the manufacture of atomic weapons and the establishment of an international authority that would have a monopoly on nuclear research and development. If violations were charged against a member of the UN Security Council, the alleged violator would not be allowed to exercise its veto power in the Council. In addition, the Security Council would be allowed to impose, by majority vote, sanctions on violators.

The Soviet Union opposed the Baruch Plan, for several reasons. First, if accepted, the plan would have prohibited the USSR from ever developing nuclear weapons; in essence, the Soviet Union would have been frozen in a position of strategic inferiority vis-à-vis the United States. Second, perhaps recalling their treatment by their American and British allies in World War II, Soviet leaders believed that the international authority would be dominated by Western leaders who would be hostile toward the USSR. Last, the Soviets believed that the Baruch Plan would open Soviet borders to Western inspectors, some of whom would be spies. The Soviet Union had lost twenty-five million citizens in World War II and viewed outsiders with suspicion.

The Soviet representative to the UN, Andrei Gromyko, presented a Soviet counterproposal that called for the destruction of all stocks of nuclear weapons within three months of the signing of the agreement. Only after the destruction of all nuclear weapons would sanctions for violations of the agreement be established. Such sanctions would be administered by the UN Security Council and would be subject to the veto of any permanent member. This proposal was unacceptable to the United States.

The Baruch and Gromyko plans, the first efforts by the United States and USSR to achieve nuclear disarmament, failed for two principal reasons. First, the Soviet Union was unwilling to accept permanent inferiority relative to the United States, and second, the two sides had very different approaches concerning the verification of any potential agreement. When these negotiations failed, policy makers focused on finding means to manage the new, revolutionary weapons of mass destruction rather than turning them over to international control.

USE NUCLEAR WEAPONS TO DETER THE USE OF OTHER STATES' NUCLEAR AND CONVENTIONAL FORCES

If nuclear weapons could not be eliminated, they would have to be controlled. One of the oldest means of controlling weapons, as old as humanity, is to deter their use; the Roman maxim "If you want peace, prepare for war" is the quintessential statement of deterrence. The new weapons made deterrence all the more important.[18]

Nuclear strategists defined deterrence as the possession of sufficient power to inflict unacceptable damage on a potential aggressor. They considered the concept to be based on several fundamental assumptions. First, states were postulated to be the only important actors in international relations. Second, decision makers were presumed to be rational—that is, they would make decisions on a cost-benefit basis seeking to maximize benefits and minimize costs. In this sense, all decision makers, whatever their nationality, ideology, or ethnicity, would reach the same decisions when confronted with the same data. Third—and this is the fundamental assumption of deterrence—if a threat is sufficiently large and believable (or "credible," in the lexicon of deterrence theory), resort to war will be rejected. Fourth, deterrence views the severity of threats as a function of destructive capability—the greater the destructive capability, the greater the threat. According to this assumption, the number of nuclear weapons possessed by a state matters.

Over time, strategists (mostly civilian and American) developed theoretical notions related to deterrence. The mission of deterrence was important; it concerned the types of conflict that states sought to deter. When the Eisenhower administration announced its policy of "massive retaliation," by which the United States would "retaliate, instantly, by means and at places of our own choosing," many felt that this threat was not believable. Criticism came from a number of sources, including the strategic studies community (including B. H. Liddell Hart, Henry Kissinger, and William Kaufman), the military (Gen. Maxwell Taylor), and the political realm (John Kennedy).[19] During the 1960 presidential campaign, Senator Kennedy said:

> Under every military budget submitted by this [Eisenhower] Administration, we have been preparing primarily to fight the one kind of war we least want to fight and are least likely to fight. We have been driving ourselves into a corner where the only choice is all or nothing at all, world devastation or submission—a choice that necessarily causes us to hesitate on the brink and leaves the initiative in the hands of our enemies.[20]

After Kennedy became president in January 1961, his administration announced a new nuclear deterrence strategy, "flexible response."

Another important aspect of nuclear deterrence concerned the object of threat. In the Kennedy administration, there were debates among those who thought that people and cities were the most efficacious objects of threat, a targeting policy referred to as "countervalue," and others who thought that military bases and defense plants were the best targets, referred to as "counterforce" doctrine.

The last notion that was debated concerned the number of nuclear weapons needed to ensure effective deterrence. Early in his administration, President Kennedy ordered his secretary of defense, Robert McNamara, to determine how many nuclear weapons were enough to provide effective deterrence against a Soviet attack. McNamara had recruited a group of bright, young quantitative analysts, his "whiz kids," and they had determined that it was necessary to be able to kill 25 percent of the Soviet population and destroy 40 to 50 percent of the Soviet nation's industrial capacity to provide for effective deterrence. McNamara told the president that this level of destruction could be accomplished with two hundred intercontinental ballistic missiles (ICBMs) and that to be sure that all two hundred targets would be destroyed, two missiles would be assigned to each. The president then asked McNamara if he intended to request four hundred missiles from the Congress. McNamara responded that he recommended the president request a thousand ICBMs; if the president requested a smaller number, the administration would be "politically murdered."[21]

Throughout the Cold War, the United States and the Soviet Union had their nuclear weapons pointed at one another; they were, to use Robert Oppenheimer's analogy, like two scorpions trapped in a bottle. Despite the horrific potential for destruction in the Cold War era, deterrence was relatively straightforward. If the United States or the Soviet Union were attacked with nuclear weapons, the source of the attack could be identified and a retaliatory attack could be ordered.

With the advent and growth of nonstate actors in international relations, deterrence is no longer as simple and straightforward, a fact noted by President George W. Bush in his 2002 policy statement, *The National Security Strategy*: "New deadly challenges have emerged from rogue states and terrorists. None of these contemporary threats rival the sheer destructive power that was arrayed against us by the Soviet Union. Traditional concepts of deterrence will not work against a terrorist enemy whose avowed tactics are wanton destruction and the targeting of innocents."[22]

The president pointed to the challenges to deterrence theory raised by the emergency of terrorism. First, terrorists do not have territory that can be attacked. Second, they do not have an identifiable population that can be attacked. Third, terrorist leaders may not conform to the rational decision-making model on which deterrence theory is based.

PLACE QUANTITATIVE AND QUALITATIVE LIMITATIONS ON NUCLEAR WEAPONS: ARMS CONTROL

Nuclear weapons dramatically reduced the time required to cause death and destruction. Prior to the advent of missiles, it took hours for bombers to go from the United States to the USSR or vice versa. In August 1957, the Soviet Union tested the first ICBM. Thereafter, it would take thirty minutes for a missile to travel from the Soviet Union to the United States. Suddenly, the United States, which had been physically isolated from the destructiveness of Europe's wars, was vulnerable to attack, a fact that was underscored by an influential strategist, Albert Wohlstetter, in a noteworthy article arguing that American bombers were vulnerable to a preemptive attack.[23] Wohlstetter's warning struck a raw nerve with Americans, who remembered the surprise attack on Pearl Harbor. In the new world of intercontinental ballistic missiles, there were a number of ways in which nuclear war could start, including a surprise attack, as a result of an accident, or escalation from a conventional conflict.

In 1961, several books were published that called for the limitation of nuclear weapons.[24] These books constituted the foundation of a theory of arms control, whose essential feature, according to Thomas Schelling and Morton Halperin, was "the recognition of the common interest, of the possibility of reciprocation and cooperation even between potential enemies with respect to their military establishments."[25]

Until the Cuban missile crisis, nuclear war seemed to be a hypothetical possibility, the nightmare of nuclear strategists; however, in October 1962 the United States discovered a clandestine attempt by the Soviet Union to install nuclear missiles in Cuba, ninety miles from the shores of the United States. In response, President Kennedy demanded that Moscow remove the missiles. For a tension-filled thirteen days, the United States and USSR were on the brink of war. The crisis was resolved only when the United States made a public pledge not to sponsor an invasion of Cuba and a private pledge to remove its intermediate-range ballistic missiles from Italy and Turkey. It was as if Kennedy and the Soviet premier, Nikita Khrushchev, had gone to a precipice, looked into the abyss of possible nuclear war, and backed away.

In the aftermath of the Cuban missile crisis, the United States and USSR signed an agreement calling for the installation of a "hot line" between Washington, D.C., and Moscow. This provided the superpowers' leaders the ability to communicate quickly, reliably, and secretly, a capability that had been missing throughout the Cold War until then. A second arms control agreement was negotiated in a three-month period by the three existing nuclear powers: the United States, the USSR, and the United Kingdom. That instrument, the Limited Test Ban Treaty, prohibited its signatories from conducting nuclear tests in the atmosphere. At a minimum, this was a significant "clean air act,"[26] although many thought that it was more important as one of the first significant arms control agreements in the Cold War.

Other countries became concerned about the threats posed by various types of weapons and moved to place limits on them. For example, in the 1960s a number of states were concerned about the possible spread of nuclear weapons and negotiated the Non-Proliferation Treaty (see chapter 5 for details). In 1969 the United States and USSR opened negotiations to limit long-range nuclear weapons, the Strategic Arms Limitation Talks (SALT). The first SALT agreements—the Anti-Ballistic Missile (ABM) Treaty and an interim agreement on offensive arms—were signed in 1972, to be followed by a new round of negotiations called SALT II that resulted in an agreement in 1979. This agreement was signed, but not ratified, by the United States.[27]

The Strategic Arms Reduction Treaties, known by the acronym START, were two agreements designed to reduce the numbers of long-range nuclear weapons in the arsenals of the United States and the Soviet Union. In July 1991, President George H. W. Bush and his Soviet counterpart, Mikhail Gorbachev, concluded the first Strategic Arms Reduction Treaty (START I), which called for a one-third reduction in the number of nuclear warheads and bombs held by the United States and USSR.

When the Soviet Union disintegrated in December 1991, the status of the START I Treaty was called into question, because former Soviet long-range nuclear weapons were stationed in what had now become four independent states: Russia, Ukraine, Belarus, and Kazakhstan. The three non-Russian states agreed to ratify the START I Treaty and either destroy or turn over their nuclear weapons to Russia by 1999.

In January 1993, President George H. W. Bush and Russian President Boris Yeltsin of Russia signed the second Strategic Arms Reduction Treaty (START II), which called for reductions of 50 percent in the levels of weapons allowed by START I. If and when START II is fully implemented, the United States and Russia will be left with between 3,000 and 3,500 strategic nuclear weapons. To enter into force, START II must be ratified by the United States and Russia; further, Belarus, Ukraine, and Kazakhstan must ratify START I and the Non-Proliferation Treaty. The two START treaties call for the most significant reductions in long-range nuclear warheads and bombs of any arms control agreements ever concluded. If effectively implemented, they will result in the United States and Russia holding approximately one-quarter of the number of nuclear weapons previously possessed.

The George W. Bush administration adopted an approach to Russian-American strategic nuclear arms control that was radically different from those of previous administrations. Whereas the START I treaty was more than seven hundred pages long, the Strategic Offensive Reductions Treaty signed in Moscow in May 2002 was only three pages long and contained no verification means. It declared that the total number of strategic weapons was not to exceed 2,200 as of December 31, 2012.

During the Cold War, arms control had three principal objectives: (1) to reduce the probability of war occurring, (2) if war occurred to reduce the damage caused by war, and (3) to reduce the economic cost of preparing for war.[28] These objectives informed arms control efforts from the late 1950s to the end of the Cold War. To what extent are these objectives relevant in the post-9/11 environment?

Arms control remains vitally important, particularly concerning efforts to limit the spread of weapons of mass destruction. Russian-American efforts to limit their weapons, while not as important as they were during the Cold War, remain vital. During the Cold War, nuclear weapons threatened to cause a global cataclysm. That threat is no longer as great, although the capability remains. However, the possibility that weapons of mass destruction could be used is greater today than during the Cold War.

USE NUCLEAR WEAPONS TO FIGHT AND WIN WARS

Since the beginning of the nuclear age, some strategists and political leaders have argued that nuclear weapons are capable of accomplishing a number of different missions and that they should be used in support of U.S. national priorities. In the extreme, some have argued that the United States should have the capability to fight a nuclear war and prevail. This is referred to as a "nuclear war-fighting" strategy. The Reagan administration proposed this strategy and sought the capabilities to support it. Advocates of this approach argue that nuclear weapons can be used to compel as well as to deter other states; they point to the Soviet withdrawal from Iran in 1946 and the Korean armistice of 1953 as cases in which the threat of nuclear weapons played a role.

The option to use nuclear weapons for political or military purposes requires a large number and variety of weapons so that a number of different contingencies can be addressed. Advocates of this approach argue that even though nuclear weapons are the most powerful weapons ever invented, they do not increase a state's influence unless they are, in some sense, used. Paradoxically, to prepare to use nuclear weapons best ensures their nonuse. If, however, their use becomes necessary, the most militarily effective weapons should be used.

Opponents of this approach contend that the very act of envisioning the use of nuclear weapons, the most destructive weapons ever devised, makes their use more likely. In addition, if states deploy their weapons so that they are usable, they must make them usable within a short period of time. This "hair-trigger" situation is exceedingly dangerous.

The option of "fighting and winning" a nuclear war characteristic of the strategic policy of the Reagan administration has been resurrected by the George W. Bush administration in its call for a new class of nuclear weapons, "bunker busters."[29] In 2002, the administration called for funds to explore the possibility of developing a new earth-penetrating warhead that would be used to attack and destroy underground command bunkers. The administration argued that the conventional "bunker buster" bombs would not penetrate deeply enough to destroy some targets and that new nuclear weapons were needed to accomplish this mission. In addition, the administration called for research on new tactical nuclear weapons. Both of these initiatives would require that the United States resume testing nuclear weapons, which it has not done since 1988.

LIVING WITH NUCLEAR WEAPONS

Nuclear weapons are the most destructive weapons ever invented and used. As noted scholar John Steinbruner has said, "Even with the potential for a major strategic engagement with nature looming in the background, the pattern of nuclear weapons deployment remains the largest and most imminent physical threat to any and all human societies."[30] Because of the awesome potential of these weapons, a number of options have been proposed for dealing with them, ranging from never using them to employing them in contemporary military operations.

Arms control is an appropriate strategy only for those states whose relations are a mixture of cooperation and conflict; without cooperation arms control is impossible, but without conflict it is unnecessary. It was the genius of those responsible for the development of the arms control approach that within an extremely conflictual relationship they were able to build a useful theory on as narrow a basis for cooperation as the mutual desire to avoid nuclear war. The post–Cold War objectives of arms control will differ somewhat from the objectives associated with the initial arms control approach, because the underlying assumptions about the mixture of cooperation and conflict in international relations have changed. Where the desire to cooperate extends no farther than measures designed to avoid nuclear war, all that can reasonably be expected of arms control is assistance in preventing the parties from stumbling into a war that neither wants. But once a more cooperative relationship has been developed, the possibilities greatly increase.

Ivo Daalder has drawn upon this distinction in suggesting that the future of arms control may lie with "a cooperative approach, applicable to states with largely compatible political and security interests" rather than "a competitive approach, applicable to states with fundamentally different political and security interests." While "competitive arms control" has as its primary objective preventing war, "cooperative arms control" seeks to "transform political relations in a manner conducive to creating a pluralistic security community."[31]

Proponents of the arms control approach must also extend their focus beyond the nation-state to encompass nonstate actors in a world increasingly influenced by such actors. While the principal fear and focus of the Cold War concerned the

Soviet-American nuclear balance, today the focus is on the possibility of nuclear or other weapons of mass destruction falling into the hands of terrorists or rogue states. Concepts like deterrence and coercive diplomacy developed during the Cold War are only partially applicable to a world in which states are no longer the only, or even the major, political actors. In this new environment, it is vital to develop new ways of thinking about issues of security so that, as strategist Herman Kahn put it many years ago, the living will not envy the dead.

RECOMMENDED READING

Printed Sources

Brodie, Bernard. *Strategy in the Missile Age*. Princeton, N.J.: Princeton University Press, 1959.

Bundy, McGeorge. *Danger and Survival: Choices about the Bomb in the First Fifty Years*. New York: Random House, 1988.

Freedman, Lawrence. *The Evolution of Nuclear Strategy*, 3rd ed. New York: Palgrave Macmillan, 2003.

Larsen, Jeffrey A., ed. *Arms Control: Cooperative Security in a Changing Environment*. Boulder, Colo.: Lynne Rienner, 2002.

Mandelbaum, Michael. *The Nuclear Revolution: International Politics before and after Hiroshima*. Cambridge: Cambridge University Press, 1981.

Morgan, Patrick. *Deterrence Now*. Cambridge: Cambridge University Press, 2003.

Rhodes, Richard. *The Making of the Atomic Bomb*. New York: Simon and Schuster, 1986.

———. *Dark Sun: The Making of the Hydrogen Bomb*. New York: Simon and Schuster, 1996.

Websites

Arms Control Association: www.aca.org

National Defense University: www.ndu.edu.org

Natural Resources Defense Council: www.nrdc.org

Henry L. Stimson Center: www.stimson.org

Stockholm International Peace Research Institute (SIPRI): www.sipri.org/

Union of Concerned Scientists: www.ucsusa.org.

4

Bugs and Gas: Biological
and Chemical Weapons

Two weeks after 9/11, a letter containing a suspicious white powder arrived at NBC News in New York. After the powder was determined to be anthrax, over 1,300 NBC employees were tested for exposure and infection. One week later, in Boca Raton, Florida, Robert Stevens, a photo editor at American Media, entered the hospital with a high fever. Three days later he was dead of inhalation anthrax, America's first anthrax victim in a quarter of a century. Tests indicated that the strains of anthrax used in the two incidents had been identical.[1]

On October 14, 2001, a letter containing anthrax was opened in Senator Tom Daschle's office at the Capitol. After testing determined that approximately thirty congressional staffers had been exposed to anthrax, the House and Senate recessed while congressional office buildings were decontaminated. Mail addressed to Congress was held up for months as the U.S. Postal Service put in place an expensive system to irradiate all letters and packages sent to Capitol Hill, the Department of Defense, the CIA, and other government offices. Meanwhile, numerous postal workers in New Jersey and in the Washington, D.C., area were testing positive for exposure to anthrax. Two who worked in the Washington postal facility that handled congressional mail died in late October.

Initially, most Americans assumed the anthrax-laced letters were a new phase in the terrorist attack on the United States. In mid-October 2001, Vice President Dick Cheney even suggested that the anthrax might be linked to Osama bin Laden. Laboratory analysis, however, revealed that the anthrax sent to Senator Daschle's office had come from a strain developed in the United States and that the fineness of the particles were such that the sample could have been produced only in a highly sophisticated lab.

As evidence gathered by the FBI increasingly pointed in the direction of some disgruntled military lab worker at either the U.S. Army's Dugway Proving Ground in Utah or Fort Detrick in Maryland, the trail seemed to grow cold. Nine months after the U.S. Postal Service was virtually shut down along the East Coast due to bioterrorism, no prime suspects had been publicly identified. Barbara Rosenberg, director of the Federation of American Scientists' biological weapons monitoring program, suggested that the problem was not that the FBI knew too little but that it knew too much.[2] She speculated that the investigative trail led in a direction that, if pursued, would reveal that the United States had been violating both its international commitments under the Biological Weapons Convention and domestic law by secretly pursuing biological weapons research. Rosenberg's controversial hypothesis has still not been proved—or disproved. It is possible that the case simply reveals the extraordinary difficulty in tracing the origins of a well-conceived biological weapons attack.

The post-9/11 anthrax cases revealed an extremely potent new source of insecurity in a world that, for Americans at least, already seemed more threatening than ever before. Many Americans stocked up on Cipro and other antibiotics recommended for the treatment of anthrax. Many others rushed to doctors to check up on cold and flu symptoms that in previous autumns would have been stoically endured at home. Some stopped opening the mail. Ultimately, five people died as a direct result of the anthrax attacks. But the randomness of the fatalities (which included an elderly woman in Connecticut), the apparent lack of any effective preventative measures, and the failure of the FBI to find the perpetrator raised the frightening specter of a future in which the most powerful country on earth might be unable to protect its citizens from biological warfare.

The world was, in many ways, a very different place when chemical weapons first made an impact on modern warfare. Soon after World War I began with the assassination of the Archduke Franz Ferdinand in Sarajevo, chemical attacks began. In August 1914, it was tear gas used by the French against the Germans. Two months later, the Germans employed against the French a crude chemical compound that caused violent sneezing. These early experiments in chemical warfare were, however, mere child's play compared with what was to follow. In April 1915, in the Second Battle of Ypres, Germany used chlorine gas with devastating effect. Among the ten thousand casualties caused by the attack, five thousand died. In September 1915, at Loos, the British attempted to retaliate with chlorine gas of their own, but a shift in the wind caused the British to suffer as much from the attack as the Germans did.[3]

Undeterred by similar setbacks on all sides, the combatants escalated the use of chemical weapons. Chlorine gas was followed by phosgene, a gas with ten times the lethality of chlorine gas. Then came mustard gas, the most awful chemical agent used in the Great War. Mustard gas caused vomiting and serious blisters, both internally and externally. Those exposed to mustard gas often died agonizing deaths. Most survivors were seriously incapacitated—often blinded—for life.

In all, chemical weapons caused almost 1.3 million casualties, including close to a hundred thousand deaths, during World War I. It was a horrific experience that helped to create a strong taboo among states against the use of chemical weapons. But as devastating as man-made gases were during the Great War, disease quickly reasserted itself as the more efficient killer.

Typhus, which is sometimes called "war fever" because of its common association with wartime conditions, spread through Eastern Europe and Russia during and after the war. The disease, a form of rickettsia spread by body lice, was one of the principal causes of the destruction of Napoleon's Grand Army on its ill-fated march into Russia. Of the 422,000 French soldiers who began that campaign, only ten thousand remained to return to France. In 1915, 150,000 people died of the disease in Serbia alone. From 1918 to 1922, typhus infected as many as thirty million people and claimed as many as three million victims in Eastern Europe and Russia.[4]

As the war came to an end in 1918, pandemic influenza began circling the globe. Known as the Spanish influenza, not because of its place of origin (which was China) but because it affected 80 percent of the population of Spain, the pandemic quickly killed as many as one hundred million people around the world.[5] It first hit the United States when two sailors reported ill in Boston. Spreading rapidly up and down the East Coast, the flu eventually affected almost a quarter of the U.S. population. Half a million Americans died, hospitals were filled to overflowing, and, in Baltimore and Washington, there were shortages of coffins.[6]

The pandemic was by no means confined to the United States or even to the Northern Hemisphere. Between September and November 1918, 5 percent of the population of Ghana died of influenza. Almost all of the thirty-eight thousand people living in Western Samoa got the flu in November and December of 1918; 7,500 died of it.[7] What does the use of poison gas in World War I have in common with the spread of the Spanish influenza following the war—other than, of course, extreme lethality? In a better world, one in which technological advances were not linked so often to security threats, perhaps there would be no link. Unfortunately, the same motives that led the Germans, French, and British to use, collectively, over a hundred thousand tons of gas in World War I would lead others to begin using bugs as weapons. After all, there is no need to manufacture gas (not to mention conventional bombs and bullets) if one can spread among the enemy population a disease that will be just as effective at sowing death and destruction. Some in the world today continue to operate on the basis of this proposition—and they know a whole lot more about disease than anyone knew in 1918.

THINKING ABOUT WMD

The ominous phrase *weapons of mass destruction* (or simply WMD) refers not only to the nuclear weapons discussed in the previous chapter but to biological and chemical weapons as well. Nuclear, biological, and chemical weapons can threaten our security in ways that appear genuinely apocalyptic. There are significant differences between nukes on the one hand and bugs and gas on the other. Unfortunately, the differences are ones that complicate rather than simplify the job of seeking security against WMD.

What nuclear, biological, and chemical weapons (NBC weapons, to defense analysts) have in common is, first, the potential to kill millions of people quickly and with disturbing ease. Second, each type of weapon in the WMD category is especially difficult (some might say virtually impossible, at least when civilian populations are the target) to defend against. Third, each of these types of weapons has only limited value to those governments and armies that respect the laws of war, with their prohibitions against indiscriminate killing. In fact, as we saw in the last chapter with respect to nuclear weapons, governments have regarded nuclear weapons as being useful primarily, if not exclusively, for deterrence. However, the indiscriminate and seemingly unlimited lethality of nuclear, biological, and chemical weapons make them particularly attractive to those who neither bear the responsibility of protecting a state and its citizens nor respect the rules that sometimes keep states from committing mass murder. In other words, the very qualities that make weapons of mass destruction troublesome for states make them attractive to terrorists desiring to kill large numbers of innocents.

Western thinking about WMD and the threat such weapons pose have changed dramatically since the end of the Cold War. During the Cold War, politicians, soldiers, strategists, and many ordinary citizens worried constantly about the threat posed by WMD, particularly the large numbers of strategic nuclear weapons that the Soviet Union and the United States kept aimed at each other. With the collapse of the Soviet Union, what had seemed to be a permanent nuclear confrontation was brought to a peaceful end; for a time, defense budgets decreased and worries about WMD disappeared. Peace had arrived.

The post–Cold War sense of security was short-lived; new WMD threats quickly emerged. North Korea, one of just a handful of states that had failed to respond to the message that communist dictatorships were a thing of the past, was in pursuit of nuclear weapons and in possession of ballistic missiles. The apparent hostility and irrationality of North Korea's leadership made its possession of nuclear weapons a troublesome prospect, to say the least. Even more troubling, however, was Iraq. Where North Korea's capability and intent with respect to the use of WMD was a matter of speculation, Iraq's was a matter of fact. During the 1980s, Iraq used chemical weapons in its war against Iran and against Kurdish rebels in its own territory.[8] Iraq's defeat in the Persian Gulf War in 1991 and the subsequent imposition of United Nations weapons inspectors brought to light just how eagerly Saddam Hussein had been seeking nuclear and biological weapons to go along with his chemical weapons.

Thanks in large part to North Korea and Iraq, WMD concerns in the West during the 1990s focused on the problem of "rogue states." Fears of an apocalyptic nuclear exchange signaling the failure of deterrence between the superpowers were replaced with fears of limited nuclear, chemical, or biological attacks launched by a state led by an undeterrable dictator. As Richard K. Betts of Columbia University put it in a 1998 *Foreign Affairs* article, "There is less danger of complete annihilation, but more danger of mass destruction."[9]

In the aftermath of 9/11, WMD fears shifted again. Concern has been focused on the possibility that either a rogue state or terrorists might acquire and use WMD.

Indeed, the Al Qaeda attacks on the World Trade Center and the Pentagon were intended to, and actually did, achieve a measure of mass destruction unprecedented in the history of terrorist attacks. The weapons of mass destruction used, of course, were commercial airliners, with two hundred thousand pounds of fuel on board. In thinking about WMD, the significance of 9/11 was to remove any doubt there might have been that a terrorist organization such as Al Qaeda would use nuclear, chemical, or biological weapons if it had them. In fact, Osama bin Laden has told his followers that the acquisition of WMD is a "religious duty."

At this point, it is worth recalling our discussion in chapter 1 of threats as products of capabilities and intentions. In spite of dramatic cuts in their arsenals, the United States and Russia continue to dwarf all other international actors in their WMD capabilities. But because their intentions toward each other are now benign, their WMD capabilities pose very little threat to each other. Rogue states—or, as they have been labeled more recently by the U.S. government, "states of concern"—have vastly smaller WMD capabilities than the United States and Russia, but because we cannot assume benign intentions, they constitute a clear threat to our security. Finally, terrorist organizations such as Al Qaeda are almost certainly farther from being able to use nuclear, chemical, or biological weapons than most rogue states, and yet since 9/11 we have had little doubt about the malevolence of their intentions. As a result, the least significant WMD capability at present may be the threat we must worry about most. After all, when seeking security, we must always ask, "What if?"

CHEMICAL WEAPONS

Among those who worry about chemical and biological weapons (CBW), biological weapons are currently thought to be the more serious threat. Consequently, let us begin with chemical weapons, in an effort to ease into a topic that even the experts—or, perhaps, especially the experts—find sobering.

Poison-tipped arrows, incendiary bombs, smoke (to hide troop movements), and hot oil or sewage dumped onto attackers from castle walls were the precursors of modern chemical warfare. Chemical weapons in the modern sense, however, had to await the Industrial Age and the development of modern chemical production processes. The use of tear gas and various poison gases during World War I marked the beginning of modern chemical warfare, but it almost marked the end as well, because revulsion at the use of the new weapons was so widespread. Unfortunately, in spite of remarkable restraint by all parties during World War II (although we must not forget the Nazis' use of poison gas in concentration camps and the use of chemical agents by the Italian and Japanese armies in their imperial wars), chemical weapons have not disappeared as a security threat.

Chemical weapons can be broadly defined as toxic manufactured gases, liquids, or powders that are designed to incapacitate or kill humans. There are four basic categories of chemical weapons: (1) choking agents, such as chlorine and phosgene, which damage lung tissue and make breathing impossible; (2) blood agents, such as hydrogen cyanide, which prevent the flow of oxygen in the bloodstream; (3) blister agents, such as mustard gas, which cause chemical burns on skin and all other contacted body tissue, both internal and external; and (4) nerve agents, such as sarin and VX, which disrupt the central nervous system. Chemical weapons of all types are generally spread as liquids (especially in aerosol form) or gases (sometimes as vapors produced by a liquid compound).

Chemical weapons do not produce the same fear that biological weapons do, for several reasons. The effective delivery of chemical weapons depends in large part on environmental conditions. Chemical compounds that are delivered as aerosols or gases are easily dispersed by wind. In some cases, chemical weapons are rendered less effective, if not completely inert, by hot or cold temperatures. Furthermore (and in part because of these environmental factors), large quantities of chemical agents are often necessary to inflict even modest death tolls. A study in 1993 by the Congressional Office of Technology Assessment found that a ton of sarin might cause three to eight thousand deaths if used in *ideal* conditions in a highly populated area.[10] The Aum Shinrikyo sarin attack in the Tokyo subway system in 1995 injured or psychologically traumatized as many as five thousand people, but only twelve were killed. Admittedly, both the technology and the tactics employed in that attack were very crude, but it is worth noting that the use of chemical weapons in World War I resulted in less than one death per ton of gas.

Therefore, and although many governments have invested heavily in chemical weapons over the years, a terrorist organization seeking the maximum lethal impact would look to other weapons. On the other hand, chemical weapons are cheap and easy to produce. Large-scale manufacturing can be hidden amid legitimate commercial processes in dual-use factories. Raw materials are plentiful and easily obtained. Except when accidents occur, chemical weapons can be easily transported without detection. Furthermore, clouds of gas or unseen vapors that produce painful choking deaths, hideous blisters on exposed skin, or muscle twitching followed by rapid death are likely to be highly effective if the purpose of an attack is to induce terror in a civilian population.

Broadly speaking, there are two basic scenarios in which chemical weapons might be used. The first involves state action, most likely in connection with combat operations. The second is a terrorist attack. Actual cases of the military use of chemical weapons occurred in World War I, in various colonial wars (by the British in Afghanistan and by the Spanish and French in Africa), in Ethiopia (by the Italians during the 1930s), in China (by the Japanese during the 1930s), and in the Iran-Iraq War.

Between 1980 and 1988, Iran and Iraq fought a grim war noteworthy primarily for the number of casualties and the senselessness of the human slaughter that occurred. Altogether, the war caused over a million casualties. Perhaps not surprisingly, chemical weapons were used more extensively in the Iran-Iraq War than at any time since World War I. Iraq was the chief culprit, but Iran almost certainly used chemical weapons as well. Allegations concerning Iraqi use of chemical weapons surfaced early in the war, but international observers were unable to provide confirmation until 1984, when UN personnel determined that the Iraqi military had employed mustard gas and a nerve agent called tabun. Many other incidents were reported, but independent sources were unable to confirm most of them. Charges of chemical weapons use were part of both sides' propaganda during the war. Nevertheless, chemical attacks by Iraq were confirmed on various occasions in 1985, in February 1986, and in April 1987. In 1987, investigators found evidence of exposure to mustard gas among Iraqi troops, but it was unclear whether the exposure had been the result of an Iranian or an Iraqi attack.[11]

Beginning in April 1987 and continuing on to October 1988, at the same time that Saddam Hussein's Revolutionary Guard was fighting Iran, Baghdad conducted a campaign of extermination against ethnic Kurds in northern Iraq. Four thousand Kurdish villages were razed, and somewhere between 50,000 and 180,000 Kurds were killed. Chemical weapons were used as part of the genocidal campaign.

In March 1988, after Kurdish rebels moved into the predominantly Kurdish city of Halabja in northern Iraq, Iraqi planes dropped large numbers of chemical bombs over the course of several days. In what was likely an attack intended by Saddam Hussein both to push forward the genocidal campaign against the Kurds and to test Iraq's chemical warfare capabilities, a variety of chemical weapons, including mustard gas, sarin, tabun, and VX, were dropped on the city. An estimated three to five thousand civilians were killed in the attack; tens of thousands more were injured. Since the chemical attacks on Halabja and sixty other Kurdish towns, abnormally high rates of cancer, respiratory disease, birth defects, and infertility have been reported.[12]

The primary example of the use of a chemical weapon in a terrorist attack up until now is the March 1995 Aum Shinrikyo attack on the Tokyo subway using the nerve agent sarin. Aum Shinrikyo (Supreme Truth), an apocalyptic cult founded in 1984 by Shoko Asahara, prophesied a global Armageddon during which the group would take over and govern a Japan devastated by a U.S. nuclear attack.[13] Around 1990, when cult members were defeated in Japanese parliamentary elections and the Japanese government began to investigate some of the cult's business deals for possible fraud, the group began to pursue weapons of mass destruction.

Through businesses owned by the cult, donations from cult members, and almost certainly fraud as well, Aum Shinrikyo amassed assets believed to have been in the neighborhood of a billion dollars in 1995. The organization used its wealth as well as the scientific expertise of many young, highly educated cult members to establish labs for the production of both chemical and biological weapons. Biological weapons came first. In the early 1990s the group is believed to have produced botulinum toxin, anthrax, and Q fever. The effort to produce chemical weapons began in 1993 and, after experiments with other nerve agents, focused on sarin.

In early 1994, according to Japanese prosecutors, Aum Shinrikyo began building a manufacturing plant designed to produce up to two tons of sarin a day. Although equipment failures and police investigations prevented the group from reaching its chemical weapons production goal, the demonstrated potential was alarming.

Between 1990 and 1995, Aum Shinrikyo members attempted on ten separate occasions to disseminate biological agents in Tokyo and the surrounding areas, including U.S. Navy bases. For a variety of reasons ranging from a failure of nerve on the part of operatives to poor bacterial strains, not a single casualty resulted from any of these attacks using biological agents. Consequently, the group began to focus on chemical weapons.

The use of sarin in an assassination attempt in 1993 failed, nearly killing the assailant. In June 1994, in the town of Matsumoto, the cult targeted three judges who were set to rule in a land fraud case involving Aum Shinrikyo. Late at night, for ten minutes, seven cult members sprayed vaporized sarin at the judges' living quarters. Seven people were killed and 144, including all three judges, were injured in the attack. The cult's deadliest and most notorious attack, however, came nine months later.

On March 20, 1995, five cult members carrying eleven doubled plastic bags containing a low-grade sarin solution converged on separate subway trains on the Tokyo station closest to the Tokyo police headquarters. At the height of the Monday morning rush hour, the cultists punctured the bags on the floors of the subway cars in which they were riding and fled when their respective trains reached the station. As the sarin solution evaporated, passengers on the trains experienced vomiting, respiratory problems, seizures, and other signs of sarin poisoning. Trains containing the deadly vapors continued on their way from station to station—one for an hour and a half—before the system was closed down and cleanup began.

Twelve people died in the attack. Initial reports indicated that five thousand others were injured in the attack, but according to Japanese officials, three-fourths of the approximately five thousand people examined in hospitals following the attack showed no signs of exposure to sarin. The actual number of people with physical injuries appears to have been closer to one thousand than to the figure of 3,938 cited by Japanese prosecutors, but the larger number of people reporting to hospitals suggests that psychological trauma may have affected far more people than were physically affected.

It is possible to view the Aum Shinrikyo attack on the Tokyo subway system as evidence that chemical weapons attacks are not as easy to mount as is often supposed. In fact, there *are* significant obstacles to terrorist organizations hoping to use chemical weapons as weapons of mass destruction. Most analysts, however, view the Aum Shinrikyo sarin attack with alarm, preferring to see it as a wake-up call. The cult, after all, had invested considerable resources in developing chemical and biological weapons and, over time, learned a number of lessons about what would and would not work. Just as those charged with defending society have learned a great deal from the March 1995 chemical attack, so too have those who are interested in using weapons of mass destruction against free societies. One of the lessons that terrorist organizations may have learned from Aum Shinrikyo is that biological weapons may have certain advantages over chemical weapons.

BIOLOGICAL WEAPONS

Human beings, as a species, have waged an epic struggle against disease from the beginning. (We examine this struggle in chapter 6.) Long before modern science began to uncover the role that microbes—viruses and bacteria—play in disease, some unscrupulous warriors sought to make disease their ally. One of the most notorious cases of primitive biological warfare may have been partially responsible for the Black Death that devastated Europe in the fourteenth century.

By 1340, traders operating between China and Europe had begun to carry the rat-borne fleas by which the bubonic plague from China was transmitted. In 1343, some Genoese merchants were attacked by Tartars at the Crimean trading post of Kaffa. The merchants saved themselves from the conventional Tartar attack by retreating behind the walls of Kaffa, but before the Tartars withdrew they catapulted plague-infested corpses over the walls. Some merchants subsequently died of the plague on their way home, but others survived to transmit the disease to Constantinople, Genoa, and Venice. From these commercial hubs the Black Death spread all over Europe, by 1351 killing at least one-quarter of Europe's population.[14]

Some native Americans were victims of a deliberate effort to spread disease during the French and Indian Wars. Sir Jeffrey Amherst, the commander of British forces in the war, ordered that smallpox-infested blankets be delivered to tribes loyal to the French in the Ohio River Valley. Whether the infected blankets were directly responsible is unknown, but smallpox did devastate several tribes soon thereafter.[15]

It was not until 1870 that biologists were able to prove that microorganisms cause disease. (Oddly enough, given its current significance as a biowarfare agent, the decisive experiment involved injecting anthrax into mice.) From that time on, it was possible to contemplate biological warfare in different terms, without the need to use corpses or infected materials as carriers of disease. Eventually, the disease-causing microbes—pathogens—themselves could be isolated and "weaponized."

Modern biological weapons employ living microorganisms, such as viruses and bacteria, or toxins produced by living organisms, to incapacitate or kill. Bacteria, viruses, and rickettsia are the three categories of microorganisms used as biological agents. Each type of microorganism produces a distinctive set of diseases. Bacterial diseases, which include anthrax, plague, and tularemia (rabbit fever), generally produce flu-like symptoms initially and are treatable with antibiotics. Anthrax and tularemia are not contagious; plague is. Among the rickettsia are Q fever, which is rarely fatal, and typhus. Both are treatable with antibiotics. Viruses include smallpox and yellow fever. Following a global campaign of vaccination coordinated by the World Health Organization, smallpox was declared in 1980 to have been eradicated, but stocks of the smallpox virus were kept for research purposes by the United States and the Soviet Union. The existence of these stocks, combined with the fact that the smallpox vaccine is no longer routinely administered (or even widely available), makes many defense and public health officials worried about the reappearance of smallpox as a biological weapon.

Unlike microbes, toxins are nonliving substances. They are considered to be biological weapons because they are derived from living organisms, such as molds and fungi. Because they are not living organisms, toxins do not reproduce or spread through contagion the way other biological agents do. As a result, toxins have more in common with chemical agents than with biological agents. Some biological toxins can even be chemically synthesized.

In order to produce mass casualties, the microorganisms or toxins that make up biological weapons must be widely dispersed. Contagion—that is, the spread of disease from person to person—can play a role, at least in the case of a number of pathogens. Smallpox, for example, is highly contagious. In the case of bacteria that do not spread from person to person, or in the case of toxins, however, mass casualties can be produced only by using means of delivery that cause the biological agent to come in contact with large numbers of people. This generally means creating an aerosol spray with a liquid containing the biological agent. When prepared properly, such an aerosol is likely to be tasteless, odorless, and invisible. As a result, victims of a biological weapons attack may not know what has happened until well after symptoms have begun to develop.

The time frame for the appearance of symptoms following a biological weapons attack depends on the bacteria, rickettsia, or virus used. The incubation period for smallpox is from ten to fourteen days, and for plague from one to six days. Botulism has an incubation period of from twelve to seventy-two hours. Q fever, on the other hand, has an incubation period of from two to three weeks. Further complicating the ability of defense and public health officials to know that a biological weapons attack has occurred is the fact that disease symptoms, when they finally appear, are likely to be mistaken for symptoms that would accompany naturally occurring illnesses. Consequently, the first people to have evidence that a biological attack had occurred might be hospital lab technicians, public health epidemiologists, pharmacists, or even funeral directors. This is one reason that the United States government after 9/11 attempted to vaccinate all emergency-room workers with the smallpox vaccine.

Most microorganisms that might be used as biowarfare agents present special problems where "weaponization" is concerned. Some are killed by ultraviolet radiation and are therefore not suitable for use outdoors during the day. Most require extraordinarily careful handling to avoid the infection of lab workers or people living close to labs. In 1979, in Sverdlovsk (now Ekaterinburg), anthrax was accidentally released from a Soviet biological weapons lab. Sixty-four people died from what Soviet officials originally suggested was an anthrax outbreak caused by contaminated meat.

In spite of the tragedy at Sverdlovsk, anthrax is thought to be one of the biological agents best suited for use as a weapon. It is extraordinarily hardy, capable in nature of surviving in the soil fully exposed to the elements for decades. It can be freeze-dried, which means it can be milled into an extremely fine powder that, like the anthrax sent to Capitol Hill in September and October 2001, can be suspended in the air like particles of dust. In this form it can easily be inhaled. From the lungs, anthrax enters the bloodstream and is often lethal. The previously cited 1993 study by the Office of

Technology Assessment concluded that an airplane spraying 220 pounds of anthrax spores over Washington, D.C., on a calm night would kill between one million and three million people.

The potential for biological warfare using only what nature provides in the way of pathogens is bad enough, but genetic engineering offers some truly horrifying possibilities. Dr. Ken Alibeck, who was First Deputy Director of the Soviet Union's biological weapons program from 1988 until his defection to the United States in 1992, has noted that Moscow's illegal biowarfare program had genetically modified anthrax to make it resistant to treatment using antibiotics.[16] Recombinant DNA technologies take the threat to another level. Imagine, for example, being able to make the deadly Ebola virus spread itself from person to person as easily as influenza. The creation of such diabolical diseases is no longer simply a sinister fantasy.

Biological weapons pose a particularly significant threat due to certain characteristics, some of which are unique and some of which are shared with other weapons of mass destruction. First, unlike nuclear weapons, for example, biological weapons can be produced without a large supporting industrial infrastructure. A typical college or even high school laboratory could be used to produce biological weapons. This leads to a second characteristic, low production cost. Third, biological weapons are accessible to rogue states and terrorist groups, a characteristic related to ease of manufacture, low production cost, and the relative ease with which clandestine manufacture and shipment can occur. While sophisticated systems like missiles or bombs can be used to deliver biological weapons, they are not required. Thus, ease of delivery is a fourth threat-enhancing characteristic of biological weapons. Fifth, the extraordinary lethality of many types of biological weapons makes them especially worrisome. Sixth, these weapons are very small; an anthrax spore may be just one to five microns in diameter, which is one fiftieth the width of a human hair.

Because biological weapons can be produced without a significant industrial infrastructure, their proliferation is likely to be both cheaper and more easily hidden than other kinds of weapons of mass destructions. Dual-use technology makes hiding a biological weapons program easier than hiding a nuclear weapons program or, in some instances, chemical weapons production. For example, fermenters are required to produce biological weapons in large quantities, and one might be tempted to conclude that the presence of a fermenter provides evidence that someone is trying to produce biological weapons. The problem with this approach is that fermenters are commonly used in the biotechnology, pharmaceutical, and even beer-manufacturing processes.

A study produced by the Carnegie Endowment for International Peace in 2002 listed twelve countries suspected of having biological weapons capabilities and eleven suspected of chemical weapons capabilities. Both lists included China, Egypt, India, Iran, Iraq, Israel, Libya, North Korea, Pakistan, Sudan, and Syria. Russia was on the list of biological weapons suspects only.[17] Following the U.S. invasion of Iraq, which was justified by the Bush administration on the grounds that Iraq possessed weapons of mass destruction, Saddam Hussein's regime was found not to have any

WMD capabilities. Beginning in late 2004, Iran was under the scrutiny of the United States and the European Union due to suspicions that it was developing nuclear weapons. Meanwhile, North Korea announced in February 2005 that it possessed nuclear weapons.

What possible motivation could there be for the use of chemical or biological weapons? The incentives—and disincentives—are different for countries and for nonstate actors.[18] A country contemplating a CBW attack against another country must expect, first, retaliation in kind if the victim of the initial attack has access to weapons of mass destruction. Second, it must expect the strong condemnation of the international community for violating well-established norms against the use of such weapons. For nonstate actors, such as terrorist organizations, rebel armies, or individual crackpots, the calculus is different. Retaliation in kind may not be possible, particularly if the person or organization using the weapon cannot be identified. As we have noted, an intentional release of deadly microbes would be followed by an incubation period of somewhere between a few days and a few weeks before the appearance of disease symptoms. Since even the onset of observable signs of disease might initially be assumed to have resulted from natural causes, individuals or groups employing biological weapons might well have time to go deep underground before their attack becomes obvious. The problem of deterrence (or, if deterrence fails, retaliation) is made even worse in the case of cults or terrorist organizations that have an apocalyptic worldview (as Aum Shinrikyo does) or readily accept the possibility of martyrdom (as in the case of Al Qaeda). Because deterring the use of WMD by such groups seems unlikely, preventing them from acquiring (or maintaining) a WMD capability is imperative. For these reasons, soon after the 9/11 attacks, Lord Robertson, who at the time was NATO's secretary general, said, "Deterrence worked for forty years of Cold War. It failed on September 11th."

In May 1996, John Deutch, who was then Director of Central Intelligence, suggested that "proliferation of nuclear, biological, and chemical weapons and their potential use by states or terrorists is the most urgent challenge facing the national security, and therefore the intelligence community, in the post–Cold War world."[19]

ADDRESSING THE THREAT

The threats described in this chapter do indeed present an urgent challenge. For the individual citizen, responses to the threat posed by bugs and gas begin with simply learning more about the threat and preparing to deal with it. In crisis-prone areas, study after study has found that those individuals who are better informed are more likely to deal with the crisis more effectively. For example, officials who conducted studies after the 1994 Northridge quake in California found that those who prepared for the earthquake were less likely to be injured. Similar results have been found in hurricane-prone areas. Based on these findings, it makes sense to understand and prepare for chemical and biological terrorist attacks.

Unfortunately, some people in the world have been forced to prepare for such attacks. Israel is a small state surrounded by a number of threatening neighbors, and in the past there have been fears that Israel would be attacked with chemical or biological weapons. For example, in the 1991 Gulf war many feared that Saddam Hussein would use chemical weapons in the Scud missile attacks on Israel. To prepare for such attacks, the Israeli government distributed gas masks to all Israeli citizens and taught them how to use the masks effectively. Iraq did not use chemical weapons, but the Israelis were nevertheless prepared.

The attacks on 9/11 caused the U.S. government to reassess its preparations for a follow-on terrorist attack on the United States. One of the items that has been added to the homeland security agenda is civil defense preparations for a possible weapons of mass destruction attack on the United States. The greatest fear of most experts on terrorism is a WMD attack on the United States, and most favor a robust civil defense program in response. The elements of such a program include the stockpiling or distribution of protective masks or clothing; equipment and training for decontamination; vaccinations for diseases used as biological weapons, such as smallpox; stockpiling of antibiotics for the treatment of outbreaks of contagions (e.g., stockpiling Cipro to treat anthrax); planning and training of emergency personnel for dealing with the use of WMD; and public education programs to increase understanding of the dangers and possible responses to weapons of mass destruction.

None of these topics is pleasant to think about, but advance planning could literally make the difference between life and death. For example, Israeli citizens are taught how to keep one room of their homes airtight in the event of a chemical or biological attack by taping plastic over the windows and doors. Poison gases and toxic biological agents dissipate within hours; if individuals can avoid exposure during the immediate aftermath of an attack, they run a much smaller risk of suffering injury. At present, few Americans know this fact, and fewer still have made any preparations for a chemical or biological attack.

Beyond the actions of individuals and the U.S. government, the international community has addressed these issues and will undoubtedly continue to do so in the future. The 1899 Hague Convention prohibited the use in war of projectiles containing poison gas. In response to the horrors of chemical warfare during World War I, the international community negotiated the 1925 Geneva Protocol for the Prohibition of the Use of Asphyxiating, Poisonous or Other Gases, and Bacteriological Methods of Warfare. The United States and Japan failed to ratify the treaty before World War II broke out; during the war, President Roosevelt stated, "Use of such [chemical and biological] weapons has been outlawed by the general opinion of civilized mankind. This country has not used them, and I hope we never will be compelled to use them. I state categorically that we shall under no circumstances resort to the use of such weapons unless they are first used by our enemies."

The Geneva Protocol was observed but not ratified by the United States until 1975. It was supplemented in 1992 with the Chemical Weapons Convention (CWC), an international agreement that strictly limits the production and stockpiling of chemical weapons. Over 140 countries have ratified the CWC, which entered into force in 1997. Although the United States stopped manufacturing chemical weapons in 1968, thirty thousand tons of chemical agents remained in its military stockpile at the end of the Cold War. Beginning in 1996, the U.S. Army began incinerating chemical weapons in a specially designed facility at Tooele, Utah.

Although most people have never even heard of it, a treaty banning the production and stockpiling of biological weapons was signed in 1972 by President Richard Nixon. To date, this treaty has been ratified by more than 140 countries and is a significant statement by the international community opposing biological weapons.

While the Chemical Weapons Convention and the Biological and Toxin Weapons Convention may help to reduce the number of countries running chemical and biological weapons programs (and thus the number of weapons of mass destruction that could fall into the hands of terrorist organizations), neither agreement can guarantee our security against the threats posed by nonstate actors. To ensure our security, therefore, we must continue to think creatively about not only limiting the capabilities of those who might wish to do us harm but about changing their intentions as well. In the end, peace and security require more than defensive responses to the threats we perceive.

RECOMMENDED READING

Printed Sources

Falkenrath, Richard A., Robert D. Newman, and Bradley A. Thayer. *America's Achilles Heel: Nuclear, Biological, and Chemical Terrorism and Covert Attack*. Cambridge, Mass.: MIT Press, 1998.

Garrett, Laurie. *The Coming Plague: Newly Emerging Diseases in a World out of Balance*. New York: Penguin Books, 1994.

———. "The Nightmare of Bioterrorism." *Foreign Affairs* 80 (January/February 2001): 76–89.

Mangold, Tom, and Jeff Goldberg. *Plague Wars: The Terrifying Reality of Biological Warfare*. New York: St. Martin's Griffin, 1999.

Miller, Judith, Stephen Engelberg, and William Broad. *Germs: Biological Weapons and America's Secret War*. New York: Simon and Schuster, 2001.

Websites

Federation of American Scientists, Chemical and Biological Arms Control Program: www.fas .org/main/content.jsp?formAction=325&projectId=4

Centers for Disease Control and Prevention: www.cdc.gov.

5

The Proliferation of Weapons of Mass Destruction: Spreading Insecurity?

Following the first Gulf war in 1991, United Nations inspectors discovered that an Iraqi official had secretly hidden 650,000 pages of material concerning biological weapons on a chicken farm outside of Baghdad. After examining these materials, the inspectors realized that Iraq had developed both a defensive and an offensive biological weapons program, that it had weaponized biological agents and had loaded them into 166 bombs and twenty-five missile warheads.[1]

In April 1999, Ayman al-Zawahiri, Osama bin Laden's deputy and a trained medical doctor, wrote a memo to Muhammad Atef, Al Qaeda's military commander, in which he proposed a secret program to develop biological and chemical weapons:

> The enemy started thinking about these weapons before WWI [World War I]. Despite their extreme danger, we only became aware of them when the enemy drew our attention to them by repeatedly expressing concerns that they can be produced simply with easily available materials. The destructive power of these weapons is no less than that of nuclear weapons. A germ attack is often detected days after it occurs, which raises the number of victims. Defense against such weapons is very difficult, particularly if large quantities are used.[2]

In 2003, a Russian businessman offered $750,000 to any Russian weapons scientist who would provide him with weapons-grade plutonium for a foreign client. The businessman was successful in contacting residents of Sarov, a city closed to outsiders by the Russian government because it had been the home of the Soviet Union's top nuclear weapons design laboratories. Fortunately, scam artists sold the businessman a canister of mercury rather than plutonium, but the episode raised the possibility of nuclear weapons materials being sold to the highest bidder.[3]

These cases demonstrate that one does not need to be Tom Clancy or a Hollywood scriptwriter to imagine the ways in which rogue states or terrorist groups might use weapons of mass destruction to cause catastrophic destruction and many deaths. Virtually every top American governmental official from President George W. Bush down has predicted that a second major terrorist attack against the United States is all but inevitable; the question is when, not if, a follow-on attack to 9/11 will occur. In their comments on the 9/11 Commission's final report, Chairman Thomas Kean noted that every expert whom the commission met had predicted a second major attack. Although the human and economic losses caused by the attacks of September 11, 2001, were enormous, they could have been much, much worse had weapons of mass destruction been used. Imagine, for example, if the airplanes that struck the World Trade Center and the Pentagon had carried radioactive materials or, worse yet, nuclear weapons. The devastation would have been incalculably worse. According to a Harvard University study, "A bomb with the explosive power of 10,000 metric tons of TNT (smaller than the Hiroshima bomb), if set off in midtown Manhattan on a typical workday, could kill half a million people and cause over $1 trillion in direct economic damage."[4]

The goal of reducing the risks that weapons of mass destruction (WMD) will be used is pursued via two principal means, nonproliferation and counterproliferation. The Non-Proliferation Treaty, the Chemical Weapons Convention, and the Biological Weapons Convention all seek to prevent the spread of weapons of mass destruction. They are characteristic of nonproliferation. The other major approach, counterproliferation, seeks to destroy or neutralize the threat of WMD. In this chapter, we will review the historical attempts to limit the spread of WMD and the contemporary threats posed by these weapons, and suggest what could be done to limit the spread of WMD.

As noted in chapters 3 and 4, weapons of mass destruction are defined as chemical, biological, and nuclear weapons. Nuclear weapons pose the greatest potential threat in terms of destruction, but biological weapons are the most likely to be used by terrorists.[5] Some experts argue that nuclear weapons are so much more destructive than chemical or biological weapons that they should not be considered in the same category. In this chapter, however, we will consider all three types of weapons of mass destruction and what has been done to limit their spread.

THE NONPROLIFERATION APPROACH

In 1963, President John Kennedy predicted that there would be from fifteen to twenty-five states that possessed nuclear weapons by the 1970s.[6] Kennedy was not alone; many others also recognized the danger to which he drew attention. As a consequence, a number of states negotiated the Nuclear Non-Proliferation Treaty (commonly known by its acronym, NPT), which was opened for signing in 1968.[7] The NPT proposed a straightforward quid pro quo: if states that did not possess nuclear weapons agreed not to produce them, states that had nuclear weapons would assist non-nuclear-weapons states with the development of peaceful uses of nuclear energy, such as nuclear power plants and civilian research reactors. This bargain was attractive to most states; by 2004, 187 states had signed the NPT.

That is the good news; the bad news is that the small minority of states that did not sign includes Israel, India, and Pakistan, countries that are in the most volatile areas of the world. India and Pakistan have a long tradition of bitter hostility, focusing primarily on the disputed territory of Kashmir. In December 2001 the two states came close to waging war, which they had previously done; however, this time, both countries possessed nuclear weapons, which they had tested in 1998.

Pakistan is a particular concern, for several reasons. Its population of 150 million includes many supporters of Islamic fundamentalism in general and Al Qaeda and the Taliban in particular. The members of the 9/11 Commission reported that there are 859 *madrassah*s (conservative Islamic schools) teaching more than two hundred thousand young people in Karachi alone.[8] According to former National Security Council staff members Daniel Benjamin and Steven Simon, before 9/11 Pakistan's military intelligence agency, the Inter-Services Intelligence directorate, was "a kind of terrorist conveyor belt" that transported "young radicals from their schools [in Pakistan] to Afghanistan for training in camps run by or affiliated with Al Qaeda. From there, they were taken to the border with Indian-controlled Kashmir, where they slipped across to launch their attacks."[9]

Despite the overthrow of the Taliban and the attacks on Al Qaeda, there is still support in Pakistan for these groups. An obvious danger is that nuclear materials could be turned over to terrorists. Even under President Pervez Musharraf, who has supported U.S. operations against terrorists and the Taliban, one of Pakistan's nuclear weapons designers, Abdul Qadeer Khan, sold nuclear components to Libya, Iran, and North Korea and headed up what the 9/11 Commission termed "the most dangerous nuclear smuggling ring ever disclosed."[10] In addition, two of Pakistan's senior nuclear scientists, Sultan Bashiruddin Mahmood and Chaudari Abdul Majeed, are sympathetic to Islamic extremists and have met with Osama bin Laden and his deputy, Ayman al-Zawahiri, discussing nuclear weapons with bin Laden.[11] Bin Laden has stated that he is seeking nuclear weapons and that, for Muslims, it is a "religious duty" to develop them.[12] Al Qaeda has repeatedly tried to buy or steal nuclear weapons, and documents captured from Al Qaeda bases in Afghanistan reveal "a significant effort to pursue nuclear weapons."[13] In recent years, there have been two assassination attempts on President Musharaf; had one of these been successful, it is possible that the Pakistani government would have been taken over by elements sympathetic to such Islamic terrorist groups as Al Qaeda.

The Non-Proliferation Treaty stimulated the development of peaceful nuclear research programs throughout the world. Many people believed that nuclear power could help solve contemporary problems, whether in medicine, energy, or other civilian issue areas. It was believed that certain uses would be safe and separate from weapons use; however, only four kilograms of plutonium (8.8 pounds) or twelve kilograms of enriched uranium (26.4 pounds) are needed to make a nuclear bomb. By the late 1990s, there were twenty metric tons of highly enriched uranium at 13 operational civilian research facilities in more than forty countries.[14] In addit'' there were an unknown number of civilian research reactors with highly enr' uranium (HEU), and many of these had lax or nonexistent security programs. An example illustrates the danger from the research reactors around the world. Uranium just below the quality of HEU was stolen from a research reactor in Congo and wound up in the hands of the Italian mafia.[15] Although this nuclear material could not have been used to make a nuclear weapon, it would have been suitable for a radiological weapon, or "dirty bomb." The IAEA has reported that from 1992 through 2000 there were eighteen documented cases of seizure of highly enriched uranium or plutonium.[16]

The Non-Proliferation Treaty was designed to limit the spread of nuclear weapons, thereby increasing international security; however, the quid pro quo that was the heart of the treaty resulted in the spread of nuclear materials throughout the world. Much of that material is no longer secure but vulnerable to theft or unauthorized diversion. Thus, the NPT had the unintended and unforeseen consequence of increasing the danger that nuclear materials would fall into the wrong hands.

THE BIOLOGICAL AND CHEMICAL WEAPONS CONVENTIONS

Chapter 4 defines and describes biological and chemical weapons. As noted, biological weapons derive from living organisms, whereas chemical weapons come from nonliving sources.

Biological weapons are particularly horrific because they are weaponized versions of infectious diseases such as the plague or smallpox (see chapter 6). Although a number of countries experimented with biological weapons, in November 1969 President Richard Nixon unilaterally renounced biological weapons and foreswore the first use of chemical weapons. In 1972 Nixon submitted the Biological Weapons Convention to the U.S. Senate for its advice and consent, calling the agreement "the first international agreement since World War II to provide for the actual elimination of an entire class of weapons from the arsenals of nations."[17] The agreement called for the prohibition of the development, production, stockpiling, and acquisition of biological agents or toxins. Because it was assumed that there was no military utility in biological weapons, there were no verification provisions in the convention. After the Cold War had ended, President Boris Yeltsin of Russia revealed that the outbreak of anthrax in Sverdlovsk in 1979 (described in chapter 4) had resulted from an escape of anthrax spores from a biological weapons plant prohibited by the Biological Weapons Convention. There were other reports that certain Soviet labs had illegally retained stocks of biological weapons.

As we saw in chapter 4, chemical agents were used with devastating results in World War I; in fact, the deaths and injuries they produced were so appalling that chemical and biological weapons were used only sporadically thereafter. The first attempt to control biological and chemical weapons was the Geneva Protocol of 1925, an agreement that called for the prohibition of these types of weapons. Notwithstanding the protocol's provisions, chemical weapons were used by the Italians in their invasion of Ethiopia in 1931 and by the Japanese in their combat operations in China. During the Cold War, the United States and the Soviet Union developed enormous stockpiles of both chemical and biological weapons.

Opposed by the Army Chemical Corps and private chemical manufacturers, the protocol was not signed by the United States until 1975—half a century after it was first opened for signature.[18] By the 1970s and 1980s an estimated twenty-five states were developing a chemical weapons capability, including Iraq, Libya, and other countries "not known for their restraint," as former Arms Control and Disarmament Agency director John Holum put it.[19] Iraq, as noted, used chemical weapons against Iranian soldiers in the Iran-Iraq War (1980–88) and against Kurdish civilians in 1988. Faced with these uses of chemical weapons and the threat of their proliferation, the international community negotiated the Chemical Weapons Convention, which is both a disarmament and a nonproliferation treaty. Specifically, the treaty called for banning the acquisition, development, production, stockpiling, and transfer of an entire class of weapons of mass destruction. It called for the complete destruction of chemical weapons and production facilities and forbade any military preparations for the use of chemical weapons. Significantly, the Chemical Weapons Convention called for extensive verification measures, including short-notice, intrusive, on-site inspections. As of 2004, the Chemical Weapons Convention had 164 signatories, including the United States.[20]

The anthrax attacks of 2001 heightened awareness and concern over possible chemical and biological attacks. No longer were such attacks simply hypothetical possibilities; they were clear and present dangers. The genesis of the 2001 anthrax attacks on Washington has not been determined, although the evidence suggests the anthrax came from the United States rather than a foreign source.

Captured documents and interrogations indicated that Al Qaeda conducted sophisticated research on topics related to chemical and biological weapons, using open, unclassified sources.[21] Ayman al-Zawahiri was trained as a doctor in Egypt and had a sophisticated understanding of, and interest in, the development of chemical and biological weapons. In addition, by 2000 at least a dozen countries were suspected of developing biological weapons programs, including Iran, Iraq, Israel, North Korea, Syria, Libya, Russia, and possibly India, Pakistan, China, Egypt, and Sudan.[22]

What can be done to reduce the danger of the proliferation of biological and chemical weapons? Concerned that the Biological Weapons Convention had no verification or enforcement mechanisms, the international community conducted negotiations beginning in 1994 to provide for them. In the summer of 2001, the Bush administration announced that the United States was going to withdraw from the negotiations to strengthen the convention, on the grounds that the proposed protocol's verification provisions were flawed and threatened American intellectual-property rights. This refusal to participate in negotiations designed to further the security of the United States and other states had the result of reducing the security of the United States. Many experts contend that terrorists are most likely to develop and use biological weapons. Given this prediction, it would make sense for the United States to do whatever it can to strengthen the ban against biological weapons, including efforts to provide verification measures for the Biological Weapons Convention. Increased verification, at a minimum, would better enable the international community, including the United States, to identify and isolate countries attempting to develop such weapons.

THE COUNTERPROLIFERATION APPROACH

The nonproliferation approach is only effective given international cooperation. If one state or group of states supplies chemical, biological, or nuclear materials to another state or terrorist group, proliferation occurs and this approach fails. The NPT was built on the assumption that multilateral cooperation would stop the spread of nuclear weapons, but the optimistic assumption of universal cooperation has not proved to be correct. The question concerning proliferation today is not whether but when certain states or subnational actors will develop WMD.

Faced with the potential and actual spread of nuclear, biological, or chemical weapons, a second approach was developed—counterproliferation—to destroy or neutralize the threat of WMD. In contrast to the multilateral nature of nonproliferation, counterproliferation is a more unilateral approach. The United States has moved in the direction of counterproliferation during the past decade. In the early 1990s, when it appeared that North Korea was developing nuclear weapons, the U.S. government seriously considered a preemptive attack on suspected North Korean nuclear weapons sites.[23] At the same time it was making military contingency plans for attacking North Korea, the United States pursued negotiations with Pyongyang to reduce the danger of proliferation diplomatically. In 1994, the United States, Japan, and South Korea signed with North Korea an Agreed Framework that called for the three states to provide oil and build two new nuclear reactors to replace two existing reactors that produced plutonium suitable for use in nuclear weapons.[24] The North Korean threat was neutralized—at least for several years—as a result of a multilateral, nonproliferation approach.

In August 1991, Iraq attacked and occupied its Arab neighbor to the south, Kuwait. In response to Iraq's aggression and to the threat that Iraq might disrupt the world energy markets and might develop weapons of mass destruction, the United States, joined by more than thirty other countries, forced Iraq to withdraw from Kuwait and to accept inspections by United Nations teams. Inspections were conducted from 1991 to 1998. More Iraqi weapons were destroyed during this period than were destroyed during the war. In 1998, Iraq expelled the UN inspectors, and the United States became increasingly concerned that Iraq was developing weapons of mass destruction.

The Clinton administration preferred the nonproliferation approach for dealing with the issue of nuclear proliferation, although it considered a counterproliferation strategy against North Korea. With regard to Iraq, the Clinton administration adopted a nonproliferation approach. In contrast, when the George W. Bush administration entered office, its rhetoric portended a counterproliferation approach across the board.

The attacks of 9/11 significantly increased American fears and concerns about the security of the United States. The Bush administration increasingly moved toward a military-oriented policy of preemption, a position that was made explicit in several important policy statements.[25] President Bush came to believe that Saddam Hussein could not be trusted, that Iraq was developing weapons of mass destruction, and that the United States had to take forceful action—if necessary, by itself—to remove this threat. On March 20, 2003, the United States, principally with the support of the United Kingdom, attacked Iraq, with four main objectives: (1) to find and destroy Iraqi WMD, (2) to overthrow Saddam Hussein, (3) to stop and prevent any cooperation between Iraq and Al Qaeda and other terrorist groups, and (4) to establish a democratic government in Iraq, in hopes that democracy would spread throughout the Middle East.[26]

CONTROLLING ACCESS TO WMD

For almost four decades, the international community has sought to halt, or at least slow, the spread of weapons of mass destruction. In more recent years, the United States has moved from a nonproliferation to a unilateral counterproliferation policy, yet the threats posed by weapons of mass destruction persist.

Despite the fact that it is unquestionably the single most powerful country in the world, the United States cannot effectively prevent the proliferation of weapons of mass destruction by itself; it must have the cooperation and support of other countries, including those that could supply the dangerous ingredients of WMD, and of those (such as Afghanistan under the Taliban) that could harbor terrorists intent on developing WMD. Democrats and Republicans, conservatives and liberals, all agree that there is no greater danger facing the United States than the specter of terrorists armed with chemical, biological, or nuclear weapons. In his 2003 State of the Union address, President George W. Bush declared, "The gravest danger facing America and the world, is outlaw regimes that seek and possess nuclear, chemical, and biological weapons. These regimes could give or sell those weapons to terrorist allies, who would use them without the least hesitation."[27]

Although international agreements—most notably the Non-Proliferation Treaty, the Biological Weapons Convention, and the Chemical Weapons Convention—have not completely prevented the spread of weapons of mass destruction, they have created an international norm opposing WMD proliferation. In a world of two hundred states with competing interests, priorities, and policies, such a consensus has value; it sends the message that most of the world's states are opposed to the development, production, stockpiling, and deployment of weapons of mass destruction. Efforts to strengthen the agreements that undergird this consensus, such as the attempts to negotiate a verification protocol for the Biological Weapons Convention and conclude a fissile material cutoff treaty, are therefore vitally important.

Russia remains the largest potential supplier of weapons of mass destruction to rogue states and terrorist groups. As of 1993, the former Soviet Union possessed an estimated thirty-two thousand nuclear weapons and thousands of scientists with knowledge of how to build weapons of mass destruction.[28] It has been estimated that as of mid-2003 there were some eighteen thousand assembled nuclear weapons in Russia, at 150–210 sites.[29] The potential for old Soviet or Russian nuclear weapons to fall into the hands of rogue states or terrorists is colloquially referred to as the "loose nukes" problem. In 1991, Senator Sam Nunn and Senator Richard Lugar proposed legislation to provide funds to increase the safety of Russian weapons of mass destruction and to provide for their destruction. The Nunn-Lugar initiative, later called the Cooperative Threat Reduction Program, also provided funds to provide work for unemployed Russian scientists and engineers who had worked on weapons programs prior to the disintegration of the Soviet Union.[30] This program has accomplished a great deal. By the end of 2003, the program had resulted in the deactivation of 6,252 nuclear warheads and the destruction of 527 ballistic missiles, 455 missile silos, eight ballistic missile launchers, 124 bombers, 668 nuclear air-to-surface missiles, 460 submarine-launched missiles, 408 submarine missile launchers, and twenty-seven strategic missile submarines.[31] In addition, the program employed more than twenty-two thousand former Soviet weapons scientists.

Despite the success of the Cooperative Threat Reduction Program, much remains to be done. In 2001, a task force commissioned by the U.S. Department of Energy and chaired by former senator Howard Baker and presidential advisor Lloyd Cutler concluded:

> The most urgent unmet national security threat to the United States today is the danger that weapons of mass destruction or weapon-usable material in Russia could be stolen and sold to terrorists or hostile nation states and used against American troops abroad or citizens at home. The threat is a clear and present danger to the international community as well as to American lives and liberties.[32]

As of 2002, a Stanford University project had recorded 660 illicit nuclear trafficking incidents, and of these at least 370 had either taken place in the former Soviet Union or involved materials that had originated from that area.[33] In late 1998, there was an attempt to steal 18.5 kilograms of highly enriched uranium (enough to build a nuclear weapon) from Chelyabinsk, one of Russia's largest nuclear weapons facilities. This is the only known case of attempted theft or diversion involving sufficient material to make a bomb.[34] Several additional cases, however, underscore the problem of illicit diversion.

> In May 1999, 10g of 76% enriched HEU [highly enriched uranium] was discovered by Bulgarian customs officers in a car of a Turkish citizen who claimed to have obtained the material in Moldova. One year later, in April 2000, almost a kilogram (920g) of uranium to 30% [enrichment] was seized by Georgian police in the Black Sea port of Batumi. And in July 2001, three men were arrested in Paris, France, being in possession of a 5 gram sample of HEU enriched between 70 and 80%. In all three cases, the seized material is supposed to have originated in Russia.[35]

In March 2004, CIA director George Tenet noted in testimony to Congress that Al Qaeda continued to show a strong interest in the development of chemical, biological, nuclear, and radiological weapons and that "Russian WMD materials and technology remain vulnerable to theft or diversion."[36] This is problematic because Russia has a serious terrorist threat within its borders, represented by Chechen extremists who have expressed interest in using nuclear materials in their campaign against the Russian government. Reportedly, Chechen terrorists placed a canister of radiological material in a Moscow park in 1995, conducted reconnaissance on Russian nuclear warhead storage sites and transportation trains on several occasions in 2001–2002, and considered attacking and taking over a Moscow nuclear facility having significant supplies of highly enriched uranium. In October 2002, forty-one heavily armed Chechen terrorists took over a Moscow theater, demonstrating their motivation and capability to use force and die for their cause. Reportedly, the terrorists had considered taking over the Kurchatov Institute, which had enough HEU to make dozens of nuclear weapons.[37] Importantly, there are links between Al Qaeda and Chechen terrorists; if, then, the Chechens obtained weapons of mass destruction, it is possible that Al Qaeda could gain access to WMD through them.

Obviously, actual weapons of mass destruction pose the greatest danger to American security; however, the components of these weapons and the processes to produce them also pose a significant threat. Therefore, the United States should actively seek international cooperation in tracking the manufacture, import, and export of the components of WMD. Although significant steps in this direction have been taken for nuclear weapons, much remains to be done.

There are currently thousands of kilograms of military plutonium and highly enriched uranium in the countries of the former Soviet Union, enough to build between 41,800 and 83,600 nuclear weapons.[38] The United States has enough to build an additional 36,263 to 72,525 nuclear weapons. The other nuclear-weapons states have substantial supplies of HEU and plutonium. In addition, hundreds of civilian research facilities throughout the world have more than twenty thousand kilograms of highly enriched uranium and two hundred thousand kilograms of separated "civil" plutonium, which, despite their names, are usable in weapons.[39]

A recent report by the Carnegie Endowment has concluded, "Because the most difficult part of making a nuclear bomb is acquiring the nuclear material, *all weapon-usable nuclear materials should be treated as if they were nuclear weapons, and the highest standards applied to weapons should become the global norm for all such materials regardless of use or location.*"[40] There are four principal ways to prevent additional countries and nonstate actors, such as terrorists and criminal groups, from obtaining nuclear weapons. First, all stocks of nuclear weapons and weapons-usable nuclear materials should be secured throughout the world, including the United States. Physical protection of nuclear materials involves guards, gates, and guns—that is, nuclear materials and weapons should be protected by both human and physical means. In cases where it is not possible to ensure the security of nuclear materials, they should be relocated or destroyed. In fact, the United States has assisted with such measures on several occasions. In 1994, Kazakhstan shipped six hundred kilograms of highly enriched uranium to Oak Ridge, Tennessee, for secure storage, eliminating what had been the largest existing stock of fissile materials outside of Russia. In 1998, the United States removed highly enriched uranium from a vulnerable site in Tbilisi, Georgia. In addition, the United States has airlifted stockpiles of highly enriched uranium from three "dangerously vulnerable" sites in Romania, Bulgaria, and Libya, respectively.[41] In total, in 2002, comprehensive security procedures and upgrades were completed for thirty-five tons of potentially vulnerable material in Russia, an amount that equaled 6 percent of the estimated six-hundred-ton Russian stockpile.[42]

A second measure to prevent terrorists and criminal groups from obtaining nuclear weapons is to convert civilian, research, power, and naval reactors that use weapon-usable fuels to alternate fuels. The United States has sponsored a number of programs to convert highly enriched uranium into fuel for civilian nuclear-power reactors. In fact, as of 2003 half of the nuclear-generated electricity in the United States came from highly enriched uranium from dismantled Russian nuclear weapons, a quintessential "swords into plowshares" program.[43]

A third measure is to eliminate large stockpiles of weapon-usable materials. By the end of 2003, two hundred tons of highly enriched uranium from dismantled Russian nuclear weapons had been blended into low enriched uranium in accordance with Russian-American agreements. If Russian warheads contain on average twenty-five kilograms of highly enriched uranium, the two hundred tons were the equivalent of eight thousand warheads.[44] As of 2004, approximately thirty tons of highly enriched uranium was being blended down, the equivalent of 1,200 warheads per year. That is the good news; the bad news is that the HEU blend-down program is scheduled to end in 2013 and there are still over 550 tons of HEU left in Russia.

A fourth step to reduce the risk of terrorists' gaining access to nuclear materials and weapons is to halt production of all weapon-usable material. As of 2004, there was enough weapon-usable material in the world to produce more than a hundred thousand nuclear weapons. In spite of that fact, a number of states continued to produce it. Of the nine states that are known or suspected of having nuclear weapons, the United States, Russia, the United Kingdom, France, and China have halted the production of HEU and plutonium; it is believed that Israel, India, Pakistan, and North Korea continue to produce nuclear materials for weapons.[45]

More than fifty years ago, President Dwight Eisenhower first proposed the halting of the production of fissile materials that could be used to make weapons. At the Nonproliferation Review Conference in 2000, all 187 states party to the NPT called for halting the production of fissile materials by 2005. The sixty-six members of the UN Conference on Disarmament then negotiated an agreement called the Fissile Material Cutoff Treaty, to stop production of nuclear materials that could be turned into nuclear weapons. Specifically, the agreement sought to convince countries that are not covered by the Non-Proliferation Treaty—most notably Israel, India, and Pakistan—to accept some degree of oversight of their nuclear development programs.

At the end of July 2004, the Bush administration announced that the United States would support the treaty but without a means to verify compliance.[46] Critics of this position noted that the American action would cripple the attempt to stop the production of fissile materials. Dr. Frank von Hippel, a former White House science advisor and currently codirector of the Program on Science and Global Security at the Woodrow Wilson School at Princeton University, has argued that a fissile materials cutoff treaty would be "a political challenge, but it is technically feasible to establish the means to effectively monitor and verify compliance with the treaty in order to detect and deter clandestine nuclear bomb production efforts."[47] Others have noted that this "trust but not verify" approach was characteristic of the Bush administration's approach to the Strategic Offensive Reductions Treaty (or Moscow Treaty), which entered into force in 2003 with no verification provisions, and of its refusal to participate in the negotiations to strengthen the verifiability of the Biological Weapons Convention.

COOPERATION OR CONFRONTATION?

For thirty-five years from 1968 to 2003, the United States employed an approach to controlling the spread of weapons of mass destruction that placed a premium on international cooperation and diplomacy. The 9/11 attacks on the United States focused attention on the possibility of terrorist acts employing weapons of mass destruction and, consequently, increased fear that rogue states, including Iraq, might be developing and stockpiling WMD. Against this backdrop (and disregarding contrary evidence offered by UN weapons inspectors), the United States, the United Kingdom, and other allies attacked Iraq with the avowed purpose of finding and destroying Iraqi WMD. No such weapons were found.

Intelligence indicates that North Korea has several nuclear weapons and that Iran is actively working to develop them. In fact, given the evidence concerning North Korea's nuclear weapons, it would have been more in keeping with the logic of the Bush administration's policy of preemption, as described in the *National Security Strategy* of 2002, to attack North Korea before Iraq. That was not done, and now the United States must decide what to do about North Korea, Iran, and other potential or actual proliferators, as well as what to do about the very real danger of terrorists' or criminals' obtaining nuclear materials or even nuclear weapons.

Iraq was the first application of the Bush administration's military-based, preemptive policy of counterproliferation, and it raised a number of troubling questions. The rationale for the invasion was that Iraq possessed weapons of mass destruction that posed a clear and present danger to the United States. While evidence of old Iraqi WMD research programs was found; nothing to justify the prewar security concerns was uncovered. The invasion was undertaken on the basis of false intelligence assumptions, with enormous costs to both the United States and Iraq. Given the prohibitive costs of the policy of preemption, what other options exist?

An international, diplomatically based nonproliferation policy is frustrating and time consuming, but it was followed by the United States for three and a half decades. Perhaps 9/11 changed everything and demanded a dramatic revolution in U.S. strategy; that is the position of the Bush administration.[48] Just as difficult cases make bad law, however, it may be that traumatic tragedies such as 9/11 result in policies that are not sustainable or effective over the long term. A policy that patiently enlists the cooperation and support of the entire international community, less a few rogue states, is the best way to seek greater security in an insecure world.

RECOMMENDED READING

Printed Sources

Allison, Graham. *Nuclear Terrorism: The Ultimate Preventable Catastrophe.* New York: Times Books, 2004.

Bunn, Matthew, and Anthony Wier. *Securing the Bomb: An Agenda for Action.* Cambridge, Mass.: Nuclear Threat Initiative and the Project on Managing the Atom, Harvard University, May 2004.

Campbell, Kurt M., Robert Einhorn, and Mitchell Riess, eds. *The Nuclear Tipping Point: Global Prospects for Revisiting Nuclear Renunciation.* Washington, D.C.: Brookings Institution Press, 2004.

Cirincione, Joseph, with Jon B. Wolfsthal and Miriam Rajkumar. *Deadly Arsenals: Tracking Weapons of Mass Destruction.* Washington, D.C.: Carnegie Endowment for International Peace, 2002.

Perkovich, George, Joseph Cirincione, Rose Gottemoeller, Jon B. Wolfsthal, and Jessica T. Mathews. *Universal Compliance: A Strategy for Nuclear Security.* Draft report. Washington, D.C.: Carnegie Endowment for International Peace, June 2004.

Sagan, Scott D., and Kenneth N. Waltz. *The Spread of Nuclear Weapons: A Debate Renewed.* New York: W. W. Norton, 2003.

Websites

Carnegie Endowment for International Peace: www.ceip.org

Federation of American Scientists: www.fas.org

International Atomic Energy Agency: www.iaea.org

Monterey Institute for International Studies, Center for Nonproliferation Studies: cns.miis.edu

Nuclear Threat Initiative: www.nti.org

II

New Sources of Insecurity

6

Disease: The Greatest Killer?

Traditionally, security is conceived purely in state-centric military terms; however, a number of historical examples call this view into question. In his classic *History of the Peloponnesian War*, Thucydides writes not only about the military battles between the archrival city-states of Athens and Sparta but about, in excruciating detail, the epidemic that swept Athens in 430–429 BC, killing a quarter of its soldiers.[1] According to a modern historian of disease, William McNeil, in a relatively short period of time the epidemic "inflicted a blow on Athenian society from which it never recovered."[2] Thucydides himself implies that the epidemic contributed to Sparta's defeat of Athens. Many scholars consider Thucydides to be the father of the discipline of international relations, yet his progeny have focused narrowly on military aspects of conflict rather than the broader view Thucydides adopted.

Between 1347 and 1351, a catastrophic pandemic ravaged Eurasia and Africa north of the Sahara. Estimates of the number of deaths caused by the plague are necessarily rough, but scholars have suggested a mortality rate for Europe ranging from 25 to 45 percent of the population. In 1351, the Vatican put the number of plague deaths in Christian Europe at 23,840,000, which was about a third of Europe's population before bubonic plague struck in 1347. According to the medieval historian Froissart, "a third of the world died."[3] No war in human history has killed a larger proportion of the world's population.

Historians often point to the technological superiority of the European conquistadors in explaining their impressive defeat of the native meso-American Indians in the sixteenth century. However, when Spanish explorer Cortez and his men reached the New World with their European weapons, even more destructive to native peoples was the smallpox virus that they also brought to the Americas. Although smallpox had caused many deaths in Europe, the conquistadors and other survivors of periodic European smallpox epidemics had built up some immunity to the virus. The Amerindians of Mexico and Central America had no such protection; the results were devastating to the immunologically unprepared peoples of the New World. When

Cortez arrived in 1519, there were an estimated thirty million people in central Mexico; fifty years later, the indigenous population was three million, a tenth of what it had been. By 1618, the indigenous population had fallen to 1.6 million, and the primary culprit of this devastating population decline was disease.[4] In this sense, the conquistadors' most effective weapon against the indigenous peoples of the Americas was smallpox, not gunpowder.

As measured by the total number of people killed (approximately fifteen million), World War I was one of the costliest wars in human history. What most people (even those who have studied World War I) do not know is that following the war in 1918–19 a worldwide epidemic of what at the time was called "Spanish influenza" (also called swine flu) killed as many as one hundred million people, six times as many as had been killed in all theaters of World War I. This disease took four months to circle the globe; in today's more globalized world, it could do so in four days.

These examples demonstrate the dramatic impact that disease has had on human history, an impact that many historians have failed to note adequately. Disease, in short, has posed significant threats to the security of peoples and political entities throughout history, and it continues to pose a substantial threat. Indeed, given the emergence of new diseases and the possibility of terrorists employing biological weapons, disease may very well be one of the greatest, if not the greatest, threat to security at present.

In this chapter, we will describe various infectious diseases and the threats that they pose, indicate what has been done to control these threats, and describe what else can be done to address the security implications of infectious diseases.

INFECTIOUS DISEASES

Major advances in the scientific understanding of infectious diseases have occurred only within the past century. Before the twentieth century, with little understanding of the way infectious diseases attack their victims and spread to others, defenses were impossible. Not even simple bacterial infections of the kind associated with dirt in an open wound could be treated effectively prior to the discovery of penicillin. The timely discovery and large-scale manufacture of penicillin, in fact, made World War II the first conflict in history in which those wounded in battle had a better than even chance of surviving without the loss of a limb. As the macabre scene of a Confederate hospital in Atlanta in the classic movie *Gone with the Wind* suggests, prior to the introduction of penicillin only amputation under relatively antiseptic conditions would save the life of a soldier with a spreading infection.

The remarkable advances of modern medicine have achieved only limited success in halting the carnage of infectious diseases, and even those limited successes are in danger of being reversed. Let us note first the successes and then the very real threats.

The most deadly microbial infectious disease in history is smallpox. In the twentieth century alone, smallpox killed somewhere between three and five hundred million people worldwide. In the 1930s in the United States, approximately fifty thousand people per year were infected, and the mortality rate among victims was 30 percent. Alarmed by these losses, the international community under the auspices of the World Health Organization (WHO) sought to eliminate smallpox by vaccinating the world's people. By 1977, WHO declared that smallpox had been eradicated. However, as we have noted, both the United States and the Soviet Union kept samples of smallpox in order to prepare defenses against a possible biological attack employing smallpox; clearly, the virus had not been completely eliminated. Following the attacks of September 11, there was concern that terrorists might obtain samples of smallpox and deliberately infect the populations of target states; this possibility even became the subject of a popular television program.[5]

Worldwide, infectious diseases kill more people than all other causes combined; in 1998, a total of fifty-four million people died of infectious diseases.[6] By contrast, an estimated total of fifty million people died in World War II, which lasted from 1939 to 1945. Pestilence clearly is the most destructive of the four horsemen of the apocalypse.

During the past several decades, thirty previously unknown diseases have emerged, including HIV/AIDS, Ebola virus, Marburg fever, hepatitis C, SARS, avian flu, Hanta virus, and a virulent form of flesh-eating streptococcus. Unfortunately, there is no end in sight to the emergence of new diseases and pathogens, and the emergence of terrorism has not only heightened concern over this situation but contributed to it as well. Laurie Garrett, a Pulitzer Prize–winning journalist who focuses on public health issues, has noted that the destruction of the World Trade Towers "was a public health event" that represented "a biological event for which we had no precedent. The pH [of the dust and debris] ran between about 12 and 13, and most natural occurring respiratory assaults are acidic, with a pH down between 3 and 5. And it contained two molecules never before seen in the atmosphere of Earth, and we have no way of knowing what it will mean to all those who inhaled this as the time went on."[7]

In addition to newly emerging diseases, several of humanity's oldest and most deadly scourges are staging a comeback, including tuberculosis, cholera, and malaria. According to the World Health Organization, among the seven infectious diseases that caused the most deaths in 1998 were both new and reemerging diseases: (1) hepatitis B and C, (2) measles, (3) malaria, (4) tuberculosis, (5) diarrheal diseases, (6) acute respiratory infections, including pneumonia and influenza, and (7) HIV/AIDS.[8]

Epidemiological studies indicate that approximately twenty well-known diseases are reemerging, and this is occurring in developed as well as developing countries. For example, tuberculosis was supposed to have been eradicated in the United States by 2000, but it is staging a robust return. In 1993, WHO identified TB as a global emergency, with particular areas of the world, including Russia, India, Southeast Asia, sub-Saharan Africa, and parts of Latin America, considered particularly vulnerable.

In 1998 more than 1.5 million people died of TB, a number that excludes those who were infected with both TB and HIV/AIDS. Among people fifteen to forty-five years old, tuberculosis is the leading cause of death from a single disease. TB also causes substantial economic losses. The World Bank estimates that treating TB costs the average patient three to four months of lost earnings or 30 percent of household income.[9] Of the people infected with HIV, approximately 30 percent are estimated to be coinfected with TB, which is the leading identifiable cause of death among HIV-positive people.[10]

Malaria is another well-known disease that has devastating effects in both human and economic terms. At present, malaria is endemic in more than a hundred countries, about half of the countries in the world. Malaria annually kills more than a million people worldwide and causes three hundred million cases of acute illness.[11] Ninety percent of deaths from malaria occur in sub-Saharan Africa, mostly among children. An estimated 150,000 children per month die from malaria in Africa, a number that is approximately half that of the total number killed by the tsunami in the Indian Ocean region in December 2004.[12]

Even in the developed world, disease takes a ghastly toll. In the United States, infectious disease remains the third-leading cause of death. Many medical researchers are now worried that the overuse—and the misuse—of antibiotics may be stimulating the development of drug-resistant strains of bacteria, thus diminishing the world's capacity to overcome many common diseases. This concern raises an important and very disturbing aspect of humanity's battle with disease. Just as action-reaction processes sometimes characterize conflicts between or among countries, a pattern in which the defensive measures of one side prompt the development of countermeasures by the other side, so the human conflict with pathogenic microbes involves an unending quest for biological escalation dominance. Diseases mutate in ways that, at the risk of making them seem human, appear fiendishly clever. Thus, the influenza vaccine developed to protect the most vulnerable people in society (generally the elderly and the young) from the ill effects of one flu season are unlikely to have any effect against the influenza strains that spread through the population a year later.

The use and misuse of antibiotics also illustrates a central theme of this book—that actions taken to defend against threats often have the unintended effect of becoming threats themselves. In the case of antibiotics, drugs developed to defend against infection actually assist pathogens in developing mutations that are not affected by the antibiotic. A pertinent example of problematic pathogen evolution is multiple-drug-resistant tuberculosis found in Central Asia and Africa. In a sense, the actions taken to defend against a particular threat become threatening.

What some of the world's emerging diseases lack (so far) in numbers of victims they more than make up for in the ghastliness of their effects on human beings. Whether spread deliberately or not, an outbreak of Ebola in the United States would introduce an element of insecurity related as much to the disease's symptoms as to its contagiousness or lethality. A Zairean doctor who in 1976 was among the first to encounter the modern strain of Ebola reported his findings in these words:

> The affliction is characterized by a high temperature around thirty-nine degrees Celsius; frequent vomiting of black, digested blood, but of red blood in a few cases; diarrheal emissions initially sprinkled with blood, with only red blood near death; epistaxis [nosebleeds] now and then; retrosternal and abdominal pain and a state of stupor; prostration with heaviness in the joints; rapid evolution toward death after a period of about three days, from a state of general health.[13]

Based on contemporary descriptions of the effects of Ebola such as this and comparing them to the descriptions of the plague in Thucydides' *History of the Peloponnesian War,* some analysts believe that the plague that devastated Athens and was described by Thucydides was actually Ebola.[14]

In 1967, a hemorrhagic fever closely related to Ebola, called Marburg fever (for the German city where it was first seen), briefly made the jump from Africa to Europe when three workers at a pharmaceutical plant fell ill with flu-like symptoms. They were hospitalized, but their condition rapidly worsened; nausea, enlarged spleens, and bloodshot eyes appeared first. Then came red rashes, raw throats, and acute diarrhea. In the second week, the entire body of those affected became red in color as blood flow was blocked throughout the capillaries. This was accompanied by severe pain. Next, the vomiting of blood, the peeling of skin, and uncontrollable bleeding appeared. Several patients died, and others were left with assorted disabilities. The disease was traced to a group of monkeys that had been shipped to European labs from Uganda.[15] Not only is there no vaccine or cure for the Ebola and Marburg hemorrhagic fevers, but both are considered by public health officials to be excellent candidates for use as biological weapons.

Unfortunately, Marburg fever and Ebola are not the only diseases to jump from an animal species to humans. In 1997, there was an outbreak in Hong Kong of avian influenza virus (H5N1) that killed six of eighteen people infected with it.[16] Previous to this outbreak, scientists had thought that it was not possible for birds to infect humans. Following the initial outbreaks, millions of chickens, ducks, and other birds in Asia were killed in an attempt to destroy the virus. Yet, in 2004, forty-four confirmed human cases of avian flu were documented in Thailand and Vietnam. Of those people infected, thirty-two died. The virus has not only jumped from birds to humans but has mutated and infected cats, pigs, and tigers. There is currently no vaccine for the virus. Shigeru Omi, a top World Health Organization official, has warned that the avian flu virus could unleash a pandemic that could kill as many as a hundred million people.[17]

In December 2002, a new disease—severe acute respiratory syndrome, or SARS—was first identified in southern China. During the next two years, nine thousand cases were identified, and nine hundred people died of this new disease. Although SARS was mainly present in five Asian countries (China, Taiwan, Singapore, Vietnam, and Thailand), it had global implications. For example, the outbreak of SARS in Canada caused a downturn in American tourist visits there, with significant economic implications for Canada. Fortunately, within two years of the initial outbreak of SARS, a vaccine had been developed.

In spite of the brief incursions into the developed world that Marburg fever, Ebola, avian flu, SARS, and certain other emerging infectious diseases have made, it may be tempting to think of such diseases as someone else's problem. After all, most of these newly discovered diseases were native to Africa and Asia and, with some rare exceptions, were largely confined to these areas. Other debilitating diseases, such as cholera and malaria, are primarily found in developing countries, and the public health systems of developed countries like the United States have, with few exceptions, either beaten back these scourges or kept them at bay.

It is unwise, however, to assume that the world's bacteriological and viral problems have always been stopped at the borders or that they will be in the future. Globalization has always encouraged a robust exchange of microbes along with goods and services. Recall that it was merchants returning from Asia to Europe who carried bubonic plague in the fourteenth century. Remember too that two sailors disembarking in Boston in 1918 brought the Spanish influenza to American shores. The approach of both American and international public health officials in combating infectious disease has been, according to Laurie Garrett, based on two false assumptions: "that microbes were biologically stationary targets and that the diseases could be geographically sequestered."[18] The greater the level of exchange of persons and products in the world—that is, the greater the degree of globalization—the greater will be the possibility that deadly pathogens also will travel.

Time is of the essence. In 1350 BC the first epidemic of smallpox was identified in Egypt. It had spread to China by 49 AD, to Europe after 700, the Western Hemisphere by 1520, and Australia by 1789.[19] Thus, it took smallpox a little over three thousand years to circumnavigate the globe. By contrast, it took HIV/AIDS only about thirty years to do so. In this sense, globalization collapses time when it comes to the spread of infectious diseases.

Potential for the global spread of infectious diseases is related to the different incubation periods of infectious diseases and has a profound impact on public health. Smallpox, for example, has an incubation period from ten to fourteen days. Thanks to the ease and efficiency of international air travel, an individual who carries the smallpox virus could visit half a dozen or more of the world's major cities in the time between contracting the disease and first noticing the symptoms. Add to this disturbing reality the fact that more people than ever before are traveling long distances. In 1951, there were seven million airline passengers. The number topped five hundred million (or 1.4 million per day) by 1993, and, in spite of the slump in air travel caused by the events of 9/11, by 2013 the annual number of airline passengers is expected to surpass one billion. As the Nobel Prize-winning geneticist Joshua Lederberg puts it, "The world is just one village. Our tolerance of disease in any place is at our own peril."[20]

HIV/AIDS

Nowhere is this truth more evident than in the case of the human immunodeficiency virus (HIV) and acquired immune deficiency syndrome (AIDS). HIV/AIDS is recognized as a clear and present danger. By the end of 2004, approximately forty-two million people worldwide were living with HIV/AIDS and twenty million had died from the pandemic.[21] Since the disease was first identified just over thirty years ago, seventy million people have been infected. Three million people died of the disease in 2004 alone. Ninety-five percent of those infected with HIV are in the developing world, almost thirty million in sub-Saharan Africa alone. Every day, eight thousand people worldwide die of HIV/AIDS, and every day there are fourteen thousand new cases, over half of them among people under twenty-five years of age.[22] Within two decades, HIV/AIDS will have surpassed all other diseases, including smallpox, as the most prolific killer in history. An official of the U.S. National Intelligence Council has noted that AIDS "has already killed more people than all the soldiers killed in the major wars of the twentieth century, and equals the toll taken by the bubonic plague in 1347. The bad news about AIDS is that unless something is done in the near future, we're on a trajectory for things to get much worse."[23] The World Bank estimates that an additional forty-five million people will have become infected with HIV/AIDS in the 2002–10 period.[24]

One significant effect of the HIV/AIDS pandemic has been the creation of large numbers of "AIDS orphans." The U.S. National Intelligence Council estimated in 2004 that in some African countries "one in ten children is an orphan and the situation is certain to worsen."[25] The Joint United Nations Programme on HIV/AIDS (UNAIDS) estimates that by 2010, approximately twenty-five million children will have lost one or both parents to AIDS, creating a generation of orphans; an estimated twenty million of these children are African, including 2.7 million in Nigeria, 2.5 million in Ethiopia, and 1.8 million in South Africa.[26] An estimated 860,000 children in sub-Saharan Africa lost teachers to AIDS in 1999 alone.[27] AIDS orphans are less likely to remain in school and are more vulnerable to exploitation by sex traffickers or warlords. Many fear that the "lost orphan generation" created by AIDS deaths will exacerbate the child-soldier problem (see chapter 2). With no parents to provide for and supervise them, orphaned children are being recruited by unscrupulous warlords and guerrilla groups as soldiers. Sadly, child soldiers existed before the scourge of AIDS, but by creating millions of orphans the HIV/AIDS pandemic has made the child-soldier problem much worse. It is likely to continue to worsen far into the future. Clearly, HIV/AIDS has affected Africa the most severely; Africa is literally and figuratively the epicenter of the AIDS pandemic.

AIDS is a crisis for both the developed and the developing worlds. To date, more than 450,000 people have died of AIDS in the United States. This figure is forty-five thousand greater than the total number of Americans killed in World War II. For this reason, and because of the threat that the HIV/AIDS pandemic represents to the political, social, and economic stability of the world, in April 2000 President

Clinton declared that AIDS represented a "national security threat." The National Intelligence Council, a U.S. government advisory body, issued a national intelligence estimate in 2000 entitled "The Global Infectious Disease Threat and Its Implications for the United States." Currently the Central Intelligence Agency actively recruits medical analysts specializing in internal medicine, epidemiology, infectious diseases, and public health.[28]

Concern over HIV/AIDS is not a partisan issue. In his confirmation hearings to become secretary of state, Colin Powell noted that he, like President Clinton, viewed HIV/AIDS as a "national security threat." President George W. Bush has concluded that "AIDS is the greatest health crisis of our time."[29] Underscoring the seriousness and international nature of the issue, in 2001 both the UN Security Council and the General Assembly met in special sessions devoted to the global threat posed by AIDS.

A collaborative analysis of HIV/AIDS cosponsored by the Milbank Memorial Fund and the Council on Foreign Relations concluded, "Global HIV/AIDS is undoubtedly one of the greatest contemporary threats to mankind."[30] The former head of the World Bank, James Wolfensohn, has noted, "Many of us used to think of AIDS as a health issue. We were wrong; . . . nothing we have seen is a greater challenge to the peace and stability of African societies than the epidemic of AIDS. . . . We face a major development crisis, and more than that, a security crisis."[31]

A number of governments, international and nongovernmental organizations, and individual analysts have focused on AIDS as a security threat. P. W. Singer, for example, writing in *Survival,* the journal of the respected International Institute for Strategic Studies, has argued that AIDS poses a direct danger to national and international stability and is a threat to the militaries of countries.[32] In regard to the AIDS threat to military forces, Singer notes that studies consistently indicate that the infection rates in African military forces are around five times that of civilian populations and that during times of war infection rates can be as much as fifty times higher.[33] The average rate of infection for African militaries is 30 percent, but for some countries it is much higher. Estimates indicate that infection rates are as high as 50 percent for the Congo and Angola, 66 percent for Uganda, 75 percent in Malawi, and 80 percent in Zimbabwe. The United Nations draws many of its peacekeeping forces from the ranks of African militaries. If AIDS infection rates continue to grow, many African militaries will be unable to provide forces. Singer concludes, "AIDS is indeed a security threat and should be treated as such, with the high-level attention and resources necessary to defend against it. Fighting AIDS is not just a matter of altruism, but enlightened self interest."[34]

In an early analysis of the link between AIDS and security, the nongovernmental International Crisis Group analyzed AIDS as significant in five different senses: as a personal issue, an economic issue, a communal security issue, a national security issue, and as an international security issue.[35] On the personal level, AIDS threatens the "lives, health, family structure, and well being of individuals and entire communities."[36] In an economic sense, "AIDS puts at risk human capital and natural resource development, and business investment, which form the foundation of national economies."[37] The World Bank estimates that in the thirteen African countries with HIV/AIDS infection rates of 8 percent or more, the pandemic has cut 1 percent from gross domestic product.[38] In the poorest countries, the estimated economic cost of HIV/AIDS is as high as 2 to 3 percent of gross national income. Serious economic effects are not limited to the poorest countries; for example, the World Bank has estimated that AIDS and tuberculosis combined could cost Russia 1 percent of its gross domestic product by 2005.[39] AIDS not only affects a country's economic performance but its community and social cohesion as well. According to the British House of Commons, "Evidence suggests that in societies facing economic crisis and lack of clear political leadership the presence of AIDS with its associated stigma may cause instability. The citizens are aware of the increase in illness and death, the stigma associated with it; and the lack of leadership leads to blame."[40] AIDS has the potential to threaten both individual states' national security as well as broader international security.

Acknowledging the appalling, tragic effects of, and the threat posed by, the AIDS pandemic, in his 2003 State of the Union Address President Bush announced the establishment of the President's Emergency Plan for AIDS Relief, describing it as "a work of mercy beyond all current international efforts to help the people of Africa."[41] The president pledged that the United States would provide fifteen billion dollars over a five-year period. The program was aimed at preventing seven million new infections and sought to treat two million people infected with HIV/AIDS. In addition, the program sought to provide care for ten million people. Initially, the Bush administration identified fourteen countries (twelve of them in sub-Saharan Africa) to which aid would be directed: Guyana, Haiti, Botswana, Côte d'Ivoire, Ethiopia, Kenya, Mozambique, Namibia, Nigeria, Rwanda, South Africa, Tanzania, Uganda, and Zambia. Congress later instructed the president to add a fifteenth country outside of the Caribbean or Africa, and Vietnam was accordingly added to the list in the summer of 2004.

The Bush administration has been slow delivering on its promised aid. The requests for fiscal years 2004 and 2005 were low, and the administration has requested only $3.2 billion for fiscal year 2006.

BIOTERRORISM

The threats posed by naturally occurring diseases are substantial and frightening enough; however, the potential for terrorist use of diseases as weapons amplifies the threats. Bioterrorism was very much on the minds of the top-level members of the U.S. government even before the traumatic events of September 11, 2001. In his State of the Union Address of January 2000, President Clinton declared, "I predict to you, when most of us are long gone, but sometime in the next ten to twenty years, the major security threat this country will face will come from the enemies of the nation-state: the narco-traffickers and the terrorists and the organized criminals, who will be organized together, working together, with increasing access to ever more so-phisticated chemical and biological weapons."[42] President Clinton's national security advisor, Anthony Lake, introduced his provocative book *6 Nightmares* with a fictional scenario depicting a biological weapons attack by terrorists on the Washington, D.C., convention center.[43] Clearly, U.S. leaders were worried about pathogens being used as weapons to attack the United States and kill many Americans. They had very good reason.

As noted in chapter 4, states that are currently thought to possess biological weapons include Iran, Syria, China, North Korea, Russia, Israel, and Taiwan. In addition, the following states possibly possess biological weapons: Sudan, India, Pakistan, Egypt, and Kazakhstan.[44] The U.S. government has sought to prevent the use of biological and other weapons of mass destruction (i.e., chemical and nuclear weapons) through deterrence. In essence, the United States has proclaimed that if it were attacked by a state using WMD, it would counterattack in kind and inflict unacceptable damage on the attacking state. Such threats have proved to be efficacious against states; however, the question now is whether they will deter terrorist groups.

In the case of bioterrorism, history is not reassuring. The problem with groups like Aum Shinrikyo is that they have no territory of their own to threaten with counterattack. This led the respected strategist Richard Betts to conclude in 1998: "If a larger part of the worry about WMD these days is about their use by terrorist groups, the odds are higher that sometime, somewhere in the country, some of these weapons will go off despite the best efforts to stop them."[45] More recently, the National Intelligence Council concluded, "Our greatest concern is that terrorists might acquire biological or, less likely, a nuclear device, either of which could cause mass casualties."[46]

ADDRESSING THE THREAT OF DISEASE

Clearly much can be done to confront the threats of infectious diseases and bioter-rorism. The past can be a guide to the future. Significantly, the World Health Organization, with the cooperation of member states, was able to eradicate smallpox as a threat.[47] Of course, the use of smallpox by terrorists is possible, but as a natural infectious-disease threat it was eliminated. The way in which this was accomplished suggests how threats in this area might be reduced. The most striking aspect of WHO's effective campaign to eliminate smallpox was the cooperation of states, international organizations, and nongovernmental organizations. Indeed, cooperation by various types of international actors is key to confronting the threat of infectious disease.

The response to date to the threat of HIV/AIDS to national and international security offers both positive and negative lessons. On the positive side, the U.S. government and the international community have recognized the significance of the threat that infectious disease represents. In addition, people whom *New York Times* columnist Thomas Freidman has called "super-empowered individuals" have also recognized and addressed the threat of infectious diseases. Beginning in 2000, the Bill and Melinda Gates Foundation began making donations to improve public health around the world. The foundation is the wealthiest in the world, with an estimated thirty billion dollars in assets. To date, it has distributed almost eight billion dollars to improve global health and education; the World Health Organization estimates that 670,000 children's lives have been saved thereby and that millions more will be saved in future years.[48] Bill and Melinda Gates's actions illustrate an important theme of this book, that nonstate actors are increasingly important in international relations.

There is general consensus that HIV/AIDS represents a threat not only to public health but also to security. On the negative side, the response to HIV/AIDS has tended to eclipse the threats posed by other infectious diseases. For example, malaria still kills more than a million Africans each year and "costs Africa about $12 billion in lost production each year."[49] The leading cause of death of AIDS victims is tuberculosis, and an estimated 30 percent of African AIDS victims are coinfected with HIV and TB. As the authors of the 2004 study cosponsored by the Council on Foreign Relations and the Milbank Memorial Fund argued:

> The concerted campaign to fight malaria in the 1960s and 1970s drew resources from the larger health systems and [away] from other vital health problems. For the smallpox eradication campaign of the 1970s and 1980s, a separate delivery system was developed and then allowed to dissolve, leaving no infrastructure for later vaccination campaigns. Fighting HIV/AIDS in the same way would have a negative effect on health systems' capacity to meet other health needs, and it would have disastrous consequences for the long-term health and development of affected countries.[50]

What is needed is a comprehensive, integrated approach that focuses on multiple infectious-disease threats rather than isolating only one or a few.

Resources are vital. The contrasts between health expenditures in developing and developed states are stark. The World Health Organization estimates that health spending in high-income developed states averages two thousand dollars per person per year. The cost of treating someone infected with HIV/AIDS is between fifteen and thirty thousand dollars per year. In contrast, the average spent on health care by African countries is only six dollars per person per year. This means that the cost of providing anti-retroviral drugs—the "AIDS cocktail"—is 2,500 times the average annual amount spent on an African's health care. Clearly, it is not possible for African countries to spend what developed states spend treating HIV/AIDS victims. The generic forms of anti-retroviral drugs cost six hundred dollars per year, an amount that is still a hundred times the average per capita amount spent on health care in Africa. But this amount is far more feasible than the fifteen thousand dollars per patient spent in developed countries.

It is vital that wealthy countries make and maintain their commitment to confront the threats posed by infectious diseases. In this regard, the commitment by the United States in the President's Emergency Plan for AIDS Relief is noteworthy but must be fully funded. Studies conducted to date indicate that high-level political leadership is key to addressing the problem effectively.

Another important aspect of addressing the pandemic of HIV/AIDS concerns female literacy. Studies indicate that the number of women infected with HIV/AIDS is growing. This is due to the ways in which HIV/AIDS is transmitted. In many cases in the developing world, older males who frequent prostitutes or use intravenous drugs marry younger women and infect them with HIV/AIDS. Because two-thirds of the world's illiterate people are women, many women are unaware of the dangers of and precautions against HIV/AIDS infection. Increasing women's literacy programs is one way of addressing the problem of AIDS and other health issues. For example, women who read are more likely to be able to provide for their families and to obtain medical care for their children. Increasing women's literacy is also a means of addressing population control and economic development in that, as studies have shown, "for every three years of education that you provide a woman, it tends to reduce their own individual birth rate by one child."[51] The World Bank has found that "women with a post-secondary education are three times more likely than uneducated to know that HIV can be transmitted from mother to child."[52] Educating women can have salutary economic effects; for example, increasing the level of education and resources available to female farmers to the same level as male farmers increased crop yields as much as 22 percent.[53] In its study of the world of 2020, the National Intelligence Council stated, "A growing body of empirical literature suggests that gender equality in education promotes economic growth and reduces child mortality and malnutrition."[54]

An emphasis on literacy could also have the beneficial effect of enabling citizens in developing countries to reject erroneous claims. For example, Wangari Maathai, a Kenyan woman who won the 2004 Nobel Peace Prize, touched off a firestorm of controversy when it was reported that she told participants in an AIDS workshop in Kenya that HIV was deliberately manufactured in laboratories to kill Africans.[55] Although Maathai later insisted that she did not believe HIV was produced in labs, reports of such beliefs can have very real and tragic effects on those who are uneducated. In 2003, before the controversy surrounding Maathai developed, several politicians and clerics in northern Nigeria told their followers that Americans had put HIV in polio vaccines in order to make African women infertile. Not surprisingly, many Africans refused to be vaccinated; the result was that polio spread to eleven West African countries, leaving nearly seven hundred children paralyzed.[56] Educating people can increase their ability to distinguish between real and bogus claims.

Education is also needed in countries that are likely to be targets of bioterrorists. Richard Betts has called for extensive civil defense programs to prepare Americans for possible attacks employing weapons of mass destruction. In addition, antibiotics to treat victims of bioterrorism could be stockpiled, though at substantial cost. In the aftermath of the anthrax attacks on Washington, D.C., the U.S. government ordered nine hundred million dollars' worth of antibiotics, but these are only effective for eighteen months. Are the American people prepared to spend almost a billion dollars every year and a half to prepare for a hypothetical attack? Other measures that could be implemented to prepare for bioterrorism include the stockpiling or actual distribution of protective masks (as is already done in Israel), the purchase and distribution of decontamination equipment, public education about protection from biological weapons, and increased public health resources to deal with an attack. Narita Airport in Japan already screens transiting passengers for infectious diseases, something that could be done at airports throughout the world.

At present, as Laurie Garrett has warned, "The world is completely vulnerable to a smallpox attack."[57] Currently, only about 10 percent of the world's 6.3 billion people have been vaccinated against smallpox. The solution to this vulnerability would be to vaccinate the world's people. The last time an emergency mass vaccination took place in the United States was in 1947, when a visitor from Mexico "imported" smallpox into New York City. In less than four weeks 6.35 million New Yorkers were vaccinated, and the epidemic was stopped. In 1961, smallpox broke out in Britain, and 5.5 million people were vaccinated within thirty days. In 1971, twenty million people were vaccinated in Yugoslavia. Today, no country has the stocks of smallpox vaccine to respond so massively and quickly. Stockpiling vaccines, then, is one way to respond to this bioterrorist threat.

In December 2004, the U.S. National Intelligence Council noted the very real and substantial threat of disease in the report on its 2020 Project. The Council concluded that while terrorism could slow globalization, a widespread pandemic could stop it altogether.[58] Such a development would have profound implications for the future of civilization as we know it. For this reason, the threat of infectious disease may be the most serious that exists.

RECOMMENDED READING

Printed Sources

Betts, Richard K. "The New Threat of Mass Destruction." *Foreign Affairs* 77 (January/February 1998): 26–41.
Garrett, Laurie. *Betrayal of Trust: The Collapse of Global Public Health*. New York: Hyperion, 2000.
———. "The Lessons of HIV/AIDS." *Foreign Affairs* 84 (July/August 2005): 51–65.
———. "The Next Pandemic?" *Foreign Affairs* 84 (July/August 2005): 3–23.
Haacker, Markus, ed. *The Macroeconomics of HIV/AIDS*. Washington, D.C.: International Monetary Fund, 2004.
International Crisis Group. *HIV/AIDS as a Security Issue*. ICG Report. Washington, D.C., and Brussels: June 19, 2001. Available at www.icg.org.
Lederberg, Joshua, ed. *Biological Weapons: Limiting the Threat*. Cambridge, Mass.: MIT Press, 1999.
McNeil, William. *Plagues and Peoples*. New York: Anchor Books, 1976.
Milbank Memorial Fund and Council on Foreign Relations. *Why Health Is Important to U.S. Foreign Policy*. New York: Milbank Memorial Fund, 2001.

————. *Addressing the HIV/AIDS Pandemic: A U.S. Global AIDS Strategy for the Long Term.* New York: Milbank Memorial Fund, 2004.

Oldstone, Michael. *Viruses, Plagues, and History.* New York: Oxford University Press, 2000.

Singer, P. W. "AIDS and International Security." *Survival* 44 (Spring 2002): 145–58.

Tucker, Jonathan B. *Scourge: The Once and Future Threat of Smallpox.* Boston: Atlantic Monthly, 2001.

U.S. National Intelligence Council. *The Global Infectious Disease Threat and Its Implications for the United States.* NIE-99-17D. Washington, D.C.: January 2000.

Websites

Centers for Disease Control: www.cdc.gov
International Crisis Group: www.icg.org
National Institutes of Health: www.nih.gov
Joint United Nations Programme on HIV/AIDS (UNAIDS): www.unaids.org
Roll Back Malaria Campaign, World Health Organization: www.rbm.who.int
World Health Organization: www.who.int.

7

Cyber-Threats: How We're All Connected to the Bad Guys

Lest you be skeptical that the threats to computer systems and the computer-based infrastructure of the United States are overhyped creations of the media, consider the following actual events.

Members of the September 11 network that perpetrated the attacks on Washington, D.C., and New York communicated via the Internet using encrypted messages. Following the attacks, there was fear that the Al Qaeda network would use cyber-attacks in the future.[1] As Frank Ciluffo of the Office of Homeland Security put it, "While bin Laden may have his finger on the trigger, his grandson might have his finger on the mouse."

In late 1999 the FBI got very concerned about attempts that had been going on for more than a year to break into U.S. government computers. The FBI, which called its investigation into this case "Moonlight Maze," traced the hackers to Moscow. The FBI found that they had downloaded military technical research, such as missile guidance programs.

In February 2000, several of the largest sites on the Internet were bombarded with requests to respond. For three days, Amazon.com, eBay, CNN.com, ZDNet, E*Trade, and Excite were either slowed or shut down. Computer scientists referred to this as a "denial of service" attack; it was "the digital equivalent of a nervous breakdown."

Starting in June 2000, millions of computer users began receiving a message saying "ILOVEYOU" and containing an attachment that once opened would send itself to everyone on the address list and replicate itself. The so-called Love Bug was by far the most damaging virus ever. It infected an estimated forty million computers and cost an estimated ten billion dollars in lost productivity. It infected 80 percent of all U.S. federal agencies and departments, including the Defense and State departments.

In September 2002, Ramzi bin al-Shibh, an Al Qaeda member who was indicted as a co-conspirator for the 9/11 attacks, was captured in Pakistan. In his apartment were three satellite phones, five laptop computers, a CD burner, and more than five hundred

CDs. He apparently had lived in the apartment for months and communicated with other Al Qaeda members using satellite phones and the Internet.[2]

In November 2002, Omar Bakri Muhammed, one of Britain's most outspoken Islamic clerics, gave an exclusive interview to *Computerworld* in which he said that "in a matter of time you will see attacks on the stock market," referring specifically to the markets of New York, London, and Tokyo.[3]

These events underscore the importance of information and the vulnerability of individuals, corporations, and countries to cyber-attacks. This chapter will: (1) review the importance of information in history; (2) describe the security implications of the offensive and defensive uses of information; and (3) review the possibilities of terrorists employing cyberwar techniques.

INFORMATION IN HISTORY

Throughout history, there have been four fundamental sources of power: economic wealth, military force, ideas, and information. Almost four centuries ago, the English philosopher Francis Bacon wrote, "Knowledge itself is power."[4] Prominent leaders in the worlds of business, commerce, and defense have noted the shift in the contemporary world from the pursuit of wealth and military power to what former Citibank chairman Walter Wriston has called the "pursuit of information and the application of information to the means of production."[5] Former Secretary of Defense William Perry has written, "We live in an age that is driven by information. Technological breakthroughs . . . are changing the face of war and how we prepare for war."[6]

Successful leaders throughout history have recognized the significance of information and communications. For example, the Chinese strategist Sun Tzu wrote: "What enables the wise sovereign and good general to strike and conquer is foreknowledge."[7] Early American patriot Benjamin Franklin may very well have been the first American information warrior; he is reported to have forged documents discrediting the British during the Revolutionary War.

In the Second Punic War, Hannibal used mirrors to communicate quickly and over long distances.[8] Genghis Khan used then state-of-the-art techniques to communicate quickly and effectively—riders on horseback with spare horses. When the horse the rider was on became tired, he would switch to the next. RAND Corporation analysts John Arquilla and David Ronfeldt have written: "This gave the horsemen, in relative terms, something approximating an ability to provide real-time intelligence, almost as from a satellite, on the enemy's order of battle and intentions."[9]

One of the most significant uses of information in the twentieth century was the Allies' breaking of German and Japanese codes, which enabled the Allies to know a great deal about the location, strength, and intentions of enemy forces.[10] Franklin Roosevelt and Winston Churchill made extensive use of the Axis powers' decrypted messages—that is, the raw data that the Allies intercepted and processed. However, Churchill refused to rely on intelligence reports that had been "sifted and digested" and insisted on seeing the "authentic documents . . . in their original form."[11] Throughout the Second World War, Churchill was able to read through the intercepted messages of the Axis powers and to base momentous decisions in part on these messages.

Given the sheer number of messages today, it would be impossible for a leader to review even a small percentage of the raw "unsifted and undigested" information received by a country or large corporation in a single day. Commenting on the crisis in Lebanon in July 1982, Secretary of State George Shultz would recall, "I became aware of an acute problem with the State Department's system of crisis management. The pace of events had outstripped the traditional methods of receiving cabled messages from overseas and responding with written instructions to our posts. There simply was not time to draft, type, code, transmit, decode, process and read written telegraphic traffic."[12] Eight years later, the situation that Shultz described had become much worse; during the first thirty hours of the first Gulf war, American troops received 1,300,000 electronic messages.

In the fall of 2001, leaders in the White House were able for the first time to watch a live video feed of an ongoing battle as images of an attack on Taliban forces were transmitted by a pilotless spy plane from Afghanistan. The transmission was sent to Central Command Headquarters in Florida and then to Washington, D.C. The president now literally has the ability to see what is happening on the battlefield. Anyone confronted with this tidal wave of data could be overwhelmed without an effective means of processing it reliably and quickly and in a way that makes it usable.

These examples demonstrate that the contemporary information problem is not obtaining data but gaining intelligence and knowledge (i.e., storing, processing, accessing, and presenting information) so that it can be transformed by the leader into power. Often there is so much data that national intelligence agencies—even of the most advanced countries—cannot process all of the information available in a timely fashion; this was made tragically evident on September 11, 2001. Because of this flood of information, leaders often turn to the most accessible sources of information: the print and electronic mass media.

In the first Gulf war, information was not only a management challenge but a tool (actually, a weapon) that was used by the United States in some traditional ways. For example, in the early days of the war, to hinder Iraq's access to information and to limit its leaders' ability to communicate with one another and their military commanders, the United States took down Iraq's electrical power grid. In an information warfare tactic drawn from twentieth-century conflicts, the United States dropped twenty-nine million leaflets behind enemy lines with fourteen different messages. It is estimated that these leaflets reached 98 percent of the three hundred thousand Iraqi soldiers; one Iraqi general said, "Second only to the bombing campaign, the leaflets were the highest threat to the morale [of Iraqi troops]." The United States also used false information to confuse the Iraqis. For example, on the basis of information released by the U.S. military, CNN reported that the United States was preparing to invade Kuwait amphibiously. This caused Saddam Hussein to move forces into Iraq to prepare for an invasion from the sea. This may have been the first war in history in which the enemy leaders watched the same, nearly instantaneous reports on the war.

More recently, information has been employed as a central and very effective tool in the fight against terrorism. The information that several hundred Special Forces troops on the ground in Afghanistan provided to air-attack planners enabled the United States to decimate Al Qaeda and Taliban bases with minimal loss of U.S. forces. In addition, American special operations forces in Afghanistan printed thousands of leaflets advertising a reward that the United States offered for information related to Osama bin Laden and leaders of Al Qaeda. At a minimum, these leaflets made the Al Qaeda and Taliban leaders less secure, and they may have helped in the identification and capture of some of those leaders.

OFFENSIVE AND DEFENSIVE USES OF INFORMATION

Information has been a crucial element in warfare for as long as wars have been fought. What has changed in the contemporary era? Computers are the most significant change. Individuals, corporations, and governments are all dependent on computers and electronic information sources. Yet computers are vulnerable to attack and disruption.

The growth of information in today's world is staggering. The amount of information in the world is reported to be doubling every eighteen months. An estimated 85 percent of all the scientists who have ever lived are alive today. Computers have contributed to the exponential growth of information. According to Dr. Carver Mead of the California Institute of Technology, "The entire Industrial Revolution enhanced production by a factor of about a hundred. The microelectronic revolution has already enhanced productivity in the information-based technology by a factor of more than a million—and the end isn't in sight yet."[13] If another high-tech industry—the aircraft industry—"had undergone similar progress during the last three decades, a trip from Tokyo to Washington, D.C., would take less than five minutes, would cost two dollars, and would all be done on less than half a gallon of gas." One last indicator of change: the cost of storing, processing, and transmitting a unit of information during the past fifty years has declined by a factor of up to a hundred million or more and is projected to continue to decline over the next decade. A 2004 National Intelligence Council report noted, "Today individual PC users have more capability at their fingertips than NASA had with the computers used in its first moon launches."[14]

This is the good news, but there is a downside as well. With a relatively small investment, someone can purchase a computer system that could disrupt various national infrastructures. The principal investigator of a U.S. General Accounting Office report stated in 1996, "Countries today do not have to be military superpowers with large standing armies, fleets of battleships or squadrons of fighters to gain a competitive edge. Instead, all they really need to steal sensitive data or shut down military computers is a two-thousand-dollar computer and modem and a connection to the Internet."[15] By launching a denial-of-access attack on key military information sites, an adversary might interrupt access to information just as effectively as by destroying the electrical grid with conventional military weapons, such as bombs. Thus, a small- or medium-sized country could pose a significant threat. Dr. Martin Libicki, a specialist on information warfare at the RAND Corporation, has called attention to the potential danger:

> Imagine what a sophisticated middle income country could do with a few thousand French and/or Russian precision guided munitions (PGMs); a few unmanned aerial vehicles (UAVs)(from any of thirty countries); digital videocameras; personal computers; cellular switches, phones and pagers; GPS [Global Positioning System] and pseudolite receivers; pocket radars; and night vision goggles; plus archived Powerscene maps combining purchased space imagery and topography, all integrated by a few hundred trained engineers—a Radio Shack System-of-Systems.[16]

One U.S. government report estimates that approximately 120 of the world's two hundred states are developing information warfare techniques. And that's not all. George Tenet, former CIA director, has pointed out that terrorist groups including Hezbollah, Hamas, the Abu Nidal organization, and Al Qaeda are using computerized files, e-mail, and encryption to support their operations.[17] The National Intelligence Council has predicted, "We expect that terrorists will also try to acquire and develop the capabilities to conduct cyber attacks to cause physical damage to computer systems and to disrupt critical information networks."[18] What capabilities does the information revolution make available to those who would wage, as well as protect against, information warfare?

It is difficult for most who are not proficient in computer science to fully understand what they read about computer attacks. How many people know what "packet sniffers," "IP spoofing," "worms," and "viruses" are? In figure 7.1, we have tried to categorize various types of hardware and software according to whether they are used for offensive or defensive purposes.

The techniques on the left side of the figure are used for offensive purposes—that is, to attack another individual's, corporation's, or government's computer system. The techniques on the right-hand side of the figure are used for defensive purposes: to prevent an attack on one's own computer system. Two other dimensions of the figure that are significant are reflected in the vertical axis. The techniques at the top of the figure are more expensive than those at the bottom. In addition, there are fewer suppliers of the techniques at the top of the figure.

OFFENSIVE TECHNIQUES

At one time or another, every computer user has either forgotten a password or has tried to open another person's computer. Guessing a password is a rudimentary form of offensive computer hacking. A more serious form is password "cracking,"

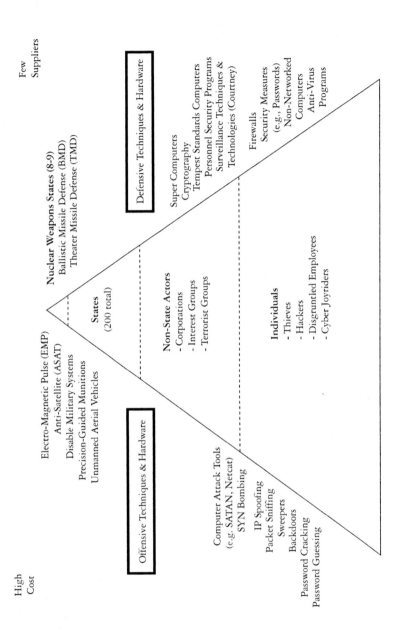

Figure 7.1. *Information Operations and Warfare Typology.*

whereby an unauthorized user utilizes a dictionary or other computer program to go through thousands or even millions of alphanumeric combinations in order to hit upon someone's password. This is the reason that some computer software security programs allow only a limited number of tries to enter passwords.

E-mail is now ubiquitous; it is hard to communicate in certain sectors without relying on e-mail. This form of communication has increased the speed, ease, and cost of communicating, and many routinely communicate with people in other countries quickly, reliably, and at little expense. The growth of e-mail illustrates one of the central paradoxes of the contemporary information revolution: e-mail has enhanced people's ability to communicate while at the same time increasing their vulnerability to communications disruptions. Recall, for example, how all communication via e-mail stops following denial-of-service attacks on networks.

E-mail can be forged, slowed down, or stopped using a number of techniques. "E-mail bombs" are used to overwhelm an e-mail server. One form of this attack is referred to as "spamming," a name that reportedly was appropriated from an old Monty Python episode in which a waitress offers her customers a choice of "spam, spam, spam, and spam!"

Messages travel across the Internet in blocks of data called "packets." An e-mail message or Web page might be broken into several packets prior to entering the network. Once the packets are received, they can be reassembled. A "packet sniffer" makes it possible to intercept packets of information as they travel across the Internet. Hackers have used sniffers to intercept user names and passwords, which can then be used for entering otherwise protected networks. In July 1995, the FBI identified a hacker who was using the Harvard University computer system to break into various U.S. Department of Defense systems, including the Naval Research Laboratory, the Los Alamos National Laboratory, and the Naval Command, Control and Ocean Surveillance Center. In order to find the offender, the FBI used a packet sniffer to scan for messages that came from the hacker, who was using the alias "Gritón" (which means "screamer" in Spanish). The FBI was able to identify an Argentine university student, Julio Cesar Ardita, who plead guilty to wiretapping and computer crime charges.

Every packet of information traveling on the Internet has a source and a recipient, indicated by the Internet Protocol (IP) addresses assigned to all computers on the Internet. Another offensive use of computer technology is called "IP spoofing," which involves forging the source address of a message so that it appears to have originated somewhere else. In a typical IP spoofing attack, the false source is trusted by the recipient, thus allowing the sender entry into a network.

The most notorious computer attacks in the past several years have consisted of "worms" and "viruses." Both of these types of attacks infect computers (hence the medical metaphor) and spread over entire networks. Computers operate strictly according to the instructions that they receive from human operators or from other computers. Such instructions can be changed ("infected"), causing the computer to operate in unexpected or even destructive ways. According to Professor Dorothy

Denning, "The main difference [between worms and viruses] is that a worm is an autonomous agent that spreads entirely on its own, whereas a virus attaches itself to other software and spreads with that software."[19] Viruses need to attach themselves to other programs, and the way that this is typically accomplished is through what is referred to as "social engineering." The "Love Bug" attack cleverly used people's natural curiosity and desire for affection to cause millions to open a message with the subject heading "ILOVEYOU." Once opened, the "Love Bug" virus attached itself to every addressee in the address list of the recipient computer. Social engineering is, in short, a euphemism for a con or subterfuge.

According to Homer, Greek soldiers hid inside a large wooden horse that the Trojans brought inside the gates of their city. Once inside Troy, the Greeks left the horse and defeated the surprised Trojans. Today, a "Trojan horse" is "used to denote any object placed within opposition territory as to conceal its subversive nature." For example, Trojan horse software can be programmed to perform some undesirable and unanticipated action, such as the deletion of files or the erasure of an entire disk. Two specific types of Trojan horses are "logic bombs" and "time bombs." Logic bombs are triggered by a specific event; if the execution occurs at a preset date or time, it is referred to as a "time bomb."

Several examples will illustrate the pernicious effects of Trojan horses. At George Mason University in the Washington, D.C., area in February 1997, someone inserted a Trojan horse into the main university server. Whenever anyone started up Netscape Navigator, the Trojan horse program sent an e-mail message to the university's computer security organization. The e-mail attack was discovered when automated replies were returned to students who had unknowingly sent a protest e-mail. A more destructive Trojan horse could be used militarily. For example, a Trojan horse program could be inserted into military computers in order to disable those computers.

Those who study information operations define "hacking" as "activities conducted online and covertly that seek to reveal, manipulate, or otherwise exploit vulnerabilities in computer operating systems and other software."[20] Hackers generally do not have political agendas; they try to break into computer systems for the challenge, for the same reason that climbers scale mountain peaks—because they are there. In contrast, "hacktivists" combine hacking with political activism. Thus, a number of activist groups use the Internet both offensively as well as defensively in support of their causes. For example, the Zapatista National Liberation Army (EZLN) has used the Internet to garner support for its guerrilla-like insurgency in the Mexican state of Chiapas.[21]

In addition to the techniques described above, hacktivists commonly attempt to break into computers in order to access stored information. The federally funded Computer Emergency Response Team Coordination Center (CERT/CC) reported 2,134 computer security incidents—break-ins and hacks—in 1997. This number rose to 21,756 in 2000, 52,658 in 2001, and 137,529 in 2003.[22] For the period 1988–2003, there were a total of 319,992 incidents. Viruses and worms have grown at similarly impressive rates. Message Labs, which scans clients' e-mails for viruses, noted that one in 1,400 messages in 1999 contained viruses. The infection rate doubled in 2000 to one in seven hundred; in 2001, one in three hundred messages were infected.[23] The cost of viruses is growing significantly; in 2003, Computer Economics, Inc., estimated that the cost of viruses on American businesses in terms of lost revenue and repair costs equaled thirteen billion dollars. The figure increased to seventeen billion dollars in 2004.[24] Clearly, hackers, cyber-joyriders, and hacktivists are responsible for most break-ins and viruses. Increasingly, however, criminals and terrorists are turning their attention to computer networks.

HOW TERRORISTS USE THE INTERNET

As early as 1990, the prestigious National Academy of Sciences began its report on computer security by declaring, "We are at risk. Increasingly, America depends on computers. . . . Tomorrow's terrorist may be able to do more damage with a keyboard than with a bomb."[25] The Federal Bureau of Investigation now takes the cyber-threat seriously; it ranks cyber-crime as its third-biggest priority, following terrorism and espionage.

Terrorists have used the Internet in recent years in seven overlapping ways. First, terrorism is a form of psychological warfare that seeks to instill fear in its opponents, and clearly the Internet can be and has been used to disseminate fear. For example, the Iraqi insurgents captured a number of American and foreign workers and beheaded them when their demands were not met. Horrific images of the beheadings were posted on the Internet for anyone to see.

A second use of the Internet by terrorists is to seek publicity and to disseminate propaganda. Virtually all of the world's major terrorist groups have had active websites with information related to their organizations and causes. Typically, these websites attempt to justify their reliance on violent methods and to recruit supporters. One of the websites consistently identified with Al Qaeda is alneda.com, which translates as "the call" or "the calling." It has presented official statements from leaders of Al Qaeda. U.S. intelligence officials also believe that this site was used to transmit secret messages to Al Qaeda operatives around the world.[26]

Third, terrorists use the Internet to obtain information on potential targets. Dan Verton, the author of *Black Ice: The Invisible Threat of Cyberterrorism*, notes, "Al Qaeda cells now operate with the assistance of large databases containing details of potential targets in the United States. They use the Internet to collect intelligence on those targets, especially critical economic nodes, and modern software enables them to study structural weaknesses in facilities as well as predict the cascading failure effect of attacking certain systems."[27] The President's Commission on Critical Infrastructure Protection identified eight critical infrastructures: telecommunications, banking and finance, electrical power, oil and gas distribution and storage, water supply, transportation, emergency services, and government services.[28]

Like many nonprofit and political organizations, terrorist groups use the Internet to raise money, a fourth use of the Internet by terrorists. As reported on a Council on

Foreign Relations website, terrorismanswers.com, Osama bin Laden has "established companies to provide income and charities that act as fronts. In addition to protection schemes, credit card fraud and drug smuggling are other possible sources of money."[29] According to testimony by Dennis Lormel, the head of the FBI's Terrorist Financial Review Group, "an Al Qaeda terrorist cell in Spain used stolen credit cards in fictitious sales scams and for numerous other purchases for the cell."[30]

Fifth, terrorists use the Internet for recruitment and training purposes. Many web-sites focus on Islamic issues throughout the world; such websites contain download-able videos of fighting in Chechnya, Afghanistan, and Iraq, and videos of prominent Al Qaeda leaders, such as Osama bin Laden and Ayman al-Zawahiri. Islamic *jihadi* groups also use the Internet to distribute training materials concerning bomb-making, kidnapping, assassination, encryption, and poison. One of the most notorious of these training manuals is the *Encyclopedia of Jihad,* which is more than a thousand printed pages in length.

Sixth, as a number of students of terrorism have noted, modern terrorists have adopted a decentralized, networked form of organization, in contrast to the hierar-chical organization of many government agencies. The Internet literally makes this form of organization possible; it provides the capability for anyone to communicate with others in the rest of the world quickly, cheaply, and securely. Terrorists can not only communicate with each other using the Internet but also share information.

Seventh, the Internet provides terrorists with the ability to plan and coordinate quickly, cheaply, and securely. Al Qaeda has used a sophisticated form of encryption called steganography, which involves hiding messages inside graphic files, such as photographs.

What can be done to protect against cyber-terrorism?

Individuals and corporations can take a number of widely known actions to increase their security, but what can countries do to increase the security of their citizens?

Ironically, a recent proposal by computer security executives is to establish a backup communications network in the event that the Internet is disabled.[31] This is ironic because the forerunner of the Internet was invented by the Advanced Research Projects Agency (ARPA) of the Department of Defense in order to provide a redundant communications capability in the event of a nuclear attack. Now, the United States has become so dependent on the Internet that it needs to invent a backup system for the backup system.

Others have suggested organizational reforms in the structure of the United States government. Of course, the creation of the Department of Homeland Security ef-fected the most extensive shake-up of the American government since the passage of the National Security Act of 1947, which created the Department of Defense, the Department of the Air Force, and the Central Intelligence Agency. Several critics have suggested that an assistant secretary position focusing on cyber-security should be established within the Department of Homeland Security.

One of the most obvious safeguards against the compromising of computer systems is physical security—simply to restrict access to computers, to lock them up. In mid-2000, officials at the Los Alamos National Laboratory in New Mexico discovered that a number of computer disks containing nuclear weapons secrets were missing. The disks included information meant to assist its special Nuclear Emergency Security Team (NEST) to find, identify, and disarm a homemade or stolen nuclear bomb. Eventually, the disks were inexplicably found behind a copy machine five weeks after they had disappeared. Of course, as the brouhaha over the "lost disks" revealed, even procedures requiring physical security of sensitive information does not mean that they will be observed or implemented effectively.

Throughout the Cold War, the U.S. government routinely screened anyone who worked with nuclear weapons for psychological problems, criminal backgrounds, and mental instabilities. In one ten-year period, fifty thousand people were disaffiliated with nuclear weapons work due to personal problems with alcoholism, drug use, or psychosis. This could be viewed as good news or bad: good in the sense that people were tested and not allowed to work with nuclear weapons if personal questions were raised; bad in the sense that an average of five thousand people per year in this ten-year period were disaffiliated.

Personnel security programs are an important means of assessing people's suitability for working with data. Background checks and psychological testing can assist companies to identify and weed out potential employees who might not be trustworthy. Sun Microsystems, for example, rejects about 9 percent of all applicants as a result of its screening procedures. Despite such efforts, however, computer specialists indicate that "insiders" are a frequent cause of computer problems and attacks. Disgruntled employees have sabotaged both hardware and software, and such actions can be devastating to an organization. One disgruntled employee who was terminated by a Texas insurance company used a logic or time bomb to delete 168,000 sales commission records. Fortunately for the company, the files were restored from backup tapes, but the threat to corporations is clear.

A second means to increase security is to conduct surveillance on employees. According to a survey of workplace practices conducted by the American Management Association, 35 percent of all companies and 81 percent of financial institutions keep tabs on their employees by recording their telephone conversations and voice mail, checking their computer files, or videotaping them while they work. A number of programs exist to provide this capability, including Professional Edition, WebSense, SurfWatch, and LittleBrother. These programs allow supervisors to review employees' computer usage and retrieve the results of their searches.

A third means to combat unauthorized intrusions into and control of their systems is to hire former hackers, who can assess the security and vulnerabilities of a corporation's information systems. Some of the largest corporations and financial institutions have adopted this strategy in combating hackers.

What else can countries do?

Of course, countries can adopt the safeguards described above for individuals and corporations. Countries can also learn from history and apply the lessons to the present. At the end of World War II, the United States recruited German rocket scientists, the most prominent of whom was Wernher von Braun. These scientists became some of the most important in the American military and space programs. In a similar fashion, the U.S. government could recruit the most capable hackers. In the aftermath of September 11, that recruitment task becomes less difficult; clearly, in the post–September 11 environment the terrorists pose a greater threat than "the government." Although some critics argue that this is like hiring the fox to guard the chickens, who better than an adept hacker knows the vulnerabilities of an organization? Some governmental organizations are given the task of assessing the vulnerability of government computers to attack. The Defense Information Systems Agency of the Department of Defense conducted thirty-eight thousand attacks against unclassified DOD computers from 1992 through 1996; it was able to gain direct access to 4.4 percent of the computers and to 65 to 88 percent of others through indirect means. The U.S. Air Force Information Warfare Center tested the security of 1,248 computers and gained access to 23 percent of them.

The U.S. Army has created a specialized reserve unit in Vermont focusing on defensive information warfare. The U.S. government could create additional military reserve units in high-tech areas such as Silicon Valley, Route 128 around Boston, and the Research Triangle in North Carolina. In addition, accomplished hackers, presumably without criminal records, could be offered direct commissions in the military services, just as individuals with underrepresented and much-needed skills have been offered direct commissions in the past. At present almost all of the psychological operations units in the U.S. military are composed of reservists. Why couldn't cyber-operations units be created? A variant of this approach would be to establish a national voluntary force of high-tech workers to mobilize quickly in case of a national emergency. The "NetGuard's" objectives would include repairing damaged communications systems, restoring computer operations, and supporting recovery efforts in the aftermath of such attacks as those of September 11.

Countries like the United States that are dependent on complex information systems have devoted attention to the need to protect their information infrastructures, which the President's Commission on Critical Infrastructure Protection defines as "the framework of interdependent networks and systems comprising identifiable industries, institutions and distribution capabilities that provide a continuous flow of goods and services essential to the defense and economic security of the United States, the smooth functioning of government at all levels, and of society as a whole." A study sponsored by the Central Intelligence Agency of global trends and future threats to the United States concluded, "Increasing reliance on computer networks is making critical U.S. infrastructures more attractive as targets." Both the President's Commission on Critical Infrastructure Protection and the National Research Council have recommended efforts to protect the nation's critical information networks. RAND analyst John Arquilla has commented that the U.S. government "has constructed a kind of Maginot Line. It has tried to build leakproof firewalls and safe areas. . . . But, as the French discovered in 1940, even the best fortifications can be outflanked and penetrated."[32] Given the leakiness and penetrability of the U.S. infrastructure, how can it best be protected?

Individuals, corporations, and governments can also encrypt their important information. Of course, encryption is a controversial topic, because criminals and terrorists can use the same encryption programs that law-abiding citizens use. Available evidence indicates that members of the Al Qaeda network encrypted their messages to one another. As we have seen, there is evidence that terrorists have used steganography, a sophisticated method to embed messages in digital media files. According to a former French defense ministry official, the terrorists behind a plot to blow up the U.S. embassy in Paris used steganography.[33]

Following the attacks of September 11 and the subsequent military action against the Taliban and Al Qaeda network in Afghanistan, the United States became concerned about the vulnerability of its military systems to disruption, for, as an Air Force lieutenant colonel has pointed out, "Information systems now serve as both weapons and targets of warfare."[34] The U.S. military is more effective than any other national military force in the world, and this effectiveness is due in part, if not primarily, to the employment of advanced technology. But what would happen to this most advanced military if its access to information and advanced technology were blocked? What if access to Global Positioning System information were blocked? What if the computers used to schedule air attacks and other sorties were infected with viruses or worms? The specific answers to these questions are not as important as the general point: that the U.S. military is highly dependent on both software and hardware and that its capabilities could be significantly degraded without firing a shot or dropping a bomb. Not only that, but the bad guys are potentially connected to anyone with a computer and a network connection. That is the age in which we now live.

RECOMMENDED READING

Printed Sources

Arquilla, John, and David Ronfeldt, eds. *In Athena's Camp: Preparing for Conflict in the Information Age*. Santa Monica, Calif.: RAND Corporation, 1997.

———. *Networks and Netwars: The Future of Terror, Crime and Militancy*. Santa Monica, Calif.: RAND Corporation, 2001.

Denning, Dorothy E. *Information Warfare and Security*. Reading, Mass.: Addison-Wesley, 1999.

Latham, Robert. *Bombs and Bandwidth: The Emerging Relationship between Information Technology and Security*. New York: New Press, 2003.

Rattray, Gregory J. *Strategic Warfare in Cyberspace*. Cambridge, Mass.: MIT Press, 2001.

Verton, Dan. *Black Ice: The Invisible Threat of Cyber-Terror*. New York: McGraw-Hill Osborne Media, 2003.

Websites

Computer Emergency Response Team Coordinating Center (CERT/CC): www.cert.com
Department of Homeland Security: www.dhs.gov
Institute for Security Technology Studies at Dartmouth College: www.ists.dartmouth.edu
Institute for National Strategic Studies: www.ndu.edu
Institute for the Advanced Study of Information Warfare: www.psycom.net

8

Drugs and Thugs: Trafficking and International Security

On December 26, 2004, an earthquake measuring 9.0 on the Richter scale shook the ocean floor near the Indonesian island of Sumatra. The earthquake, the fourth most powerful recorded since 1900, triggered a massive tsunami that rippled outward from the earthquake's epicenter at a speed of roughly five hundred miles per hour, engulfing coastal areas throughout the Indian Ocean basin.[1] Three weeks after the disaster struck, estimates put the total number of people killed or missing at over 270,000, but given the fact that many victims were washed out to sea and many villages were completely destroyed, the full death toll may never be known.[2]

Governments around the world responded almost immediately by pledging humanitarian assistance. The dollar amounts were modest at first but quickly increased as state after state reacted to public criticism of their tightfisted policies. Eventually, the governments of the world pledged over four billion dollars in grants and loan assistance, with more promised in the form of debt relief for countries affected by the tsunami.[3]

Far more remarkable, however, was the response of private citizens around the world and the way the generosity of individuals, shared via the Internet, allowed nongovernmental organizations (NGOs) to swing into action with unprecedented speed. Within a week of the disaster, for example, Doctors Without Borders (Médicins sans frontières) announced on its website that the organization had already received as much money from online donations as it could spend in the affected region, given the limitations of its infrastructure and personnel.[4] Private donations were estimated in mid-January 2005 to have amounted to approximately three billion dollars.[5]

The global response to the disaster illustrated many of the most salient features of what we commonly call "globalization." People all over the world were able to see immediately, via video images transmitted via satellite and the Internet, the impact of the tsunami. They were able to respond through a widespread and well-developed network of NGOs (including the International Committee of the Red Cross, World

Vision, Catholic Relief Services, and many others) by making credit card contributions through websites. Funds (in the form of electronic data) were sent halfway around the world, converted into the local currencies, and made available for the purchase of food, water, clothing, medicines, and building material almost instantaneously. And, while governments (largely through the military assets they were able to deploy to the region) played an enormously helpful role in the distribution of aid, much of the initial outpouring of humanitarian assistance bypassed governments completely. In short, the global response illustrated all at once the three democratizations (of technology, finance, and information) that Thomas Friedman claims are at the heart of globalization.[6]

Globalization, however, is a two-edged sword. Just as the democratization (or, simply, the spread) of technology, finance, and information has facilitated global humanitarianism, so has it promoted global crime. The same basic factors that enable the Red Cross to raise and distribute hundreds of millions of dollars in aid in a matter of weeks allow Colombian drug lords or Russian arms traffickers to launder similar amounts of money in an equally brief period of time. Globalization allows consumers in the advanced industrialized states to buy clothing manufactured in Bangladesh, computers assembled in Indonesia, and insurance policies sold by telemarketers in India, but it also allows consumers—sometimes the very same consumers—to buy heroin manufactured from poppies grown in Afghanistan, antiquities illegally exported from Egypt, and even young girls kidnapped and trafficked from Thailand.

TRAFFICKING AND TRANSNATIONAL CRIMINAL ORGANIZATIONS (TCOs)

While globalization has created the environment, it is *trafficking* that raises security issues. Trafficking is simply illegal trade. The term refers both to commerce involving legal goods (such as cigarettes or computers) traded illegally (by, for example, evading taxes or contravening export or import restrictions) and to commerce involving illegal goods (such as narcotics or human beings) when traded in any manner whatsoever.

Trafficking, although dramatically expanded by it, is not a product of globalization. In fact, both in the form of the illicit trade of legal goods and in the form of commerce in illegal goods, trafficking is an ancient activity that has involved, at various points in history, the bones of saints, Dutch tulips, and literature on birth control.

Although the list of legal and illegal items of trade has changed over time, even today a wide variety of commodities is trafficked. The list includes enriched uranium, endangered species of both plants and animals, stolen art, human organs, and illegally copied software (along with the commodities—and lives—we will be focusing on in this chapter). Although it is impossible to know exactly how much wealth is generated by criminal enterprises, most experts believe that drug trafficking and arms trafficking are the two most lucrative forms of trafficking. In fact, drug trafficking is believed to rank behind only the global trade in petroleum as a source of wealth. Human trafficking is generally thought to rank third, with the illicit trade in cultural property (art, antiquities, etc.) ranking fourth in total value.

Behind most of the trafficking that occurs are transnational criminal organizations (TCOs). Some of the biggest and most influential TCOs are well known—the Mafia, the Colombian drug cartels, the Japanese *yakuza,* and the Russian mobs, for example—but many more operate entirely in the shadows. What is perhaps most remarkable about TCOs is the extent to which their power has increased. All operate beyond the sovereignty of any state—that is, outside the law—but that has always been true of criminal enterprises. What is different now is that TCOs actually challenge the sovereignty of some states in areas well beyond the illegal activities that form the core of their identity. To put it differently, TCOs have come to control territory, extract rents (i.e., taxes) in areas under their control, provide services for local populations, and even wage war. All of these are functions that we have historically associated with sovereign states.

The wealth of some TCOs—especially certain drug cartels—has permitted them to arm themselves with sophisticated weaponry and other technologies capable in some instances of matching those wielded by states. For example, Pablo Escobar of the Medellín cartel is reported to have tried to purchase surface-to-air missiles (SAMs).[7] Although some improvements are occurring, states generally have been ill adapted to addressing the problems that TCOs present. As Roy Godson and Phil Williams note, "Governments are equipped and experienced in dealing with security threats from other governments. They are neither comfortable nor familiar with threats that are nonmilitary in character, that target society and the economy rather than the state per se, and that cannot be dealt with through traditional state-centric policy options."[8]

Different forms of trafficking raise different sorts of security issues. Human trafficking, for example, presents what is most commonly regarded as a human rights issue rather than a security issue. In the United States, responsibility for combating human trafficking rests with the Department of State and the Department of Justice, a clear indication that the issue has not been "securitized." Of course, to those trapped in modern forms of slavery, human trafficking is a security issue of the highest order. To security analysts, this form of trafficking could be said to raise security issues only in the context of the emerging concept of human security, according to which most, if not all, of those matters that affect the security of individual human beings (as opposed to those that affect the state only) are securitized. It is fair to ask, though, whether enslavement associated with war (as in Sudan) may move human trafficking toward inclusion as a national security issue. There are some indications, including a special report on human trafficking published by the Director of Central Intelligence in 1999, that such a move is occurring in the United States.[9]

Drug trafficking, like human trafficking, generates enormous wealth for criminals but tragic consequences for many of the individuals who are caught up in drug abuse or the violence commonly associated with it. It too seems to lend itself to legal rather than military responses. Unlike human trafficking, however, drug trafficking has not only been criminalized (with responsibility for addressing drug problems in the United States vested in a variety of law enforcement agencies, including the Drug Enforcement Agency [DEA], and in the Office of National Drug Control Policy) but securitized as well. Since the late 1980s, the U.S. military's Southern Command has been assigned the task of assisting Colombia's struggle against drug trafficking and, more broadly, seeking to interdict shipments of drugs destined for the United States. The intermixing of drug trafficking and revolutionary violence in Colombia, Afghanistan, and the Golden Triangle raises security concerns as well.

The nature and fundamental purpose of the commodity being traded makes arms trafficking a national security issue. The black market trade in weapons has long been implicated as a key factor in promoting and sustaining wars and revolutionary violence. It is not necessary, in other words, to be an advocate of a broader security agenda in order to view arms trafficking as a bona fide security issue. At the same time, certain characteristics of the illegal trade in arms (such as its role in facilitating the growth in the number of child soldiers worldwide) have made the trade (both legal and illegal) a key concern among advocates of human security.

We focus on these three forms of trafficking—human trafficking, drug trafficking, and arms trafficking—both because they represent significant threats to the well-being of individual human beings across the globe and because they help to illustrate different stages in the securitization of political issues. Human trafficking represents the entering wedge: a crime and a human rights concern but not yet, at least outside the realm of human security, a fully securitized problem. Drug trafficking has made the transition, so armed forces actually stand behind at least a portion of the "war on drugs." Arms trafficking has been a security issue at least since Caribbean gunrunners supplied weapons to the Confederacy during the Civil War, but it nonetheless has much in common with other forms of trafficking.

HUMAN TRAFFICKING

The U.S. State Department estimates that six to eight hundred thousand people are trafficked internationally each year, although the number may be far higher.[10] Free the Slaves, a nongovernmental organization, estimates that twenty-seven million people worldwide are held in some form of slavery.[11] In some places, such as Sudan, the slavery is of a type not all that different from that which existed in the United States up to the end of the Civil War. Elsewhere, as in South Asia, involuntary servitude is linked to industrialization, as people—often women and children—are forced to work in sweatshops making clothes, shoes, sporting goods, toys, or other consumer products sold worldwide. However, the most lucrative form of the trade in human beings for traffickers is sex slavery. Seventy percent of trafficking victims are female; a majority of those—both women and young girls—are trafficked for the purpose of prostitution.[12] The United States is no sanctuary. In fact, the CIA estimates that up to twenty thousand people are trafficked into the United States each year, most of them young women who, lured into the country by promises of good jobs as unskilled workers, end up in forced prostitution.[13]

Human trafficking, like drug trafficking and arms trafficking, flourishes because it is lucrative. In fact, profits are estimated to be $9.5 billion per year worldwide.[14] Like the other forms of trafficking, it is facilitated by the same patterns of globalization that have fostered the dramatic growth of transnational trade in such legitimate commodities as automobiles and consumer electronics. Human trafficking, in other words, represents the underside of globalization.

The problem of human trafficking is genuinely global in its scope. The Ukrainian government says that as many as four hundred thousand Ukrainian women have been trafficked into forced prostitution over the past ten years. In Côte d'Ivoire, a child can be purchased for as little as seven dollars. In India, an estimated fifteen million children have been sold by their parents into some form of bonded labor. Thailand, a popular destination for sex tourists, has perhaps the world's largest concentration of child prostitutes, many of whom were sold into the industry by their parents.[15] Over 2.3 million females in India, including an estimated five hundred thousand children, work as prostitutes.[16]

Traffickers not only treat human beings as commodities to be bought and sold but prey on the worst forms of human tragedy. People in crushing poverty are the most vulnerable to the false promises that traffickers use to ensnare their victims. Likewise, when children are sold to owners of sweatshops or brothels, it is often a desperate attempt by parents to sustain themselves and their remaining children. Not surprisingly, child labor is most prevalent in the world's least developed countries. Economic security, in other words, provides a measure of protection against some forms of slavery.

The exploitation of tragedy on the part of human traffickers reached disturbing new lows in the aftermath of the South Asian tsunami disaster. In Aceh, Sri Lanka, and elsewhere, human trafficking networks attempted soon after the tragedy to sell orphans to prospective adoptive parents and to sweatshops. Governments in the region responded by restricting travel by children, posting guards at some orphanages, and accelerating efforts to locate relatives of children orphaned by the disaster.[17]

As noted earlier, globalization helps to explain certain elements of human trafficking. International travel has become (in historical terms) inexpensive and simple. The increasing wealth of many of the world's people has dramatically expanded markets for domestic laborers (especially maids and nannies, who, even if not trafficked, are sometimes vulnerable to exploitation or enslavement by unscrupulous employers), for consumer goods that are sometimes manufactured in sweatshops, and for sex tourism. And yet, at the same time, boundaries and other traditional barriers thrown up by sovereignty may provide certain protections to traffickers. Phil Williams explains the situation this way: "Where market opportunities are lucrative, criminal organizations, large and small, ignore borders and typically violate or transcend national sovereignty; where they need safe havens they hide behind borders and exploit sovereignty."[18]

There is no question that human trafficking is an egregious abuse of human rights and a serious issue in international relations, but is it, in any sense, a security issue? The answer, as with many of the issues we consider in this book, is twofold. First, as we have noted, to those who lose their freedom and, in many cases, their lives as a consequence of trafficking, there can be no more serious and immediate threat to their security. Only those of us who are completely unaffected by human trafficking would even think to ask the question in the first place.

But, as with the issues of environmental and economic security and in the case of disease, the determination by governments that an issue constitutes a security problem (that is, the securitization of an issue) is often driven more by realist, state-centered calculations than by humanitarianism. In these terms, human trafficking differs significantly from drug trafficking and arms trafficking, although perhaps not as much as is commonly believed.

Drug trafficking and arms trafficking are considered security concerns in part because of the connection of each to violence and even warfare. Perhaps even more significantly from the standpoint of the traditional understanding of security, drug trafficking and arms trafficking have a demonstrated capacity to undermine states and threaten the stability of governments. Drug profits have sustained revolutionary and paramilitary organizations, while arms sales have altered power balances in both inter- and intrastate conflicts. Human trafficking, however tragic its impact on its victims, appears not to destabilize governments or to promote large-scale violence. Consequently, traditionalists have seen no reason to securitize the issue.

DRUG TRAFFICKING

Worldwide there are two hundred million users of illicit drugs supporting an industry that, by some estimates, generates almost as much revenue each year as the petroleum industry. (As with all illegal commercial activities, an accurate accounting of drug trafficking revenues is difficult to obtain, but retail drug sales are believed to be worth roughly four hundred billion dollars per year, making drugs second only to oil in terms of global revenues.)[19] By far the most popular illicit drug—globally and in the United States—is marijuana; over 40 percent of Americans over the age of twelve report having tried it at least once in their lives.[20] Marijuana, however, does not arouse great concern on the part of government authorities, because its health effects are relatively benign (that is, in comparison to the effects of opiates and narcotics), it provides relatively little incentive for the commission of additional crimes, has relatively low profit margins, is bulky and therefore relatively difficult to transport in large quantities, and, in general, provokes less fear. Cocaine (with 14.1 million users worldwide) and heroin (9.5 million) are far less popular than marijuana, but their highly addictive nature and the enormous profit margins they generate for traffickers, among other factors, make them the focus of many governments' drug policies.

Demand for illicit drugs is fed by a global network of production and distribution. It is this network, linked as it is to transnational criminal organizations (TCOs), corrupt or impotent governments, rebel groups, and sometimes terrorists, that makes drug trafficking a major transnational problem. But is it a security issue?

One way to answer this question is to note the way the United States has approached drug trafficking since 1982, when President Reagan brought together the heads of eighteen federal agencies in an effort to attach new weight to the federal government's drug-control efforts. National drug policy, which is directed by a "drug czar" who heads the Office of National Drug Control Policy that was created within the Executive Office of the President in 1989, has not only been "securitized" but militarized as well.

In 1989, the Department of Defense was designated the "single lead agency" in America's war on drugs. With the Cold War winding down, defense dollars began to be shifted into an effort to stem the tide of illegal drugs entering the United States. From the beginning, however, drug interdiction efforts were focused on a single aspect of drug trafficking, namely, the flow of cocaine from South America into the country. Cocaine, at that time, was the most visible drug problem facing Americans. By 1989, there were at least eight million cocaine addicts in the United States, including a significant number of well-known entertainment and sports personalities, so it is not surprising that cocaine produced in the Andes should have been the focus of the early war on drugs.

Responsibility for the military component of the war on drugs rests with the Miami-based Southern Command (SOUTHCOM), which provides military support, primarily in the form of ships and aircraft, to the Joint Interagency Task Force (JIATF). This group, in turn, brings together not only the Defense Department but the Coast Guard, the Customs Service, the Drug Enforcement Agency, and other federal agencies with responsibility for drug control efforts.

Aside from the fact that it largely ignores a wide range of drugs coming from other parts of the world (including heroin from South Asia), the war on drugs has a number of other characteristics that seem certain to reduce its chances of success. First, efforts to suppress drug production in one area inevitably create incentives for production in another area. Even the successes achieved in Colombia in the disruption of the Medellín and Cali cartels have merely spurred the creation of scores of smaller cartels. Second, the focus on production rather than consumption is problematic in and of itself. It means that the United States is widely perceived as treating its drug problem by lashing out at poor countries around the world rather than by taking responsibility for ending drug use at home. Intervention to destroy drug crops or arrest drug traffickers in places such as Colombia or Afghanistan can arouse resentment at what appears to be another form of imperialism as powerful countries attempt to solve their drug problem "over there" on the supply side rather than at home on the demand side. Furthermore, to destroy coca plants or poppies is, generally, to destroy the livelihoods of poor farmers and not the obscene profits of middlemen.

Declaring war on drugs does not, of course, guarantee that the problem will be treated as a security issue or, more to the point, that it should be. Antidrug policies necessarily involve efforts to reduce both supply *and* demand. When the demand comes from one's own citizens, the idea of a war on drugs, even if only metaphorical, seems inapt.

Regardless of how one views the American war on drugs, there are plenty of reasons to treat drug trafficking as a security issue. First, drug traffickers regularly and persistently employ violence to intimidate government officials, battle with rival traffickers over access to markets and supplies, and facilitate business in many other ways. The term "narcoterrorism" was, in fact, coined to describe the use of violence by drug syndicates against government officials, journalists, and others.

Beyond the actual use of violence by traffickers, drug trafficking presents itself as a security issue for other reasons. Profits from drug trafficking are commonly used to purchase weapons. This means not only that arms trafficking and drug trafficking are frequently linked but that drug cartels and other TCOs are sometimes better armed than the police and even the military forces of many states in which they operate. Drug profits support rebel groups and terrorist organizations as well. In Colombia, FARC (the Revolutionary Armed Forces of Colombia) has funded its long-running effort to overthrow the government with drug money—as much as three hundred million dollars a year. The anti-Taliban Northern Alliance in Afghanistan funded its operations with heroin profits until the United States stepped in to provide support after 9/11. In Lebanon's Bekaa Valley, terrorist training camps have long operated side by side with fields cultivated with opium and cannabis. Finally, although considerable evidence suggests otherwise, there have long been suspicions that Al Qaeda profited from opium sales in the months leading up to 9/11.[21]

In addition to these direct security ramifications, drug trafficking is closely tied to many other global problems that raise security concerns. Beginning with their effects on consumers and working backwards, we may note first that drugs have serious health consequences. Beyond the direct and readily observable health impact of illicit drugs like cocaine and heroin, the spread of HIV/AIDS is associated with intravenous drug use. The societies in which drug abusers live and work must bear a variety of costs associated with the issue. In 2000, illicit-drug-related health care costs in the United States were almost fifteen billion dollars. Productivity losses amounted to over $110 billion.[22] Crime is also closely correlated with illicit drug use.

For Colombia, the problems associated with drug trafficking and the revolution it sustains are staggering. Two million Colombians, out of a total population of thirty-six million, have been displaced by guerrillas or drug traffickers. Only Sudan and the Congo have more internal refugees.[23] Although murder and kidnap rates have declined in recent years, Colombia's rates for these crimes remain among the highest in the world.

In spite of the overthrow of the Taliban and the continuing presence of American troops in Afghanistan, opium production is booming there. Afghanistan accounted for 87 percent of global opium production in 2004, up from 76 percent the previous year. A report by the United Nations argued that the drug trade, which accounts for a staggering 60 percent of Afghanistan's gross domestic product, threatens to undermine democracy and strengthen terrorist organizations.[24]

ARMS TRAFFICKING

Arms trafficking differs from human trafficking and drug trafficking in some ways that are important to note at the outset. First, the illegal trade in weapons is overshadowed by a vast legal—that is, government-sanctioned—trade in arms. (The legal global arms trade in 2002 is calculated to have been worth between $26.3 and $34 billion.)[25] Selling weapons, unlike selling human beings or nonmedicinal drugs, is not illegal in and of itself. Consequently, arms traffickers must either compete with states (or legal corporations operating with state sanction and, commonly, subsidies) or find niche markets in which legitimate arms merchants do not operate. In most instances, this means that traffickers sell to the only buyers with whom legal dealers will not do business: rebel armies, terrorist organizations, drug traffickers, and other actors that threaten states and international order.

Second, the impact of arms trafficking on security is neither indirect nor incidental. While it may be facile to suggest that weapons alone cause wars, the widespread availability of weapons is undoubtedly an important factor both in making the resort to war feasible and in sustaining conflicts that are already under way. Over two-thirds of the world's legitimate arms sales (and, almost certainly, an even higher percentage of illicit sales) are directed toward developing states, a fact that both reflects and contributes to the war-proneness of the developing world.[26] Small arms, which are favorites of traffickers due to their widespread availability, their popularity with consumers, and their portability, are thought to be responsible for over half a million deaths each year.[27]

Finally, arms traffickers have the perverse ability to turn conflict resolution and disarmament to their advantage as postwar demilitarization in one part of the world makes available a supply of weapons for sale elsewhere. The end of the Cold War, for example, resulted in the reduction of standing armies throughout NATO and the Warsaw Pact. While many weapons were destroyed or stockpiled in government arsenals, an unknown (but probably large) number of weapons entered into circulation via arms traffickers. As a result, arms traffickers may function as arbitrageurs of war and peace in the world.

Arms traffickers are middlemen; they sell but do not manufacture weapons. Consequently, the arms that are available on the black market almost invariably were transferred first in legal transactions. Many such transactions were designed to support the security policies of states. This is particularly evident in the case of the United States, which accounts for almost half of all legal arms transfers in the world.[28]

During the 1980s, billions of dollars worth of weapons were channeled into Afghanistan in order to aid Afghan rebels (the *mujahidin*) in their war against the Soviet Union. When the Soviet Union withdrew in 1989, vast quantities of weaponry disappeared. Much of it wound up on the black market. Among the most disturbing aspects of this situation was the disappearance of an unknown number of Stinger missiles onto the market. These shoulder-fired surface-to-air missiles, covertly supplied by the United States, had been used with devastating effect by the *mujahidin* against Soviet aircraft. Roughly 2,300 Stingers had been delivered to the Afghan rebels; six hundred were unaccounted for when Kabul fell to the Taliban. The CIA estimated that about one hundred had been purchased by the Iranians. The remainder were either in the hands of the Taliban, Afghan warlords, or were circulating, via the black market, all over the Middle East and Africa.[29]

Given the threat posed by surface-to-air missiles in the hands of terrorists, the CIA in 1996 authorized an effort to buy back the Stingers wherever they could be found. In early 1997, a CIA official approached the Taliban with an offer to buy the fifty-three Stingers believed to be in the Taliban government's possession. In spite of the generous terms being offered by the CIA, the Taliban refused to sell the missiles, insisting that they were being kept for use in a future conflict with Iran.[30] Soon after, Osama bin Laden began to court the Taliban.

Stingers, however, are not the only shoulder-fired antiaircraft missiles currently being trafficked. In November 2004, a U.S. government official revealed that American intelligence agencies had tripled their formal estimate of shoulder-fired surface-to-air missile systems believed to be at large worldwide. The revision was based on a determination that at least four thousand of the weapons in Iraq's prewar arsenals cannot be accounted for. The new government estimate says that a total of six thousand of the weapons may be outside the control of any government, up from a previous estimate of two thousand. It is not known how many of the missiles are in the hands of terrorist organizations. However, the price on the black market is said to be five thousand dollars. That the price is so low means that the black-market supply of antiaircraft missiles is plentiful and that they are within the reach of almost any organization that might be interested in purchasing them.[31]

Many experts believe that the widespread availability of shoulder-fired missiles combined with the increasing difficulty of carrying bombs onboard commercial airliners means it is only a matter of time before terrorists attack civil aviation in the United States, perhaps even in a coordinated attack involving planes taking off or landing at many different airports. At Los Angeles International Airport, the threat has prompted the addition of more security fencing and additional patrols in the area surrounding the airport, but officials acknowledge that the enormous urban area surrounding the airport makes surveillance extremely difficult.[32]

In most of the world, trafficking in small arms presents a greater security concern. Weapons like the American-made M-16 rifle or the Russian-made AK-47 have been the primary instruments of the many intrastate conflicts that have plagued the globe since the end of the Cold War. They are inexpensive and widely available, making it easy for aggrieved groups to take up arms against governments or other nonstate actors. These same characteristics facilitate illicit trade and make regulation more difficult to enforce. Their ease of use and small size make small arms ideal for use by untrained combatants and even child soldiers. Making the problem even worse, the end of the Cold War was accompanied by both a loss of superpower control over the trade in small arms and the creation of a tremendous surplus of weapons. Furthermore, the existence of transnational criminal organizations trafficking in drugs and persons provided a ready-made network of dealers for the illicit weapons trade. In short, a broad convergence of factors brought the issue of small arms trafficking to the fore during the 1990s.[33]

Arms trafficking is commonly fed by the profits generated by other forms of illegal commerce. Colombian drug cartels, for example, have been major purchasers of weapons for many years. In Sierra Leone during the 1990s, a rebel group called the RUF armed itself through the sale of diamonds mined and illegally exported from the country. Sierra Leone's bloody civil war, which was characterized by extraordinary levels of gratuitous violence that included hacking off the limbs of thousands of noncombatants, was sometimes described as a war about nothing, since the rebels often appeared unconcerned with political objectives. More important than any political objectives, however, was the fundamental economic objective of gaining and maintaining control of the country's diamond mines, since the wealth available from diamonds was the only means the rebels had of supporting their insurgency.

In Sierra Leone, Colombia, Afghanistan, Burma, and many other places in the world, trafficking in one commodity tends to facilitate, and often finance, trafficking in other commodities. Rebel groups, transnational criminal organizations, and even terrorists understand that the distribution networks, methods of transportation, and money laundering systems that make drug trafficking possible often work just as well for arms trafficking (and vice versa). What this means is that addressing trafficking in all its forms requires dealing with networks. But it also requires an understanding of markets.

Trafficking, like legal trade, involves market transactions for which both interested buyers and sellers must exist. There is, in other words, both a supply side and a demand side. As with most unregulated market transactions, the terms of trade are adjusted as supply and demand fluctuate. This means that a drop in demand brought about, for example, by vigorous enforcement of laws that make it illegal to travel abroad to engage in sex with a child or by a public education campaign that succeeds in reducing the number of cocaine users will, *ceteris paribus* (all other things being equal, as cautious economists like to say), cause the price of the commodity in question to decrease. Prices will also fall when supply increases faster than demand, as might happen when thousands of weapons become expendable at the end of a war or favorable growing conditions produce a bumper crop of the opium poppies from which heroin is derived.

The very existence of trafficking, which we defined at the outset as illegal trade, indicates that simply legislating against slavery, drug abuse, or selling weapons without an export license is inadequate. Enforcement is necessary too, but not because enforcement, no matter how vigorous, is likely to eliminate trafficking. At best, enforcement simply imposes additional costs on traffickers. The seizure of a shipment of drugs or weapons reduces (usually by a very small amount) the total supply available. By the laws of supply and demand, prices increase and, in the end, the industry as a whole (if not the individual seller) profits just as much as it would have in the absence of the seizure. Looked at another way, the costs imposed by law enforcement are, for traffickers, just one of the costs of doing business, costs that ultimately will be paid by consumers.

Some argue, on the basis of the fundamental economics of trafficking, that decriminalization (perhaps in combination with taxation) is the solution. If every step taken to stamp out trafficking merely makes it more profitable for the traffickers who survive (or those who choose to get into the business when they see the enormous profits to be made), then antitrafficking efforts are like punching a pillow or squeezing a balloon: an indentation here causes a bulge there. The problem is exacerbated by the fact that the world is divided into two hundred separate sovereign states; some have considerable capacity, along with the will, to develop and enforce laws against trafficking, and some do not. In the end, our ability to address trafficking may depend to a considerable degree on collective action. The international community, in this as in so many other respects, is only as strong as its weakest member.

RECOMMENDED READING

Printed Sources

Berdal, Mats, and Monica Serrano, eds. *Transnational Organized Crime and International Security: Business as Usual?* Boulder, Colo.: Lynne Rienner, 2002.

Farer, Tom. *Transnational Crime in the Americas.* New York: Routledge, 1999.

Richard, Amy O'Neill. *International Trafficking in Women to the United States: A Contemporary Manifestation of Slavery and Organized Crime.* Intelligence Monograph. Washington, D.C.: Center for the Study of Intelligence, Central Intelligence Agency, November 1999.

Trafficking in Persons Report 2004. Washington, D.C.: U.S. Department of State, June 2004.

Williams, Phil, ed. *Illegal Immigration and Commercial Sex: The New Slave Trade.* Portland, Ore.: Frank Cass, 1999.

Websites

Office of National Drug Control Policy: www.whitehousedrugpolicy.gov/

The Protection Project: www.protectionproject.org/

United Nations Office on Drugs and Crime: www.unodc.org/unodc/index.html.

III

Political and Social Conditions of Insecurity

9

The State of the State: National Security after 9/11

Immediately after the 9/11 attacks, Richard Perle, then chairman of the Defense Policy Board, said, "This could not have been done without help of one or more governments. . . . Someone taught these suicide bombers how to fly large airplanes. I don't think that can be done without the assistance of large governments. You don't walk in off the street and learn how to fly a Boeing 767."[1]

Perle was not alone in mistakenly assuming that there had to be a state behind the most destructive attacks on American soil in history. President Bush, Deputy Defense Secretary Paul Wolfowitz, and other high-level administration officials sought to link Al Qaeda specifically to Iraq after 9/11. Richard Clarke, the National Security Council official in charge of counterterrorism efforts, recounts a conversation with President Bush on the evening of September 12. The president, having previously been assured by the CIA and others that Al Qaeda was solely responsible for the attacks, said to Clarke and others in the Situation Room of the White House, "I want you, as soon as you can, to go back over everything, everything. See if Saddam did this. See if he's linked in any way."[2] The Bush administration's search for evidence of a direct link between Iraq and Al Qaeda continued right up to the beginning of the war with Iraq in March 2003. Evidence of contacts, including a Czech report (later discounted) of a meeting between hijacker Mohamed Atta and an Iraqi diplomat in Prague, were touted as "ties" or "links." In fact, on February 5, 2003, Secretary of State Colin Powell, addressing the United Nations Security Council in an effort to gain international support for the American war in Iraq, said, "Iraqi officials deny accusations of ties with Al Qaeda. These denials are simply not credible."[3]

While the Bush administration was clearly attempting to make a credible case for including military action against Iraq in the "global war on terrorism," key officials also seem to have been trapped in an outmoded worldview that made it difficult, if not impossible, to envision significant threats to the security of the United States emanating from nonstate actors. States have long been considered central to what security is all about, both as the primary objects of security and as the primary threats to the security of other states.

Until recently, most studies of international security focused on the state and on the problem of war. During the Cold War, in fact, the term *security studies* referred almost exclusively to the study of the military and the use of force in international politics. Stephen Walt, for example, said that "security studies may be defined as the study of the threat, use, and control of military force."[4] Much of security studies, in fact, was devoted even more specifically to problems related to nuclear deterrence and arms control. The centrality of the state can also be seen in the ubiquity of the term *national security*. (As students of international relations will know, the term *national* commonly substitutes for the term *state* or *nation-state,* as in *the national interest* and *national defense.*) When the United States reformed its defense and foreign policy apparatus after World War II, it did so through a legislative initiative called the National Security Act of 1947. One of the major creations of that act (as amended in 1949) was the National Security Council. In 1952, President Truman created the National Security Agency as the focus of activities related to electronic intelligence.

The same emphasis on the state can be seen in other countries as well. The chief intelligence agency of the Soviet Union for most of its history was the Komitet Gosudarstvennoy Bezopasnosti (KGB), or Committee for State Security. Today, the main security agency of the People's Republic of China is the Ministry of State Security. Indeed, this pattern is almost universal. It is state (or national) security that preoccupies virtually every government in the world.[5] This fact alone makes it important to examine the state and the closely related phenomenon of war as part of our survey of security.

STATES AND SECURITY: AN AMBIVALENT RELATIONSHIP

For more than 350 years, states have been the fundamental constituents of global society. Peoples seeking to establish political communities in which to enshrine their most cherished values have aspired to the creation of states. The Wilsonian principle of self-determination, which holds out the promise that every nation should be able to incorporate itself in the form of a state, has become a part of international human rights law.[6] It has also become extraordinarily popular, at least if the growth in the number of states (and the tremendous human costs incurred to achieve that growth) is any indication.

At the beginning of the twentieth century, there were fifty-five independent states in the world; today the United Nations has 191 member states.[7] The dismemberment of colonial empires proceeded so rapidly following World War II that the Trusteeship Council, one of the six main organs of the United Nations and a body dedicated to the oversight of dependent territories, was able to suspend its operations in 1994. The Trust Territory of the Pacific Islands, a strategic trust administered by the United States until 1990, was the last to appear on the agenda of the Trusteeship Council. Its dissolution yielded three new states, each a member of the United Nations in its own right (the Federated States of Micronesia, the Republic of the Marshall Islands, and the Republic of Palau), and the Commonwealth of the Northern Marianas, which remains a part of the United States.

States exist, and their number continues to increase, because they have proven themselves adept at protecting and promoting certain fundamental values. The values that we most commonly look to the state to provide are order, rights, collective goods, and security from external threats.

To many theorists, the most important function of the state is to establish order or, in the words of the U.S. Constitution, to "insure domestic Tranquility." Thomas Hobbes was especially concerned with this point. In a world where the use of force or the threat of force is a constant, people must organize to protect themselves. Beginning in Western Europe at the end of the medieval period and gradually spreading across time and territory to encompass the entire globe, the effort to organize for mutual protection has produced a system of roughly two hundred autonomous states. Over time and in a variety of legal instruments, ranging from the Peace of Westphalia of 1648 to the United Nations Charter of 1945, the state has been legitimated in its role as society's primary manager of force.

It is important to emphasize that the state's role is to manage or control the use of force, not to eliminate it. Force, after all, may be necessary both to secure order within the state and to protect against external threats. States may legitimately use force to promote certain additional aims, such as the defense of norms, including respect for human rights and the prohibition against aggression, adopted by the society of states. Nor is the state's role merely to arbitrate among those who use force. It does not simply establish rules for duels and feuds and insurrections. It seeks to eliminate substate violence while preserving the possibility of state violence, if for no other reason than to quash substate violence in order to prevent the anarchy that prompted Hobbes to posit the need for a Leviathan. The problem, of course, is that the state's use of violence on behalf of security is subject to abuses of many kinds, including violations of the human rights of the state's own citizens and aggression against other states, abuses that are often rationalized by governments as necessary to deal with security threats. The power of the state can be—and often has been—a force for tremendous evil when it has not been subjected to adequate checks, when it has been wielded by unscrupulous rulers, and when it has been placed in the service of inhumane projects. One need think only of the forced collectivization of agriculture in Stalinist Russia, Hitler's Final Solution, or Mao's Cultural Revolution (among many cases) to understand the pitfalls of a system in which states possess what approaches a monopoly on the legitimate use of force. The dimensions of the problem are illustrated by R. J. Rummel's findings that during the twentieth century more people died at the hands of their own governments than were killed in all of the century's wars combined.[8]

Controlling the state's use of force within its own borders is primarily a matter of constitutional arrangements and personal virtues. Beyond its borders, however, the state's use of force is limited by international law, international organizations, and, ultimately, the power of other states. In the more serious cases of the state's abuse of power internally, other states, acting under the authority of international norms and institutions, may be the only means of control available. This, in fact, was the rubric under which NATO intervened in Kosovo, to cite one example.

To summarize, the state occupies a privileged position with respect to the use of force in the contemporary world. Simply put, the state may kill; other actors may not. Of course, the state is an institution—a legal abstraction even—so to say that the state may kill and others may not is to say that only those acting under the authority of the state (soldiers, policemen, executioners) may legitimately use violence.

We may say, then, that the fundamental divide in the world, at least from the standpoint of security, is between those for whom the resort to force is legitimate (i.e., states and their agents) and those who have no such right. The way the world is organized, terrorists, criminal gangs, and disgruntled individuals have no right to employ violence. This is what Hobbes had in mind in presenting Leviathan as the necessary substitute for the "war of each against all."

Of course, to suggest that the dividing line between legitimate users of force and illegitimate ones is the line that separates the state from all others is a bit too simple. It denies the legitimacy of revolutionary violence, including the American Revolution, the French Revolution, and many more recent revolutions, at least some of which have been democratic in both intent and outcome. It leaves individuals and peoples everywhere without effective recourse against injustice when that injustice is cloaked with the authority of the state. It also grants the state too much authority. Even states, after all, cross the line when using force unjustly.

Nonetheless, the Hobbesian insight concerning the state and its relationship to the security of individual human beings is an important one for us to consider in thinking about states and war. It can help us to understand the centrality of the state (and national security) in the traditional paradigm, and it can alert us to a number of important ways that the new security agenda affects states.

THE CHANGING STATE OF THE STATES SYSTEM

Our concern, however, is not only with the way that new conceptions of security affect states. States, and perhaps more importantly the international system that states constitute, are changing in ways that impact our understanding of security.

Perhaps the most obvious change of the past century is the dramatic growth, mentioned earlier, in the number of members of the states system. The almost fourfold increase in the number of sovereign states from the twentieth century's beginning to its end was the result first and foremost of the fragmentation of multiethnic empires in Europe and Asia (including the breakup of the Austro-Hungarian and Ottoman empires after World War I and of the Soviet Union at the end of the Cold War) and of successive waves of decolonization in Africa, Asia, Oceania, and the Caribbean.

As the number of states has increased, the willingness of states to join together in international organizations has also increased. The first intergovernmental organizations (to regulate navigation on the Elbe and Rhine rivers) were formed in the first half of the nineteenth century, in response to the demands of the increased commercial interactions of Europe's states. The 2004/2005 edition of the *Yearbook of International Organizations* lists 1,743 intergovernmental organizations (not including another 593 dissolved or inactive IGOs, over two thousand multilateral treaties establishing regimes, if not institutions, and another two thousand or so entities that are sometimes counted as IGOs).[9]

As the number of intergovernmental organizations has increased, so has the willingness of states to join. The League of Nations, the first IGO to aspire to universal membership, never counted the United States among its members; it rejected Liechtenstein, San Marino, and Monaco as too small to be able to fulfill the obligations of membership; and it suffered the withdrawal of sixteen states (including Japan and Germany), as well as the expulsion of the Soviet Union in 1939. The United Nations, on the other hand, has achieved something very close to universal membership.[10]

The delegitimization of colonialism and the concomitant growth of the size of the society of states have produced a system in which the gap between the strongest and weakest members of the states system, regardless of how strength is measured, has become enormous. Military expenditures by the United States fall just short of an amount equal to the military expenditures of every other state in the world combined.[11] In economic terms, while gross domestic product per capita tops thirty thousand dollars in the ten wealthiest states in the world, in one hundred of the world's states GDP per capita measures five thousand dollars or less.[12] The tiny South Pacific state of Tuvalu has a GDP of twelve million dollars, a sizeable portion of which is derived from a deal negotiated in 2000 to lease the country's Internet domain name (".tv") over a period of twelve years for fifty million dollars.[13] Whereas at one time such differentials would have invited the absorption of the weak into the empires of the strong, today the rules of international society expressly forbid such "solutions" to the weak state/strong state divide.

This leads to another important change in the states system: the persistence of "failed states." Because the security implications of failed states appear so significant today, this issue will be considered separately below.

The increasing democratization of the world's states is another profound change that has significance for our assessment of states and war in the twenty-first century. In 1900, monarchs ruled thirty of the world's sovereign states; today, Freedom House classifies only ten states as monarchies; six are either on or adjacent to the Arabian Peninsula.[14] One hundred years ago, no country in the world met the criteria for democracy, according to Freedom House. At the end of the twentieth century, 119 countries containing almost 3.5 billion people qualified as democracies.[15] There are, of course, many complexities that are obscured rather than revealed by these statistics, and it is important to recognize, as Samuel Huntington notes, that history is not only "messy" but assuredly "not unidirectional."[16] Nevertheless, the changes that these numbers document are profound, particularly when one considers the concept of the "democratic peace."

The democratization of states has gone hand in hand with the feminization of states. In 1900, only one country in the world (New Zealand) had extended the right to vote to all of its women. Today, there are only three states that still deny women the right to vote: Brunei and the United Arab Emirates (neither of which allows men *or* women to vote) and Saudi Arabia.[17] In 1900, not a single state in the world allowed women to stand for election to national offices. At the end of the century, women occupied one in eight seats in the lower houses of the world's national legislatures and 8.7 percent of the world's cabinet positions.[18] Although women occupied the top positions in only eight of the world's governments at the conclusion of the twentieth century, never before had so many women served as president or prime minister at one time.[19] The representation of women in governments around the world is appallingly low and progress has been incredibly slow, but the world is nonetheless very different from the way it was a century ago. Furthermore, it appears that the presence of women in democratic governments, even in small numbers, has had significant effects.

Noting the "pronounced gender gap with regard to foreign policy and national security issues," Francis Fukuyama has suggested that there is a connection between the widely observed "democratic peace" and the feminization of politics. We know that democracies do not fight each other, but we do not know exactly why this is the case. It may be, Fukuyama suggests, that part of the answer lies in the fact that "developed democracies . . . tend to be more feminized than authoritarian states, in terms of expansion of franchise and participation in political decision making. It should therefore surprise no one," he continues, "that the historically unprecedented shift in the sexual basis of politics should lead to a change in international relations."[20]

But there are more subtle changes afoot that call into question many of our old ideas about security. Robert D. Kaplan, in an essay reflecting on the meaning of Fort Leavenworth in the nineteenth century and at present, suggests that the territorial nation-state, which, for centuries has been the focus of most thinking about security, is on the way out.[21] Richard Rosecrance, assessing changes in the nature of the state, also argues that land is becoming less significant in international relations. His thesis is that developed countries, at least, are rapidly becoming "virtual states" in which private-sector management and research functions are centralized in the territorial state while production is moved overseas to a group of "body nations" (such as China, Mexico, and India) that provide manufacturing for the world.[22] Land, particularly in those situations in which oil deposits lie under it, may remain significant to states that are economically dependent on resource extraction, but its importance is on the decline for others.

The diminishing importance of territory has already manifested itself in the delegitimization of wars of conquest and policies of imperialism. Models of political and economic success have been offered by states, such as Singapore and Taiwan, without significant territory. Of course, noting these facts is not to suggest that the territorial state is already obsolete. For the present, territory and population remain the physical base of the state, so that security calculations must continue to take both into consideration.[23]

WEAK STATES, FAILED STATES, AND COLLAPSED STATES

One of the problems with the traditional approach to the understanding of states and security is that the dramatic differences among states have often been underappreciated.[24] The false assumption that states are all fundamentally the same, at least with respect to their security interests, was especially prevalent during the Cold War, when the overwhelming majority of students of security studies focused on the United States, the Soviet Union, and their allies. Not surprisingly, given this focus, it appeared that states were principally concerned with external threats to their territorial and political integrity. To put it differently, national security required a capability to deter or defend against a military assault or espionage aimed at a coup d'état.

Because states vary widely in size, military might, political stability, and, perhaps most importantly, coherence (that is, literally, their ability to stick together), their security interests diverge in ways that the traditional understanding of national security fails to capture. The "ethnocentric obsession with external threats to state security" overlooks the fact that weak states are often concerned primarily with internal threats that commonly attend the creation and development of new states.[25] Sir Michael Howard wrote over a decade ago that "the problems of the twenty-first century will not be those of traditional power confrontations. They are more likely to arise out of the integration, or disintegration, of states themselves, and affect all actors on the world scene irrespective of ideology."[26] He could have said the same of the problems of the late twentieth century. Indeed, the historical record since 1945 suggests that security threats (understood narrowly as the threat of war and its effects) have been particularly significant in the developing world, where war has attended the creation and consolidation of new states (as in Pakistan, Vietnam, Algeria, and East Timor, to name but a few examples). Far more fighting occurred in the world of weak states in the last half of the twentieth century than in the world of the strong states, and most of that fighting took the form of intrastate conflict rather than interstate conflict.

Weak states are problematic for a number of reasons. First, they fail to provide the basic security that states are supposed to offer their citizens. They fail, in other words, to offer a respite from the "state of nature," in which, according to Hobbes' famous description, "the life of man [is] solitary, poor, nasty, brutish and short."[27] As a consequence, there may be little protection against crime (including violent crime), little opportunity for education, little economic opportunity, and little access to health care.

Second, by failing to protect their citizens or to offer assistance with basic needs, weak states may burden their neighbors with refugees. According to the United Nations High Commissioner for Refugees, at the end of 2003 there were 9,672,000 refugees in the world. Stateless persons, internally displaced persons, and asylum seekers brought the total to 17,084,100 "persons of concern." Remarkably, that total was the lowest in a decade. The three largest "producers" of refugee populations in 2003 were Afghanistan, Sudan, and Burundi.[28]

Third, by failing to extend the rule of law over all of their territories, weak states may provide safe havens for terrorists, transnational criminal organizations, international fugitives, and other actors that are a menace to international society. This problem in particular has turned a key assumption of national security on its head.

For most of the history of the modern states system, national security has required assessing and responding to the threat—defined as a product of capabilities and intentions to do harm—posed by the strongest states in the system. The balance-of-power approach to security assumes that, for their own protection, states will arm themselves and form alliances in order to meet the threats posed by powerful potential enemies. Since the end of the Cold War, however, national security has required that strong states deal with passive threats posed by the weakest states in the system.

Today, with its Cold War rival Russia in decline and with the People's Republic of China the only potential contender for superpower status, the United States stands unchallenged, the world's only hyperpower. The Persian Gulf War of 1991 demonstrated clearly the superiority of the American military over what was, at the time, thought to be a formidable Iraqi army. Events during the remainder of the 1990s, however, indicated that the U.S. military might not be capable of dealing as well with weak states as with strong states.

In country after country during the 1990s, the United States was confronted with humanitarian disasters that created pressure (in part as a consequence of media coverage and the public opinion it generated) for intervention. A more active post–Cold War UN Security Council both encouraged and assisted the interventionist impulse, with mixed results, in the former Yugoslavia, Somalia, Rwanda, Haiti, and elsewhere. During his eight years in office, President Clinton was alternately criticized for doing too little—for failing to stop genocide in Rwanda, for example—and for doing too much—for conducting "foreign policy as social work."[29]

Each of the opportunities for intervention during the 1990s—those that were seized and those that were avoided—had at its core a state in which the most basic functions of government—establishing a minimal public order and providing basic services—had broken down. The problem for strong states in the post–Cold War world had become weak states, not the threat posed by other strong states. It was exemplified in one form or another by Afghanistan, Cambodia, Haiti, Côte d'Ivoire, Liberia, Rwanda, Sierra Leone, Somalia, Sudan, and Zaire. In fact, the problem arose so often that some felt a new taxonomy—dividing cases among the categories of "weak states," "failed states," and "collapsed states"—was required. It was the phenomenon of the failed state and its implications that more than any other transformed post–Cold War optimism about the triumph of democracy and the "end of history" into pessimism about "the coming anarchy."[30]

Robert Kaplan, one of the most influential pessimists, described the problem in a bleak account, published originally in 1994, of the situation in West Africa. "Even in the quiet zones [of Liberia, Guinea, Ivory Coast, and Sierra Leone] none of the governments except the Ivory Coast's maintains the schools, bridges, roads, and police forces in a manner necessary for fundamental sovereignty." It was not just West Africa, though, because Kaplan regarded the region as a microcosm of a much broader phenomenon:

> West Africa is becoming a symbol of worldwide demographic, environmental, and so-cietal stress, in which criminal anarchy emerges as the real "strategic" danger. Disease, overpopulation, unprovoked crime, scarcity of resources, refugee migrations, the increas-ing erosion of nation-states and international borders, and the empowerment of private armies, security firms, and international drug cartels are now most tellingly demonstrated through a West African prism.[31]

For those who live in (or near) failed states, "national security" must seem an ironic concept since the state is, whether directly or indirectly, the very cause of insecurity. Rather than providing protection against anarchy, failed states permit and sometimes even abet society's slide into the Hobbesian state of nature. Wars for control of territory or resources (such as the diamond mines of Sierra Leone) or for ethnic advantage or revenge are both common and extraordinarily devastating. An estimated eight million people, primarily civilians, have been killed in failed-state conflicts since the end of the Cold War. Another four million people have been driven from their homes by such conflicts. Tens, or perhaps even hundreds, of millions more have been affected in other profound ways, especially by the denial of basic needs such as food, shelter, and health care.[32]

For the United States, the security issue related to failed states moved from the mar-gins to the center as a consequence of 9/11. Two failed states, Sudan and Afghanistan, hosted Osama bin Laden and Al Qaeda training facilities in the years prior to 9/11. The American experience in another failed state, Somalia, in the October 1993 battle of Mogadishu (recounted in Mark Bowden's *Black Hawk Down* and described in chapter 10) was read by bin Laden as an example (along with Vietnam, Lebanon, and Afghanistan) of the ability of insurgents in a weak state to drive out a superpower.[33] In short, failed states, once a cause of debates in the United States over the nation's moral responsibilities and the proper configuration of the military, became a cen-tral concern, due to the platform they provided for the operation of Al Qaeda and, potentially, other transnational terrorist organizations. The first major operation of the "global war on terrorism," consequently, was the war to overthrow the Taliban regime that had hosted bin Laden in Afghanistan. And lest there be any doubt about Afghanistan's status as a failed state in the fall of 2001, Barry Bearak indicated the true situation with this memorable line in a *New York Times* story on the possibility of war there: "If there are Americans clamoring to bomb Afghanistan back to the Stone Age, they ought to know that this nation does not have so far to go. This is a post-apocalyptic place of felled cities, parched land and downtrodden people."[34]

STATES AND INDIVIDUALS

In law and in fact (at least among those states that are strong enough to conform to our understanding of what a state is), one of the most salient characteristics of the modern state has been its monopoly on the legitimate use of force. The ability to use force is, in the final analysis, what the state relies upon to ensure the social order that is its principal raison d'être. This same ability to use force protects the social order not only from internal threats—the criminal acts of individuals and the acts of rebellion of disaffected groups—but from external threats—the aggressive acts of other states—as well. Generally, the former was a matter of law enforcement and, for well-developed states at least, posed less of a threat to the security of the state's citizens than war, because of the inevitably superior firepower of the state in comparison with individual criminals or criminal gangs. The latter, on the other hand, posed the threat of large-scale death and destruction and the potential loss of most, if not all, of the core values shared by citizens of the state.

Individuals have always possessed some of the instruments of force on which the state's internal order depended and have, therefore, always been able to mount a threat to that order. More destructive weapons—battleships, bombers, missiles, and so on—have generally been outside the reach of individuals. Changes in the technology of war and, perhaps more importantly, the spread of some of the most destructive technologies threaten now to alter in a very fundamental way the relationship between states and individuals with respect to the use of force. Put simply, the state's monopoly on the legitimate use of force has, if we drop the term "legitimate," been lost. "Super-Empowered Angry Men," to use the term coined by Thomas Friedman, can now take on the state, if not on equal terms, at least on terms that are far less favorable even to the strongest of states. As Stephen P. Cohen notes, terrorists such as Ramzi Yousef and Osama bin Laden "used to believe that they had to overthrow their own governments and get control of their own states before they could take on America. Now they just do it directly on their own as individuals."[35]

The 9/11 attacks (which simulated the use of weapons of mass destruction) and the anticipated spread of WMD to terrorists represent advances in the leveling of state and substate capabilities not seen since the demise of feudalism. Transnational terrorism, however, is not the only activity that exemplifies the growing capacity of substate actors to challenge the security of states. The sale of illicit drugs generates almost as much revenue each year as the petroleum industry. As we noted in chapter 8, profits from drug trafficking are commonly used to purchase weapons, sometimes to the extent that drug cartels or other transnational criminal organizations (TCOs) come to be better armed than the military forces of many states in which they operate. But drug profits are not only used to buy weapons. They also fund rebel groups and terrorists organizations, which then pose a direct challenge to the survival of the state. It was, in part, the growing power of drug traffickers relative to states, including the United States, that prompted President Bush to militarize the effort to suppress international drug trafficking by announcing a "War on Drugs" in 1989 and ordering the U.S. Southern Command to devote resources to the prosecution of that effort.

NATIONAL SECURITY AND TRANSNATIONAL THREATS

Perceptions of national security are changing slowly. At the beginning of September 2004, the *Washington Post* reported that Pentagon officials were considering a major shift in strategy, one that, if adopted, would require significant changes in American force structure. The shift then being contemplated was based on the view that traditional conceptions of national security have become outmoded as a consequence of the 9/11 attacks. As the *Post* story put it, "The plan's working assumption is that the United States faces almost no serious conventional threats from traditional, state-based militaries."[36] Worrying about states is out; worrying about substate actors is in. The final report of the 9/11 Commission explains the foundations of this shift in perspective and is worth quoting at some length:

> In the post-9/11 world, threats are defined more by the fault lines within societies than by the territorial boundaries between them. From terrorism to global disease or environmental degradation, the challenges have become transnational rather than international. That is the defining quality of world politics in the twenty-first century.
>
> National security used to be considered by studying foreign frontiers, weighing opposing groups of states, and measuring industrial might. To be dangerous, an enemy had to muster large armies. Threats emerged slowly, often visibly, as weapons were forged, armies conscripted, and units trained and moved into place. Because large states were more powerful, they also had more to lose. They could be deterred.
>
> Now threats can emerge quickly. An organization like Al Qaeda, headquartered in a country on the other side of the earth, in a region so poor that electricity or telephones were scarce, could nonetheless scheme to wield weapons of unprecedented destructive power in the largest cities of the United States.[37]

The dramatic rise of transnational threats associated with the increased capabilities of substate actors and their ability to operate out of failed states (or ungoverned territories in weak states) is transforming traditional assumptions underlying national security. States have long been viewed as the principal threats to the security of other states, but state-based challenges are increasingly perceived as emanating from the weakness rather than the strength of states. When states fail to carry out their fundamental purpose of establishing order in society, the security of their own citizens is, as it always has been, endangered. But transnational actors are now making state failures a threat to citizens in other states as well.

RECOMMENDED READING

Printed Sources

Fukuyama, Francis. *State-Building: Governance and World Order in the 21st Century*. Ithaca, N.Y.: Cornell University Press, 2004.

Mandelbaum, Michael. *The Ideas That Conquered the World: Peace, Democracy, and Free Markets in the Twenty-first Century*. New York: PublicAffairs, 2004.

Rosecrance, Richard N. *The Rise of the Virtual State: Wealth and Power in the Coming Century.* New York: Basic Books, 1999.

Rummel, R. J. *Death by Government.* New Brunswick, N.J.: Transaction, 1994.

Websites

CIA, *The World Factbook 2004*: www.cia.gov/cia/publications/factbook/

Freedom House: www.freedomhouse.org/

Global Policy Forum: Nations and States: www.globalpolicy.org/nations/index.htm.

10

Ethnic Conflict and Security:
Ancient Hatreds?

Since the end of World War II, there have been at least ninety conflicts that can be classified as "civil wars."[1] In the twelve years from 1990 to 2002 there were fifty-six major armed conflicts in forty-four locations throughout the world, and most of these were civil wars.[2] At the beginning of the twenty-first century there were more than twenty major armed conflicts in the world, and most of these were civil wars. In World War I, 10 percent of the casualties were civilians, and 90 percent were military personnel. In World War II, about half of the casualties were civilian, and half were military. The casualties of current conflicts are the mirror image of the First World War: 90 percent are civilians, and 10 percent are military.

The respected International Institute for Strategic Studies in London has calculated that the twenty-eight major conflicts in the 1991–2004 period consisted of twenty-four civil wars and four international, state-to-state wars. The civil wars resulted in two-thirds of the fatalities (approximately three million), and the international wars resulted in the deaths of one-third (1.65 million).[3] Given these facts, it is not surprising that current UN Secretary General Kofi Annan has noted, "In the world today intrastate conflict is the face of conflict."[4]

Despite the fact that civil wars are confined to the territory of one state, they have effects on the residents not only of the warring country but of surrounding states as well. Links between poverty and armed conflicts are very strong. Of the twenty poorest states in the world, 80 percent have suffered a major conflict during the previous decade and a half.[5] It is also costly to assist those affected by international conflicts. In 1994 the cost of assisting victims of internal wars was estimated to be $7.2 billion.[6]

As residents of a country engaged in a civil war seek to flee the conflict, they often go to neighboring countries, taxing the latter's ability to provide for both their citizens and refugees. Refugees are often placed in camps in crowded conditions, without adequate food, clean water, or proper sanitation. These conditions, in turn, encourage infectious diseases and their spread.

While the frequency and pervasiveness of internal conflict is not in doubt, the causes are. Clearly one of the most important developments that has contributed to the increasing outbreak of internal conflict is the decline of state sovereignty. In recent times governments have lost control of weaponry, capital, and information, and power has migrated from the public to the private sector. In some states, such as Colombia, state sovereignty has been directly challenged by organized criminal organizations. Beyond the erosion of sovereignty, however, what are the causes of intrastate conflict?

In his ambitious study of *The International Dimensions of Internal Conflict*, political scientist Michael E. Brown argues that one must distinguish between underlying and proximate causes of intrastate conflict. The former include such factors as weak states, elite politics, widespread economic problems, and problematic group histories. Proximate causes include factors such as "internal, mass-level factors (bad domestic problems); mass-level problems (bad neighborhoods); external, elite-level factors (bad neighbors); or internal, elite-level factors (bad leaders)."[7]

Some journalists and popular writers ascribe intrastate and ethnic conflict to "ancient hatreds" between various groups. For example, in his book *Balkan Ghosts*, which reportedly influenced President Clinton's views on Bosnia, writer Robert Kaplan portrayed the root cause of the conflict as the mutual antipathy of the major ethnic groups in Bosnia. Academic analysts, however, tend to discount this explanation of the cause of internal conflict, for several reasons.[8] First, academic analysts tend to dismiss any monocausal explanation; even if "ancient hatreds" play a role in causing internal conflicts, they cannot "account for significant variation in the incidence and intensity of such conflict."[9] Second, even if ethnic hostility exists, it may not result in groups' killing one another. For example, the three major ethnic groups existed peacefully for decades in Yugoslavia before they began killing one another; something besides "ancient hatred" was clearly at work when they finally did. According to political scientists David Lake and Donald Rothchild, "By itself, ethnicity is not a cause of violent conflict. Most ethnic groups, most of the time, pursue their interests peacefully through established political channels. But when linked with acute uncertainty and, indeed, fear of what the future might bring, ethnicity emerges as one of the major fault lines along which societies fracture."[10]

Ethnic "fault lines" are very much in evidence. Members of ethnic groups identify with one another because of their shared national origin, tribal affiliation, social organization, or common language, religion, or race. Demographers estimate that there are somewhere from three to five thousand ethnic groups in the world today.[11] One study has identified 233 ethnic groups as targets of discrimination or as having organized for political assertiveness; this constitutes between 5 and 8 percent of the world's total number of ethnic groups.[12] Of the two hundred states that exist today, fewer than twenty—about 10 percent of the world's total—are ethnically homogeneous, "in the sense that ethnic minorities account for less than five percent of the population."[13] In some states since 1989, ethnic fault lines have resulted in the disintegration of states—Czechoslovakia, Yugoslavia, the Soviet Union, and

Table 10.1.   Ethnic Groups Pressing for Independence

Ethnic Group	State
Kashmiris	India
Kosovars	Yugoslavia
Tamils	Sri Lanka
Uigurs	China
Tibetans	China
Kurds	Iraq, Turkey, Syria, Iran
Chechens	Russia
Palestinians	Israel

Ethiopia. In a number of other states, a significant potential for ethnic conflict exists, as table 10.1 demonstrates.

Ethnic groups often have ties to states outside of the countries in which they reside. In some cases states provide economic, and sometimes even military, aid to ethnic groups in other countries. For example, during the Soviet occupation of Afghanistan, the government of Saudi Arabia provided substantial aid to the Muslim *mujahidin* who were fighting the Soviets. When ethnic groups receive aid from foreign governments, domestic disputes can turn into international conflicts.

If "ancient hatreds" between or among ethnic groups do not fully explain the causes of internal conflict, what factors do? In an ambitious study of the causes of and means to prevent deadly conflict, the Carnegie Corporation of New York identified nine sources of conflict.[14] First, irresponsible leaders such as Pol Pot in Cambodia or Idi Amin in Uganda have caused unspeakable human suffering. Second, historical intergroup tensions (as distinct from ancient hatreds), as among the Serbs, Croats, and Bosnians in the former Yugoslavia have contributed to the outbreak of conflict in the former Yugoslavia. Third, population growth taxes the limits of some states and results in competition for scarce resources. Fourth, increasing crowding in cities, a function of both population growth and urbanization, contributes to the outbreak of conflict. Fifth, economic deterioration can worsen intergroup relations, as was the case in Rwanda. Sixth, environmental degradation can increase intergroup tensions. Seventh, repressive or discriminatory policies have worsened the relationships among various groups. Eighth, corrupt or incompetent governance may contribute to internal conflict. Lastly, technological development that increases the gap between rich and poor can also increase the gap between or among various domestic groups. Taken together, these factors constitute a "recipe for conflict."

Since 1945 there have been more than fifty United Nations peace-support operations; thirty-two of these operations were established in the decade from 1988 to 1998. As of July 2005, there were sixteen active UN peacekeeping operations, as shown in table 10.2.

The cost of UN peacekeeping increased significantly during the early 1990s due to the large-scale operations in Yugoslavia and Somalia. The annual cost of UN

Table 10.2.   UN Peacekeeping Operations as of July 2005

Region	Peacekeeping Operation
Africa	Sierra Leone, Congo, Côte d'Ivoire, Ethiopia/Eritrea, Liberia, Burundi, Western Sahara, Sudan
Americas	Haiti
Asia	India/Pakistan
Europe	Cyprus, Georgia, Kosovo
Middle East	Golan Heights, Lebanon, UN Truce Supervision Organization

Source: www.un.org/Depts/dpko/missions/.

peacekeeping personnel and equipment peaked at 3.6 billion dollars in 1993, more than twice the cost of regular UN operations. These costs fell to 1.4 billion dollars in 1996 and 1.3 billion dollars in 1997. The total estimated peacekeeping costs for the United Nations in 1998 were under one billion dollars. For 2005–2006, peacekeeping is budgeted at 3.2 billion dollars.[15] As of May 2005, the United States owed the UN 893 million dollars in peacekeeping dues, by far the largest amount owed by any member state.

Peacemaking seeks to go beyond peacekeeping's objective of simply keeping opposing sides separated, by seeking a brokered solution to conflict. This may involve conciliation, mediation, the offering of "good offices," possibly even the deployment of military forces to establish law and order. In recent years, the UN secretary general has sent personal envoys to a number of conflict-prone areas to try to negotiate peaceful resolutions.

Peace enforcement is a more recent notion that the international community should act through the United Nations and other international organizations to end intrastate and ethnic conflicts even when the opposing parties do not request assistance. These actions are sometimes referred to as "Chapter VII operations," because that section of the UN Charter refers to such actions, authorized by the Security Council, as blockade, enforcement of sanctions, forcible disarmament, and direct military action. Peace enforcement has been used in relatively few, recent cases, including the Persian Gulf War, Somalia, Rwanda, Haiti, Bosnia-Herzogovina, and Albania. None of these enforcement operations was under UN control; rather, all were directed by single states or regional international organizations. For example, in Bosnia-Herzogovina, a multinational military force of the North Atlantic Treaty Organization (NATO) succeeded an existing but largely ineffective UN peacekeeping operation.

CASE STUDIES IN PEACE OPERATIONS

Given the increasing frequency of intrastate and ethnic conflict, it is likely that the demand for peacekeeping, peacemaking, and peace enforcement will continue into the foreseeable future. The effects of some conflicts have been ameliorated by the intervention of outside nongovernmental organizations, international organizations, and states. What can we learn from recent peace operations? In this section, we will focus on peace operations in Somalia, Bosnia, Rwanda, Kosovo, and Sudan.

Somalia

Somalia, in the Horn of Africa, has had a troubled history since its founding in 1960. In 1969–70, a Marxist government headed by Gen. Mohammed Siyad Barre took power and opened Somali ports to the Soviet Union. In 1974 a pro-Soviet faction took over in Ethiopia, and the USSR shifted its support in the region to this new government. Somalia, in turn, provided support for insurgent forces fighting for independence of the Ogaden region of Ethiopia. The situation worsened, and in 1977 Ethiopia and Somalia went to war. Assisted by Cuban troops, Ethiopia defeated Somalia, and Somalia turned to the United States for aid. Throughout the 1980s, intermittent conflict between Ethiopia and Somalia continued, with disastrous results for the people of Somalia. Disease and famine were common, and many Somalis left the country. Exhausted by more than a decade of fighting, the belligerents signed a peace agreement in 1988. In 1991, Siyad Barre left the country, and the fourteen major clans of Somalia began to fight one another for control.

In March 1991, the UN intervened in Somalia in order to assist an estimated two hundred thousand refugees in the capital city of Mogadishu and to bring supplies to the more than four million Somalis who were threatened with famine. In April 1992, the UN Security Council established the United Nations Operation in Somalia (UNOSOM), which consisted of fifty observers whose mission was to provide humanitarian aid and promote the end of conflict in Somalia. The UNOSOM observers were not able to achieve their mission, due to continued fighting among the clans. The UN secretary general, Boutros Boutros-Ghali, requested that the United States assist with the delivery of relief supplies. President George H. W. Bush ordered Operation Provide Relief, which during a five-month period (August–December 1992) airlifted twenty-eight thousand metric tons of critically needed relief supplies into Somalia.[16]

The security situation worsened, and in November 1992 a ship fully laden with relief supplies was fired upon and thereby prevented from delivering its cargo. Photos of emaciated children accompanied the story about the ship, and public pressure to "do something" mounted. In response, the UN established a multinational coalition, the "Unified Task Force" (UNITAF), which was to be led by the United States. President Bush ordered the initiation of Operation Restore Hope, with the dual mission of providing humanitarian relief and restoring order to Somalia. Significantly, this was the first time in its forty-seven-year history that the UN had dispatched troops with rules of engagement that authorized its troops to shoot anyone interfering with the relief effort. Eventually, UNITAF involved more than thirty-eight thousand troops from twenty-one different countries; of these, twenty-eight thousand were Americans.

UNITAF was relatively successful in stabilizing the political situation and distributing food to those who most needed it. Plans called for the termination of UNITAF and the establishment of a permanent peacekeeping force. In March 1993, the UN Security Council established UNOSOM II. Significantly, this was the first-ever UN peacekeeping operation mandated under the Chapter VII peace-enforcement provisions of the UN Charter. The mandate of UNOSOM II went well beyond that of UNITAF and called for UN forces to engage in "nation building." The local Somali warlords viewed the new UN mandate as threatening to their power, and on June 5, 1993, the forces of one of them, Mohammed Aideed, attacked and killed twenty-four Pakistani peacekeepers. The next day, the United Nations passed a resolution calling for the apprehension of those responsible for the killings. Several elite U.S. Army units—Rangers and the Delta Force—were flown to Mogadishu to apprehend General Aideed. On October 3, the U.S. units received a report that Aideed had been sighted. They attempted to arrest Aideed but were ambushed. Eighteen American soldiers were killed and seventy-five wounded in the bloodiest battle of any UN peacekeeping operation since the 1960 Congo crisis. Pictures of mutilated bodies of American soldiers were broadcast around the world, and the U.S. public demanded the withdrawal of American forces, which President Clinton ordered.

Somalia is often cited as the first post–Cold War peacekeeping failure, but such a criticism is not accurate. First, the attack on U.S. forces came during UNOSOM II, which was essentially a peace-enforcement operation and not a peacekeeping operation. Thus, if anything, Somalia was a failure to achieve nation building rather than to keep the peace. Second, analysts have estimated that UN and U.S. actions in Somalia from 1992 to 1995 saved 250,000 to five hundred thousand lives. In human terms, it is difficult to consider this a failure. But Somalia affected the way that Americans and the UN viewed peacekeeping operations, as was to become evident in the Bosnian and Rwandan cases.

Bosnia

Bosnia-Herzegovina, in the Balkans, was at one time part of Yugoslavia. For centuries the Balkan region was the battleground of empires; in the fifteenth century the Ottoman Empire defeated the Serbs at the Battle of Varna, and the region fell under control of the Muslim Ottomans. During the eighteenth and nineteenth centuries the Russian and Austro-Hungarian empires made inroads into the Balkans and increased their influence. By 1806 Serbia had established an independent kingdom. The Treaty of Berlin in 1878 gave control of Bosnia-Herzegovina to the Austro-Hungarian Empire; however, Serbians, based on ethnic and historical reasons, considered Bosnia-Herzegovina to be theirs. So did the Croatians, the second-largest ethnic group in the region. Not only conflicting claims concerning Bosnia but religion as well divided the Serbs and Croatians; the Serbs were Orthodox, and the Croatians were Catholic. Complicating the problem was the existence of a large third ethnic group in Bosnia—Bosniaks—that is predominantly Muslim.

In 1908 Austria-Hungary annexed Bosnia, an action that catalyzed the Balkan Wars of 1912–13. The assassination of the heir apparent of the Habsburg Empire,

Archduke Ferdinand, and his wife by a Serbian nationalist during a visit to Sarajevo, the capital of Bosnia, in June 1914 lit the fuse that ignited World War I. The result of the ensuing four years of war was fifteen million dead across Europe and beyond.

At the end of World War I, the Kingdom of Serbs, Croats, and Slovenes was established; it was characterized by competition and hostility among its ethnic groups. Throughout the interwar period, the dominant ethnic groups engaged in terrorist activities against one another. These activities were reinforced rather than interrupted by the Axis invasion of Yugoslavia in 1941. The Croats and the Croatian terrorist organization, the Ustasha, allied themselves with the Nazis and killed five to seven hundred thousand Serbs. In turn, the Serbian terrorist organization, the Cetniks, sought to kill as many Nazis and Croats as possible. Josip Broz Tito, a Croatian communist, led the partisans and sought to create an effective resistance to the occupying Nazis. At the end of the war, Tito and his partisans proclaimed the Federal People's Republic of Yugoslavia and thereafter, to sustain it, sought to dampen the nationalistic feelings of the major ethnic groups it contained. But these feelings were deep-seated and long-lasting.

Tito ruled Yugoslavia for thirty-five years. He was able to maintain the unity of the state by a combination of effective leadership and brute force. When Tito died in 1980, many predicted the death of Yugoslavia, a prediction that took a little more than a decade to come true. In April 1987, Muslims, who constituted three-quarters of the population of a southern "autonomous region" of Serbia—Kosovo—challenged Serbian control. The Yugoslav president sent Slobodan Milosevic to Kosovo to quell the ethnic disturbance. Instead, Milosevic, a Serb, concluded, as he was to report, "The situation in Kosovo was intolerable. . . . They [Muslim Albanians] murdered Serbs; they defiled our [Serb] graves."[17] Following his visit to Kosovo, Milosevic embarked on a campaign for a "Greater Serbia," which he extended to Bosnia, where he formed an alliance with the Bosnian Serb leaders, Radovan Karadzic and Gen. Ratko Mladic. In June 1991, Croatia and Slovenia (Yugoslavia's richest and most Western republics) declared their independence. The United Nations imposed an arms embargo on the former Yugoslav republics. In retrospect, this gave a major advantage to Serbia, which controlled the former Yugoslav army; the militaries of Croatia and Bosnia were left at a significant disadvantage. In December 1991, Germany extended formal diplomatic recognition to Croatia and Slovenia.

The first UN peacekeepers were sent to the former Yugoslavia in March 1992. By then conflict had spread throughout the country, and a new, horrific euphemism for genocide had been introduced into the lexicon of politics: "ethnic cleansing." This referred to tactics designed to "expel or frighten people from one ethnic group into abandoning territory coveted by another. It can include the use of terror tactics, mass rape and summary execution."[18] The number of UN troops in the former Yugoslavia was not sufficient to prevent the mass killing of innocent noncombatants. What had been inconceivable—a repetition of the horrors of the Holocaust—had happened again. When UN forces proved incapable of stopping the killing, NATO imposed "no fly zones" and attacked Serb positions on several occasions. But these actions too proved ineffective in stopping the killing.

On the afternoon of July 10, 1995, Bosnian Serb soldiers attacked Srebrenica, a city that the UN had declared a sanctuary for some forty thousand people who sought refuge from the war. The UN peacekeepers in the city were hopelessly outnumbered and had to watch as some six thousand people were rounded up and killed. One account of the carnage reported:

> The Muslim men were herded by the thousands into trucks, delivered to killing sites near the Drina River, lined up four by four, and shot. One survivor, 17-year-old Nezad Avdic, recalled that as he lay wounded among the dead Muslims, a Serbian soldier surveyed the stony, moonlit field piled with bodies and merrily declared: "That was a good hunt. There were a lot of rabbits here."[19]

Following the attack on Srebrenica, Serb forces threatened other "safe" areas. In addition, the Serbs shelled the main marketplace in Sarajevo, killing more than fifty innocent civilians. In August three American diplomats died tragically when their armored personnel carrier went off the treacherous road into Sarajevo. These events catalyzed the American and European response: the deployment of sixty thousand soldiers to Bosnia to implement a new peace agreement negotiated in Dayton, Ohio, by Serbian president Milosevic, Croatian president Franjo Tudjman, and Bosnia Muslim leader Alia Izetbegovic. The provisions of the agreement were implemented in November 1995. During the four years of the war in Bosnia an estimated two hundred thousand people had been killed and two to three million displaced from their homes. Since the signing of the Dayton Accord, there have been no significant instances of genocide in Bosnia.

Rwanda

Rwanda is one of the poorest countries in the world. In 1993, annual per capita gross domestic product (GDP) equaled $290. Fifty percent of Rwanda's total GDP was derived from the agricultural sector, and coffee and tea historically made up 50 percent of total exports.[20] In 1987, the International Coffee Agreement collapsed, causing the price of coffee to decline to 50 percent of its 1980 value. This precipitous drop in price had a disastrous effect on the Rwandan economy and served as the backdrop for subsequent events.

For the past four centuries, two tribes—the Tutsi and the Hutu—had jointly inhabited the area now known as Rwanda. The Tutsi, primarily cattle herders, were wealthier than the more numerous Hutu farmers. The area, comprising present-day Rwanda and Burundi, was controlled for a time by Germany and then Belgium from 1916 to 1962. In 1962, Rwanda and Burundi gained their independence from Belgium and became separate states. President Gregoire Kayibanda, a Hutu, ruled Rwanda autocratically until 1973, when Maj. Gen. Juvenal Habyarimana, also Hutu, staged a coup and took over the government.

Relations between the Tutsi and Hutu periodically flared into open conflict, most notably in 1963, 1966, 1973, and 1990–93. With each episode of violence, more Tutsi fled Rwanda for surrounding states. By 1992, approximately 8 percent of Rwanda's population of Tutsi was living in exile. Some of these exiles formed armed groups that staged sporadic raids into Rwanda. In February 1993, the Tutsi militia in exile launched an offensive that displaced 650,000 Rwandans. Negotiations were conducted and eventually resulted in a comprehensive peace agreement, which was signed in Arusha, Tanzania, in August 1993. The Arusha Accords called for the creation of a coalition government that would incorporate Tutsi in the government and the army and would provide for the reintegration of Tutsi refugees into Rwanda. Implementation of the accords was slow and problematic; the UN secretary general expressed his concern over the "increasingly violent demonstrations, roadblocks, assassination of political leaders and assaults on and murders of civilians, developments that severely overstretch the resources and capabilities of the national gendarmerie."[21]

On April 6, 1994, six days after the secretary general issued his report, President Habyarimana of Rwanda and the president of neighboring Burundi were killed when two missiles hit their plane as it approached the airfield at Kigali, the capital of Rwanda. The missiles had been fired from a military base controlled by the Rwandan Presidential Guard, elements of which opposed Habyarimana's negotiation with the Tutsi. The assassination unleashed a killing spree not seen since the days of Nazi Germany. In the ensuing three months an estimated five hundred thousand to a million people were killed, and almost five million people were forced to flee for their lives.[22] The Carnegie Commission on Preventing Deadly Conflict noted, "This has been one of the most horrifying chapters in human history."[23]

What could have been done to stop this carnage? Following the conclusion of the Arusha Accords, the UN established a peacekeeping force to support implementation of the agreements. This force, which eventually reached a strength of 2,500 troops, was commanded by a Canadian, Lt. Gen. Romeo Dallaire. The force was stretched to the limit by the daily logistical demands of sustaining itself and by a series of emergencies, such as a coup in Burundi and the resulting refugee crisis.[24] General Dallaire sought authority for an augmented force operating under Chapter VII ("peace enforcement") of the UN Charter rather than Chapter VI ("peacekeeping"), in order to: (1) stop the genocide, (2) conduct a peace enforcement mission, (3) assist in the return of refugees, (4) deliver humanitarian aid, and (5) assist in the cessation of hostilities. General Dallaire estimated that with five thousand troops and a mandate under Chapter VII, he could have prevented most of the killing.[25] Why then were his requests not approved? General Dallaire's requests came in the aftermath of the disastrous Somalia intervention, and both the UN and the U.S. government were hesitant to involve themselves in another possible disaster. In addition, the UN, the U.S. government, and NATO were trying to figure out what to do about the situation in the former Yugoslavia. As a result, there was little support for sending more troops to Rwanda.[26] Thus Rwanda became, according to former Assistant Secretary of State for African Affairs Chester Crocker, "the first victim of the post-Somali backlash."[27]

Kosovo

Tito established Kosovo as an autonomous province in 1974 in order to decrease the power of Serbia. Kosovo is about the size of the state of Connecticut and at the beginning of 1999 had approximately two million residents, 90 percent of them Albanian Kosovars and 10 percent Serbs. For their part, Serbs have long considered Kosovo to be sacred territory, because of an important battle fought (and lost) against Ottoman Turkish forces in 1389. In addition, there are some Orthodox monasteries in Kosovo that the Serbs highly value.

As noted earlier in this chapter, Slobodan Milosevic came to Kosovo in April 1987 and began his campaign for a "Greater Serbia" here. In 1989, he revoked Kosovo's autonomous status and imposed repressive Serbian rule. This situation was similar to the system of apartheid that existed in South Africa, except in the case of Kosovo, an ethnic-religious rather than racial minority controlled the other 90 percent of the population.

Bordering on Kosovo is the poorest country of Europe, Albania, whose population is ethnically identical to Kosovo's. The Albanian economy collapsed in 1990–91. It rebounded modestly in 1993–95, then collapsed again in 1997 due to financial "pyramid" schemes that had swept the country. The resulting social unrest led to more than 1,500 deaths, widespread destruction of property, and the looting of Albanian army and police weapons-storage depots. Military weapons including powerful combat assault rifles, such as the Kalashnikov AK-47, became available.

Many of these weapons made their way across the Albanian-Kosovar border into the hands of Kosovars who wanted independence from Serbia. For the first time, members of the Kosovo Liberation Army (KLA) had the means to challenge their Serbian oppressors, and they increasingly and more blatantly attacked the Yugoslav army and Kosovo police, both of which were almost exclusively Serbian.

Faced with an increasingly militant and effective resistance and having staked out Kosovo as sacred to the Serbs, Milosevic ordered his forces to crack down on the KLA and restive Kosovars beginning in early 1998. Milosevic ordered the army into Kosovo that summer; by September these forces had destroyed an estimated five hundred villages.

Members of NATO observed Serbia's actions with concern and increasing alarm. In Bosnia, two hundred thousand people had died and two to three million had been made homeless; most informed observers believed that the Serbs were the principal cause of these losses. Leaders of both NATO and the United Nations were concerned that the Serbs might attempt to "ethnically cleanse" Kosovo as they had in Bosnia.

In June, NATO threatened air strikes but did not follow through. In September, the United Nations passed a resolution calling for a cease-fire and the resettlement of the estimated 270,000 refugees. At the end of September, a group of eighteen ethnic Albanian children, women, and elderly people were found massacred; the prospect of a repetition of the horrors of Bosnia was very real.

In October, a U.S. diplomat, Richard Holbrooke, who had brokered the Dayton Accord, arrived in the area to meet with Serbian and Kosovar leaders. As a result of these meetings, Milosevic agreed to a cease-fire, with withdrawal of Serbian forces from Kosovo, and the deployment of two thousand unarmed observers from the Organization for Security and Cooperation in Europe.[28]

A new round of talks was convened in February 1999 at Rambouillet, France. The Kosovar representative to these talks agreed to a plan that called for (1) increased autonomy for Kosovo, which would remain a part of Serbia; and (2) the deployment of twenty-eight thousand NATO troops to Kosovo to police the agreement. Milosevic refused to sign the agreement, and NATO delivered an ultimatum—sign the Rambouillet agreement or face air strikes. Milosevic continued to refuse to sign, and on March 24, 1999, NATO began bombing targets in Serbia, Kosovo, and Montenegro. The NATO attacks against Serbia were the largest use of military force by the allies since the end of World War II.

As the nineteen members of NATO attacked, Serbian forces increased their own attacks on the Albanian Kosovars, who fled the Serbian onslaught in desperation. Within two weeks of the beginning of the bombing campaign, an estimated five hundred thousand Kosovars had fled the country. The allied bombing, as had bombing during World War II, seemed to stiffen resistance.

Darfur, Sudan

Sudan, a sub-Saharan country in Africa, is one-quarter the size of the United States (2.5 million square kilometers) and as of 2003 had an estimated population of thirty-three million.[29] The gross domestic product for Sudan in 2003 was thirteen billion dollars and the per capita GDP three hundred dollars, making Sudan one of the poorest countries in the world.

Three provinces in the western part of Sudan make up the Darfur region, of approximately 150,000 square miles—about the size of France. There are five to six million people in this region.

Sudan is Africa's largest and ethnically most diverse country; more than ninety tribes live in Sudan, the three major ones being the Fur, Massaleit, and Zaghawa.[30] About two-thirds of the population is Muslim, 25 percent are animists, and 10 percent are Christian. In the northern part of the country, the Muslims predominate; most of the Christians live in the south.

For centuries, Sudan was inhabited by small groups of tribally based kingdoms and principalities. In 1820, Egypt took over and unified the northern part. In 1898 local Sudanese sought to gain independence from Egypt, but Egyptian and British military forces put down this revolt. For almost sixty years, Sudan was under the control of Britain and Egypt. In 1956, Sudan gained its independence. Since then, Muslims have controlled the government.

In 1969, a group of military officers staged a coup and took over the government. Col. Gaafar Muhammad Nimeiri became prime minister and abolished parliament and all political parties. In 1983, Nimeiri, a Muslim, announced that he would institute traditional punishments based on Islamic law (Shari'a), including public lashings, amputations, and beheadings. This decision was controversial even among some Muslims and led to a civil war between the northern Muslim and southern Christian sections of the country, a conflict that continues to the present.

In 1985, Gen. Suwar al-Dahab led a military coup that deposed Nimeiri and attempted to broker a peace agreement with the Sudanese People's Liberation Army, led by Col. John Garang de Mabior. Garang and his followers called for the abolition of Islamic law, which the government refused. Conflict between northern and southern forces continued. In 1989, a coup brought Gen. Omar Hassan al-Bashir to power; he remains in power at this writing.

In 1993, the leaders of Eritrea, Ethiopia, Uganda, and Kenya, under the auspices of the Intergovernmental Authority on Development (IGAD), a jointly sponsored regional organization, launched a peace initiative among the parties. In 2000, Egypt and Libya presented a proposal for a cease-fire, but this like previous proposals was unsuccessful. In 2001, President George W. Bush appointed former U.S. Senator John Danforth to be his envoy to explore possibilities of achieving peace in a country that had been at war for twenty years.

The cost of war in Sudan has been horrific. Since the north-south civil war began in 1983, according to the U.S. State Department, "an estimated 2 million persons have been killed in the violence or have died from the effects of humanitarian needs; approximately 4 million have been displaced internally as a result of fighting between the Government and insurgents in the south. In addition, more than 1 million persons have been internally displaced within Darfur and 200,000 refugees have fled to Chad."[31] Because displaced Sudanese are fleeing to adjacent countries, the problems in Sudan are being exported. The situation in Sudan has been described as "Rwanda in slow motion."[32]

Traditionally, nomadic tribes from the north would herd their animals from the north to the more temperate south during the dry season and then go back to the north with the rains. A serious drought caused the nomads to go farther and farther to the south in search of water and pasturelands for their animals. When the rains did not come, many nomads chose to stay in the south, causing conflict between the farmers in Darfur and the nomads from the north. Exacerbating the conflict was the ethnic difference between the two groups: the nomads of the north were Arabs, and the Darfur farmers were African. Arabs controlled the Sudanese government and were sympathetic to the plight of their nomadic kinsmen.

Facing incursions from the Arab nomads, in 2003 two armed groups in Darfur, the Sudan Liberation Movement and the Justice Equality Movement, formed a loose alliance and began staging attacks on government posts in Darfur. In response, the government implicitly authorized Arab militias called *janjawiid* to attack, rape, and kill in Darfur. A United Nations report of February 2004 described the actions of the *janjawiid*: "In an attack on 27 February [2004] in the Tawilah area of northern Darfur, thirty villages were burned to the ground, over 200 people killed and over 200 girls and women raped—some by up to 14 assailants and in front of their fathers who were later killed. A further 150 women and 200 children were abducted."[33]

The international community, including the United States, has responded to the crisis in Darfur. In June 2004, Secretary of State Powell visited Sudan, and the following month Secretary General Kofi Annan traveled there. On July 23, 2004, the U.S. Congress passed a unanimous, bipartisan resolution that characterized the actions in Sudan as genocide. A number of nongovernmental groups have also called what is happening genocide, including Justice Africa, Physicians for Human Rights, the Committee for Refugees, and Africa Action. In November 2004, the U.S. representative to the United Nations and former special envoy to Sudan, Ambassador John Danforth, called a special meeting of the Security Council to meet in Nairobi, Kenya, only the fourth time in its history that it had met outside of New York. The African Union has deployed eight hundred troops to Darfur and has plans to increase the size of its force to 7,500 troops. Following months of inaction, the West followed up on its expressions of concern in June 2005 as NATO defense ministers meeting in Brussels agreed to provide logistical assistance and training to African Union forces.

REDUCING ETHNIC CONFLICT IN THE WORLD

Kofi Annan, who previously served as Under-Secretary of the Department of Peacekeeping Operations, has argued that conflict prevention and disease prevention can be thought of in similar terms. A number of other leaders, academics, and researchers agree.[34] The Carnegie Commission on Preventing Deadly Conflict has argued, "Just as in the practice of good medicine, preventing the outbreak, spread, and recurrence of the disease of deadly conflict requires timely interventions with the right mix of political, economic, military, and social instruments."[35] In 1994, the Carnegie Corporation of New York funded a major review of the causes and potential prevention of deadly conflict in the world. A commission of sixteen eminent leaders and scholars with long practical and academic experience in dealing with conflict resolution and prevention supervised the study, sponsoring research that it felt was needed in understudied areas of conflict prevention. An international advisory council of more than forty distinguished practitioners and scholars assisted. The annual reports, the final report, and specialized studies of the commission are all available to the public at the commission's website, www.ccpdc.org. Given the importance of the commission's study, this section will summarize its findings.

Three fundamental conclusions constituted the core of the commission's findings. First, "mass violence is not inevitable"; violence does not emerge inexorably and inevitably from "ancient hatreds" or human interaction. Intra- and interstate conflict result from deliberate, political decisions, and these decisions can be influenced. Second, "the need to prevent deadly conflict is increasingly urgent." The growth in population, increasing economic interdependence, and the advance of technology, especially in communications and weaponry, are an often deadly mix, underscoring the need to prevent conflicts from turning massively violent. Third, successful preventive action is possible. "The problem is not that we do not know about incipient and large-scale violence; it is that we often do not act." What is needed is the early, skillful, and integrated application of political, diplomatic, economic, and military measures.

Like Michael Brown in his characterization of the "underlying" and "proximate" causes of ethnic conflict, the Carnegie Commission has described strategies for preventing violence in two categories, "operational prevention" and "structural prevention." The former includes measures that are applicable in the face of an immediate crisis; the latter includes measures "to assure that a crisis will not occur in the first place."[36]

There are four key elements of operational success in conflict prevention. First, there should be a lead actor—an international or regional organization, a country, or even a prominent individual—around which preventive efforts can be organized. Second, there should be a coherent political-military-economic approach designed to stop the violence, provide necessary humanitarian assistance, and integrate all relevant aspects of the solution to the problem at hand. Third, adequate resources are needed to support effective preventive engagement. Fourth, and particularly relevant to intrastate conflict, a plan to restore the host state's authority and responsibility is required.

Structural prevention—also called peace building—requires the development by states of international regimes, which are implicit or explicit agreements, procedures, or organizations to manage the interaction of states in various issue areas. In addition, states must work for the security, economic well-being, and justice of their citizens. Fairness is a characteristic of stable political systems, and the achievement of fairness should be the goal of governments, regardless of their form.

Many people (including the authors of this book) assumed that the genocide perpetrated by the Nazis in World War II would not be repeated. After all, the Allies had expended millions of lives and vast material resources to defeat the Nazi obscenity. Sadly, this proved to be a mistaken view, for genocide has reappeared in a number of cases: in Pol Pot's Cambodia, Idi Amin's Uganda, and more recently in Bosnia, Rwanda, the Democratic Republic of the Congo, and Sudan.

With the demise of the Cold War, intrastate conflicts have become more common. There is much that individuals, states, and the international community can do to stem intra- and interstate violence and conflict—if only they will.

RECOMMENDED READING

Printed Sources

Anderson, Scott. "How Did Darfur Happen?" *New York Times Magazine,* October 17, 2004, 52ff.

Brown, Michael E., ed. *The International Dimensions of Internal Conflict.* Cambridge, Mass.: MIT Press, 1996.

Brown, Michael E., and Richard N. Rosecrance, eds. *The Costs of Conflict: Prevention and Cure in the Global Arena.* Lanham, Md.: Rowman & Littlefield, 1999.

Carnegie Commission on Preventing Deadly Conflict. *Preventing Deadly Conflict: Final Report.* Washington, D.C.: The Carnegie Corporation of New York, 1997.

Crocker, Chester A. "The Lessons of Somalia." *Foreign Affairs* 74, no. 3 (May/June 1995): 2–8.

Dallaire, Romeo. *Shake Hands with the Devil: The Failure of Humanity in Rwanda.* New York: Carroll and Graf, 2004.

Gurr, Ted Robert, and Barbara Harff. *Ethnic Conflict in World Politics.* Boulder, Colo.: Westview, 1994.

Lake, David, and Donald Rothchild, eds. *The International Spread of Ethnic Conflict: Fear Diffusion and Escalation.* Princeton, N.J.: Princeton University Press, 1998.

Power, Samantha. "Dying in Darfur." *New Yorker,* August 20, 2004, 56–63.

Websites

Carnegie Commission for Preventing Deadly Conflict: www.ccpdc.org
International Peace Academy: www.ipacademy.inter.net/
UN Department of Peacekeeping Operations: www.un.org/Depts/DPKO
U.S. Department of State: www.state.gov/
U.S. Institute of Peace: www.usip.org/.

11

The Root of All Evil? The Matter of Economic Security

The Christian apostle Paul wrote, "The love of money is the root of all evil."[1] But is this really the case? As noted in chapter 1, traditionally policy makers and scholars have thought of security as derived from military power—bombs, bullets, battleships, airplanes, tanks, and more recently, weapons of mass destruction. At present, however, many have begun to think about the extent to which threats to the economic well-being of individuals, states, and regions constitute threats to security. Futurologist Alvin Toffler has noted, "The power of the state has always rested on its control of [military] force, wealth, and knowledge."[2] Significantly, governments have increasingly lost control of each of these three main sources of state power, and this development has profound implications for international relations.

The final report of the 9/11 Commission noted: "Terrorism is not caused by poverty. Indeed, many terrorists come from relatively well-off families. Yet, when people lose hope, when societies break down, when countries fragment, the breeding grounds for terrorism are created."[3] In the 2002 *National Security Strategy*, the George W. Bush administration noted: "Poverty, weak institutions, and corruption can make weak states vulnerable to terrorist networks and drug cartels within their borders."[4] What, we ask in this chapter, is the relationship of economics to security and power?

For many years, some analysts have focused on the relationship between a state's power and economics; the classic analysts of this relationship include Jacob Viner, Albert O. Hirschman, and Klaus Knorr.[5] Hirschman contended that political power is gained through economic inequality and that a financial, trade, or investment relationship that is more significant for a small state than a larger one gives the larger country an advantage by making the smaller country dependent on the larger country.

Before issues related to economics and security can be analyzed, some terms need to be defined and clarified. The economically developed countries—also called "developed states," "advanced industrial states," or simply "the first world"—comprise the United States, Canada, Europe, Japan, Australia, and New Zealand. During the Cold War, the communist states of the Soviet Union and Eastern Europe were referred to as the "second world." With the fall of communism in these states, this term is no longer valid; some of these states are becoming "first world" states, and others are considered to be "newly industrializing states." "Third world" countries include the developing states of Asia, Africa, Latin America, and much of the Middle East. They are sometimes referred to as "less developed countries" (LDC), but many consider this a pejorative term and avoid using it. Finally, the poorest countries of the world are referred to as "fourth world" states or the "least developed countries."

A review of world population and economic output reveals that 15 percent of the world's 6.3 billion people live in the Northern Hemisphere and produce 77 percent of the world's gross domestic product (GDP). Eighty-five percent of the world's population live in the Southern Hemisphere and produce 23 percent of the world's GDP.

Each year, the United Nations publishes the *U.N. Human Development Report* and the World Bank publishes the *Human Development Index*. Recent issues of these reports show that of the world's two hundred states, more than 60 percent are developing countries. Of these 123 states, thirty-six are classified as the poorest states in the world, with a per capita GDP of $1,219 or less and life expectancy of fifty-seven years or less. Only 68 percent of their populations had access to clean water; fewer than 50 percent can read and write.

Twenty-seven of the world's poorest countries are in Africa. In seven African countries, babies born in 2004 have a life expectancy of forty year or less, due primarily to the scourge of AIDS.[6] In short, those who live in developing countries have less money, dramatically lower life expectancies, lower infant survival rates, higher death rates from infectious diseases, lower literacy rates, and less access to safe drinking water and health care. But how are these statistics related to security?

Economic circumstances are important because poverty is a key social condition associated with war and terrorism. But, as we will see, the connection between economics and security goes well beyond the link between poverty and conflict.

ECONOMIC SECURITY: DEFINING THE ISSUES

There are many economic threats to individuals, states, regions, and even the inter-national system itself. First, long-term economic cycles pose a threat to the economic well-being of actors at every level of analysis. Second, natural disasters pose economic threats. Third, state-initiated policies and actions, particularly those of the most pow-erful members of the system, can pose a threat to the economic health of both the individual members of the system and the system itself. Fourth, the failure of states can result in economic havoc and can create significant economic threats. Fifth, the actions of nonstate actors, such as terrorist groups, can pose economic threats.

In keeping with the definition of security used in this book, we will consider economic actions that are implemented with malign intent and have a capability to do significant harm as security threats. A key question is, security for whom? As noted in the first chapter, the focus here is on the security of the United States; were one to focus on other international actors, the analysis could be quite different. Excluded in our consideration are the economic problems caused by natural disasters, such as typhoons, hurricanes, floods, and tornadoes. Included in our consideration are policies concerning energy, the environment (chapter 13), poverty, and failed states.

National Wealth and Security

Economic nationalists, such as mercantilists, emphasized the necessity of increasing a state's power by promoting exports and obtaining colonial holdings. This led to the building of strong militaries, particularly naval forces. According to Jacob Viner, mercantilists subscribed to the following propositions: (1) wealth is an absolutely essential means to power, whether for security or for aggression; (2) power is an important means to the acquisition or retention of wealth; (3) wealth and power are each proper ultimate ends of national policy; (4) there is a long-run harmony between these ends, although in particular circumstances it may be necessary for a time to make economic sacrifices in the interest of military security and therefore also of long-run prosperity.[7]

During the mercantilist period, naval power was the single most important measure of power. The drive to obtain colonies led to explorations by the developed states of undeveloped areas of the world, and navies became the means by which the European powers explored, conquered, and controlled colonies throughout the world. The mercantilist system was established by the interaction of naval forces, access to resources, and trade. No country better illustrated the growth of mercantilistic power than the British empire, the needs of which, according to historian Arthur Herman, included "access to markets, freedom of trade across international boundaries, an orderly state system that prefers peace to war, speedy communication and travel across open seas and skies—[and these] remain the principal features of globalization today."[8] As Sir Walter Raleigh noted, "Whosoever commands the sea, commands the trade; whosoever commands the trade of the world commands the riches of the world, and consequently the world itself."[9]

In many, if not most, cases this attempt to achieve greater security led to the exploitation of developing states by the developed states of Europe. For example, Great Britain established trading cities on the coast of China and began importing opium from India. The opium trade proved to be very lucrative for British merchants, if tragic for the Chinese who became addicted to opium. This trade influenced Chinese views of the West for years, even to the present day. An American naval squadron under Commodore Matthew Perry forced Japan to open its ports to trade with the United States. The *samurai* warriors of traditional Japan proved to be no match for the cannons of the American ships. Thus the economic imperative of trade threatened the security of China and Japan.

Over time, a pattern evolved: developing states typically produced primary products, such as coffee, tea, and cocoa, whereas developed states produced manufactured products, such as textiles and machinery. The classical liberal economists Adam Smith, David Ricardo, and John Stuart Mill noted that certain states have an absolute or comparative advantage in producing certain products and should specialize in them. For example, in the eighteenth century, taking advantage of the technology developed during the Industrial Revolution, Britain specialized in the manufacture of textiles. Given their climate and soil conditions, Spain and Portugal specialized in growing grapes and producing port and sherry. The classical economists noted that it would be possible for Britain to grow grapes and produce its own port and sherry, and for Spain and Portugal to build their own textile factories, but not efficient. This became the rationale for free trade.

Although free trade represented the most efficient use of what Karl Marx had called the "means of production," those in developing countries in particular contended that the pattern that was established by free trade was one of dependence and therefore disadvantageous for those in developing countries. They argued that this was because the developed states reaped the profits from converting primary products into manufactured goods.

The threats posed by the Western countries to the developing states, however, had an unforeseen consequence: in order to meet the threats, many developing states in the nineteenth century began to emulate the Western states. The first step was industrialization. Factories were established in cities, and people moved from the countryside into metropolitan centers. In the mid-1700s, about the time that Adam Smith was writing *The Wealth of Nations,* approximately 3 percent of the world's population lived in cities. That figure had increased to 29 percent by the 1950s and to 40 percent by 1995; it is projected to be 60 percent by 2025. Along with industrialization came urbanization. By 1985, the population of Mexico City was seventeen million and Sao Paolo, Brazil, fifteen million. The result was that traditional social ties and stability began to break down.

The results of industrialization and urbanization led to increased secularization and social problems, including crime, disease, and demand on social services. Some developing states, however, were able to industrialize successfully and to produce technology that enabled them to compete with and even defeat developed states. For example, in 1904–1905, having built a modern navy in the space of fifty years, Japan was able to challenge and defeat Russia, in the first defeat of a Western power by a non-Western power in history. In this case, a once-vanquished state was able to defeat its opponents by adopting the opponents' technology. Another technique that states used against opposing states was the imposition of economic sanctions.

The Threat of Economic Sanctions

Economic sanctions have been used throughout history as a means of influencing behavior and attempting to achieve greater security. According to former State Department official Richard Haass, sanctions may be defined as "mostly economic but also political and military penalties introduced to alter political and/or military behavior."[10] Actions have taken the form of "arms embargoes, foreign assistance reductions and cutoffs, export and import limitations, asset freezes, tariff increases, revocation of most favored nation (MFN) trade status, negative votes in international financial institutions, withdrawal of diplomatic relations, visa denials, cancellation of air links, and prohibitions on credit, financing, and investment."[11] Both states and international organizations have used sanctions to try to influence the actions and policies of states and corporations.

During the first four decades of its existence, the United Nations imposed economic sanctions only against Rhodesia in 1966 and South Africa in 1977. In the decade from 1992 to 2002 the United Nations imposed sanctions against Iraq (1990),[12] the former Yugoslavia (1992), Libya (1992), Haiti (1994), Liberia (1992), Rwanda (1994), Somalia, UNITA forces in Angola (1994), Sudan, Sierra Leone, Afghanistan, Eritrea, and Ethiopia.[13] In a comprehensive description and analysis of economic sanctions, Meghan L. O'Sullivan identifies 122 sanctions imposed by the United States or the United Nations on state or nonstate actors from 1990 through 2001.[14] It is clear that sanctions are a commonly employed way of attempting to achieve greater security through economic means.

There is substantial controversy over the effectiveness of economic sanctions. In work published in 1985 and updated in 1990, Gary Hufbauer, Jeffrey Schott, and Karen Ann Elliott studied 115 cases of economic sanctions imposed from 1914 to 1990 and concluded that sanctions were successful in forty (34 percent) of these instances. This study was criticized by a number of analysts as too optimistic concerning the effectiveness of sanctions.[15]

Several observations concerning the literature on economic sanctions are important. First, virtually all of the studies on sanctions focus on interstate behavior. Second, almost all focus on the actions of wealthy states toward poorer states. In this sense, sanctions are actions of the powerful toward the weak. A reversal of this traditional pattern occurred in October 1973 when the Arab members of the Organization of Petroleum Exporting Countries (OPEC) imposed an embargo on oil shipments to the countries that supported Israel in the Arab-Israeli war. Within a matter of weeks, the price of oil went from three dollars per barrel to twelve dollars, a 400 percent increase. The Arab oil embargo of 1973–74 was an economic sanction imposed by the formerly weak against the strong. Thucydides wrote, "The strong do what they will, and the weak suffer what they must." The Arab oil embargo turned Thucydides on his head.

THREATS TO THE UNITED STATES FROM FAILED STATES

Due in part to the vestiges of colonialism, developing states at the present time face a number of threats so daunting that they can result in collapse. Failed states, in turn, can pose a significant threat to the United States. In fact, in the 2002 *National Security Strategy,* the George W. Bush administration argued that for the first time in history, weak states posed more of a threat to the United States than strong states.[16] According to the conclusion of a study cosponsored by the Association of the U.S. Army and the Center for Strategic and International Studies:

> One of the principal lessons of the events of September 11 is that failed states matter—not just for humanitarian reasons but also for national security as well. If left unattended, such states can become sanctuaries for terrorist networks with a global reach, not to mention international organized crime and drug traffickers who also exploit the dysfunctional environment. As such, failed states can pose a direct threat to the national interests of the United States and to the stability of entire regions.[17]

What causes contribute to state failure? First and foremost is poverty and the need for economic development. As former State Department advisor Meghan O'Sullivan has noted, "Poor socioeconomic conditions are seen not just as being of humanitarian concern but also as having security implications that extend beyond a single country's borders."[18]

Second, many developing states suffer from an absence of national unity. Colonial powers often set boundaries solely on the basis of natural barriers, such as rivers and mountain ranges, with little or no consideration of social groupings. Thus, Nigeria contains the Muslim Hausas in the north and the Christian Ibos in the south; these groups fought a vicious and bloody civil war in the 1970s. Similarly, Rwanda was populated principally by two tribes, the Hutu and the Tutsi; the killing sprees that resulted have been described in chapter 10. This problem is not limited to Africa. Yugoslavia contained three main ethnic groups, Croats, Serbs, and Bosniaks. Modern Iraq must contend with both ethnic and religious divisions: ethnic Kurds occupy the north, Sunni Muslims dominate the central part, and Shi'a Muslims are a majority in southern Iraq. The degree to which these three groups can get along will be an important factor shaping Iraq's future.

A third problem of developing states concerns industrialization, urbanization, and secularization. As the eminent British historian Sir Michael Howard has noted, in developing states "industrialization has led to urbanization, with the resulting breakdown of traditional authority and the destruction of cultures rooted in tribal rule and land tenure."[19] The resulting loss of identity and instability can have significant effects on a country and the surrounding region. There are also the related problems of overpopulation, hunger, and public health.

One of the principal dangers of failed states is that they can become sanctuaries for the opponents of international order. United Nations special envoy Lakhdar Brahimi has argued that the events of September 11, 2001, were "a wakeup call, [that caused many people] to realize that even small countries, far away, like Afghanistan cannot be left to sink to the depths to which Afghanistan has sunk."[20] Failed states can serve, and have served, as bases of operation for terrorist groups; this was the case with both Sudan and Afghanistan for Al Qaeda.

The area of the world with the greatest number of actual or potential failed states is Africa, and the threat from African failed states is very real. As Professor Lisa Cook of Harvard University has observed, "Given the long-established pattern in which extremist groups, including Islamic militants, prey on impoverished economies and failed states, Africa seems a natural breeding ground for terrorism."[21] The United States and, more broadly, developed Western states can respond to this threat in several ways. First, African leaders who assist their citizens and the war against terrorism should be supported. In this regard, President Olusegun Obasanjo of Nigeria is noteworthy. Second, efforts to reduce poverty and strengthen the economies of African countries should be continued and strengthened; the African Growth and Opportunity Act and the Millennium Challenge Account are two recent efforts to do this. Third, HIV and AIDS are literally and figuratively crippling African countries, and efforts must be continued and strengthened to address this modern-day plague. In 2003, more than nine thousand new HIV infections and six thousand AIDS deaths were reported each day in sub-Saharan Africa. The dislocations caused by this disease, as well as by malaria, tuberculosis, and other infections, contribute to societal instability. Fourth, Africa is already unstable; there is a great need to maintain peacekeeping forces in a number of conflicts, most notably Burundi, the Democratic Republic of Congo, and Sudan.

The 9/11 Commission commented on the importance of failed states: "In the twentieth century, strategists focused on the world's great industrial heartlands. In the twenty-first century, the focus is in the opposite direction, toward remote regions and failing states."[22]

PROSPECTS FOR INCREASING ECONOMIC SECURITY

For decades at least, people in developed states have recognized the need to assist developing countries for both altruistic and self-interested reasons. As Joseph Nye has argued, "Investments [in economic development] are a clear case of coincidence between self-interest and charity."[23] Developing countries have also recognized their need for development. In 1955, twenty-nine Asian and African countries met in Bandung, Indonesia, and declared that they were not aligned with either of the Cold War's two superpowers, the United States or the Soviet Union. In 1964, seventy-seven states called for the creation of the UN Conference on Trade and Development (UNCTAD). This development caucus within the UN is still known as the "Group of 77" even though its membership has grown to 132 states. Two so-called "South Summits" of the Group of 77 have occurred, the first in 2000 in Havana, Cuba, and the second in 2005 in Doha, Qatar. Among the principal objectives of the Group of 77 are trade, monetary and institutional reforms, economic modernization, greater freedom for labor migration, the elimination of economic coercion, development aid, and debt relief.

Developed states can attempt in several different ways to prevent developing states from failing and thereby posing a greater threat. First, developed states can invest directly in developing countries. In the 1990s, Western banks invested a great deal of money in Latin America, and it was not unusual for profits to be in the double digits. Such direct foreign investment could also be risky, however. When questions were raised in 1994 about the stability of the Mexican economy and government, foreign investors called in their loans and withdrew their money. This led to a serious economic crisis. The United States and the International Monetary Fund came up with a fifty-billion-dollar bailout package (including twenty billion from the United States). The Mexican bailout proved to be a great success story; Mexico paid the United States back ahead of schedule, and the U.S. Treasury made five hundred million dollars in interest. Importantly from the American perspective, the government of Mexico did not collapse, an event that would have had profound and serious security consequences for the United States had it occurred.

A second initiative that the developed world can take to prevent the failure of states is economic aid. Such aid can be measured in absolute or relative terms. Using the former measure, the United States leads the world as the country that grants the most aid in dollars, eleven billion dollars. However, if aid is measured as a percentage of the donor country's gross national product (GNP), the picture changes dramatically. At the Monterrey Financing for Development Conference in 2002, the world's economically developed states promised to move toward the goal of donating 0.7 percent of their gross national incomes to economic aid. Only five countries in the world have met this target: Denmark (1.03 percent), Norway (0.83 percent), the Netherlands (0.82 percent), Luxembourg (0.82 percent), and Sweden (0.81 percent).[24] The United States currently devotes 0.11 percent of its gross domestic product to economic aid, the lowest percentage of any advanced industrial state. The United States has traditionally allocated aid primarily on political rather than on humanitarian grounds. In keeping with this political orientation, the United States allocated most of its economic aid in the 1960s to South Vietnam; since the 1979 Camp David peace accords, more than 50 percent of U.S. aid has gone to Israel and Egypt; and in the 1980s, substantial aid went to anticommunist forces in Central America.

Joseph Nye has called attention to the self-interested rationale for providing economic aid to developing countries: "There are many reasons for development assistance by wealthy countries, but one is to deprive terrorist leaders of such arguments by showing that our policies are aligned with the long-term aspirations of the poor."[25]

THE PROTECTION OF THE LIBERAL INTERNATIONAL ECONOMIC ORDER AS A SECURITY INTEREST

At the end of World War II, Western countries led by the United States created a liberal international economic order based on, as Susan Strange described it, "an economic structure, a certain pattern of production (labour and capital) and of exchange of raw materials, semifinished and finished goods and services, and a certain pattern of distribution for consumption."[26] The system was based on free trade and the ideas of Adam Smith, David Ricardo, and John Stuart Mill. It is not surprising that the advanced industrialized states were the primary beneficiaries of the system that they implemented.

Professor Charles Kindleberger has noted the importance of a leading power or hegemon to the effective functioning of the international economic system.[27] Any threat that harms either the United States as the hegemonic leader of the contemporary system or the international economic system itself poses a threat to the security of the developed states and to a lesser extent of the developing countries. When the United States was attacked on September 11, 2001, American governmental authorities did what few others in the world could do: they declared a self-embargo of the United States. No airplanes, ships, trucks, or automobiles were allowed to enter the country for several days.[28]

The contemporary international economic system is one based on globalization, and a key element, if not *the* key element, of globalization, is international trade. The developed states in particular are dependent on trade as the engine of globalization. Therefore, if terrorists are able to dramatically reduce, or even halt, trade, they can harm the advanced industrial states. The substantial economic damage that resulted from the September 11 attacks on the United States was one of the most significant of their effects (see chapter 13).

The post–World War II international economic system was founded on principles and institutions that promoted a liberal international system of free trade, flexible exchange rates, and a stable monetary system. The developed states were the major beneficiaries of this system, but the developing and newly industrializing countries have also, to a lesser extent, benefited from it. Threats to the processes on which this system is founded—free trade and globalization—are threats to the security of both the members of the system and the system itself. If terrorists were to cripple international trade, the world would be far less prosperous. In this sense, economic security is second only to the physical security of the homeland as a vital national interest.

Economics and security are related, but in a complex manner. Mercantilists, however, viewed the relationship as simple and straightforward: a strong navy was needed to explore, conquer, and control colonies, which became sources of raw materials that could be used for trade and manufacturing, thus contributing to the wealth of the state. The subjugation of colonies was the path to wealth and security. Of course, this system created substantial resentment, even hatred, in the colonial areas that were exploited; once given the opportunity, this resentment manifested itself in violence and in some cases revolution. As a result, a system that originally sought greater security through economics ultimately threatened the security of the developed states. The unintended result is consistent with the major theme of this book: insecurity has often resulted from the search for security.

RECOMMENDED READING

Printed Sources

Baldwin, David. *Economic Statecraft*. Princeton, N.J.: Princeton University Press, 1985.

Haass, Richard N., and Meghan L. O'Sullivan, eds. *Honey and Vinegar: Incentives, Sanctions, and Foreign Policy*. Washington, D.C.: Brookings Institution, 2000.

Hirschman, Albert O. *National Power and the Structure of International Trade*. Berkeley: University of California Press, 1980.

Knorr, Klaus. *Power and Wealth*. New York: Basic Books, 1973.

Knorr, Klaus, and Frank Trager, eds. *Economic Issues and National Security*. Lawrence: University Press of Kansas, 1977.

Pape, Robert. "Why Sanctions Do Not Work." *International Security* 22, no. 2 (Fall 1997): 90–136.

United Nations. *Human Development Report*. New York: United Nations (annual).

U.S. Central Intelligence Agency. *Economic Handbook*. Washington, D.C.: U.S. Government Printing Office (annual).

World Bank. *Human Development Index*. Washington, D.C.: World Bank (annual).

Websites

Institute for International Economics: www.iie.com

International Monetary Fund: www.imf.org

U.S. Central Intelligence Agency. *World Factbook*: www.odci.gov

World Bank: www.worldbank.org.

12

Ecological Disasters and Resource Wars: Seeking Environmental Security

In a provocative essay that first appeared in 1994, Robert D. Kaplan noted the widening gap between states enjoying the benefits of globalization and those descending into anarchy. He described many sources of insecurity in the post–Cold War world, but one attracted special attention. "It is time," Kaplan wrote, "to understand 'the environment' for what it is: *the* national security issue of the early twenty-first century." He continued, listing environmental concerns with serious foreign policy implications: "The political and strategic impact of surging populations, spreading disease, deforestation and soil erosion, water depletion, air pollution, and, possibly, rising sea levels in critical, overcrowded regions like the Nile Delta and Bangladesh—developments that will prompt mass migrations and, in turn, incite group conflicts—will be the core foreign-policy challenge from which most others will ultimately emanate, arousing the public and uniting assorted interests left over from the Cold War."[1]

The world's environmental problems are widespread, and they are, in many instances, extreme. Consider this sampling:

- Every year, approximately 160,000 square kilometers of forest—an area roughly the size of Tunisia—disappears. Of the Earth's original forest cover, only half remains.[2]
- The noted biologist E. O. Wilson has estimated that fifty thousand species become extinct every year. This comes, on average, to 137 per day.[3] While the extinction of species is a naturally occurring phenomenon, human activities have increased species extinctions by as much as a thousand times the natural rate. It is estimated that up to 10 percent of the world's species could disappear in the next quarter-century if current extinction rates are not arrested.[4]
- Each year, 6.5 *billion* tons of carbon is released into the Earth's atmosphere through the burning of fossil fuels. Another 1.6 billion tons per year is released as a consequence of deforestation.[5] Since the beginning of the industrial age,

carbon dioxide levels in the atmosphere have increased by approximately 35 percent.[6]

- One-sixth of the world's population is adversely affected by desertification, a process that reduces and ultimately eliminates the productivity of agricultural lands, thereby limiting the ability of a population to feed itself.[7] Since 1990, an estimated 14,800,000 acres of land (about twice the size of Belgium) have been lost each year to some form of desertification.[8]

Clearly the world faces many environmental challenges, but is there any evidence to suggest that these challenges amount to a security threat? Over the past quarter-century, more and more analysts who concern themselves strictly with national security have begun to acknowledge important links between the environment and security. Those who think of security in terms of the lives and dignity of individual human beings see not just links between environmental problems and national security but direct threats to human security. Today, within the new paradigm of security studies, it is essential to consider environmental security as it relates to individual humans, to states, and to the international system.

Whenever human actions pose threats to the basic rights (and especially the right to life) of human beings, a security issue exists. Environmental problems have been "securitized" as a consequence of the recognition that human alterations of the natural environment do indeed threaten the lives and welfare of humans. In some instances, the threats posed by man-made environmental disasters are direct and obvious. The explosion at the Chernobyl nuclear power plant in 1986 resulted in thirty-one immediate deaths, an increase in the incidence of cancer in exposed populations, and enormous social disruption in the vicinity of the disaster. Over two thousand people in Bhopal, India, died in 1984 as a direct result of a deadly gas leak from a Union Carbide chemical plant; another two hundred thousand were injured.[9] London's "Great Smog" tripled the city's death rate over a four-day period in December 1952. The smog, produced by a combination of a natural temperature inversion and air fouled by the residues of coal smoke, was responsible for over four thousand deaths immediately and perhaps another eight thousand over the following months.[10]

The enormous complexity of ecosystems and the difficulty inherent in tracing anthropogenic (human-caused) effects on the environment make some analysts unwilling to treat environmental problems as security issues. Such skeptics argue, for example, that London's "Great Smog" was as much the product of the cold, damp air that enveloped the city as of the large quantity of sulfur dioxide and particulate matter in the air, or that the number of cancer deaths attributable to the Chernobyl disaster is simply unknowable. Similar claims are made regarding global warming. The objections of the skeptics can be met very simply and forcefully by noting, first, that the overwhelming weight of scientific opinion regarding human-induced environmental change sees far less uncertainty than the skeptics claim and, second, that in no other area involving human welfare would uncertainty be considered a legitimate reason for failure to act.

Originally, environmental issues were added to the security agenda by those who noted the environment's relationship to national security.[11] Here, with this relatively well-developed part of the new security paradigm, is a good place for us to begin our examination of environmental security.

Seen in terms of national security, environmental problems are "securitized" in two broad categories. There are, first, environmental threats that relate directly to warfare. This category includes environmental-modification techniques used in fighting wars and damage to the environment that occurs as a consequence of warfare. The second category includes environmental threats not directly related to warfare. These may still be considered matters of national security in the case of environmental problems that threaten to cause a war. However, environmental problems that, because of their severity, threaten human lives and welfare even without the intermediate agency of war should also be included in this category and considered security issues, because of our concern for human security.

WAR-RELATED ENVIRONMENTAL THREATS

Around 2500 BC, what may have been the first use in history of environmental modification as a means of warfare occurred in the Middle East when King Urlama of Lagash ordered the construction of canals to divert water from neighboring Umma during a territorial dispute in the boundary region between the two kingdoms, which lay between the Tigris and the Euphrates. A better-known and far more dramatic instance of environmental warfare occurred around 1200 BC during the great exodus of the people of Israel from Egypt. With the pharaoh's army in pursuit of the fleeing Israelites, Moses summoned divine assistance to part the waters of the Red Sea. After the Israelites had passed safely to the other side, Egyptian soldiers were drowned when the waters of the Red Sea closed over them.[12]

Herodotus describes how Cyrus, in 539 BC, invaded Babylon by diverting the waters of the Euphrates in order to allow his troops to march into the city on the dry riverbed.[13] Over two thousand years later, in 1503, Leonardo da Vinci and Niccolo Machiavelli devised a plan (never implemented) to divert the waters of the Arno River away from Pisa during a conflict between Florence and Pisa.[14] In the Netherlands, from the seventeenth century all the way up to 1940 a defensive network was based on plans to flood large portions of the country's low-lying land.[15]

The diversion of water is not the only environmental modification technique that has been used in warfare. Smoke (sometimes in combination with naturally occurring fog or dust) has been used to screen the movements of armies and ships for centuries. In the exodus from Egypt, smoke was used to hide the movement of the Israelites from the Egyptian army pursuing them. In 1632, the Swedish king Gustavus Adolphus used smoke generated by burning wet straw to cover a river crossing by his army. During the World War I battle of Loos in Belgium, British forces used smoke candles in the course of preparing for their first gas attack. So effective was the use of smoke to cover the British infantry assault at Loos that the British army continued to use smoke screens through the remainder of the war.[16] Modern navies routinely equip their ships with the capability to produce smoke screens.

The most dramatic modern-day instance of environmental warfare occurred in 1991, during the Persian Gulf War. Iraqi forces retreating from Kuwait damaged 749 oil wells, setting 650 of them ablaze. Damaged wells burned or gushed an estimated six million barrels of oil per day. In all, six hundred million barrels of oil—equivalent to three months' worth of global petroleum consumption—was lost.[17]

Warfare (and preparations for war) can have devastating environmental impacts even when environmental resources are not being deliberately used as tools of war. The following examples merely illustrate the connection. A more comprehensive accounting of war-related environmental damage would require a volume of its own.

War sometimes has a devastating effect on other species, even to the point of threatening major species with extinction. As many as a hundred of the 250 lowland gorillas and three hundred of the four hundred forest elephants populating the Congo's Kahuzi-Biega National Park are thought to have been killed between 1996 and 1999. Poachers using automatic weapons acquired from Rwandan soldiers following the 1994 genocide in Rwanda were responsible for many of the killings, but poaching was facilitated by the devastating impact of war on both conservation efforts and tourism. Rwandan and Congolese rebels using the national park as a base of operations also slaughtered animals for food and sold ivory to pay for weapons.[18]

War can also leave serious environmental hazards in its wake. Large areas of Iraq, Kosovo, and Afghanistan are today littered with low-level radioactive waste as a consequence of the U.S. military's use of depleted-uranium weapons. Depleted uranium is a by-product of the uranium-enrichment process used to produce fissile uranium for nuclear weapons or reactors. Because depleted uranium, as a metal, is almost twice as dense as lead, it is used by the United States for tank armor and armor-piercing shells. Waste, including contaminated soil, produced by testing and training with depleted-uranium weapons in the United States falls under Department of Energy guidelines for the disposal of radioactive waste. Concern over the health and environmental impacts of depleted-uranium weapons led the Air Force in 1993 to stop using them in training exercises. (The decision was reversed in 2002.)[19] Of course, there are no environmental regulations that govern the use of such weapons in warfare. Consequently, in spite of the existence of hundreds of contamination sites in Iraq, Kosovo, and Afghanistan, as well as persistent questions among scientists concerning the long-term effects of depleted uranium on plant and animal life and groundwater, the United States has taken no steps even to assess the environmental impact of these weapons.

The ultimate, although unrealized, war-related environmental catastrophe is perhaps "nuclear winter." Jonathan Schell, in an apocalyptic best seller that described the planet's possible condition following a general nuclear war, said that the United States could become "a republic of insects and grass" and that, indeed, the climatic catastrophe produced by a nuclear war might very well mean the extinction of human life.[20] Such a condition, or something approaching it, would be produced by the layer of dust and soot thrown into the atmosphere by multiple nuclear detonations.[21]

It is not combat alone that constitutes a security-related threat to the environment. A variety of environmental problems have also resulted from preparations for war.

In 1991, a Russian environmental group reported that the Soviet Union had regularly dumped radioactive waste into the Arctic Ocean during the Cold War. After initially denying the charges, the Russian government agreed in 1992 to appoint a commission to study the matter. When the report was completed the following year, it revealed that a large quantity of nuclear material had in fact been dumped. Six nuclear reactors with fuel, ten reactors without fuel, and portions of a nuclear icebreaker containing nuclear fuel had all been deposited in the Arctic Ocean. In addition, over seventeen thousand containers of radioactive waste had been dumped between 1959 and 1992. When barrels of nuclear materials floated on the surface after dumping, sailors had been ordered to shoot them with machine guns, ensuring not only that the barrels would sink but that their contents would leak immediately into the ocean.[22]

In August 2000, the *Kursk*, a Russian submarine powered by two nuclear reactors, sank in the Barents Sea. Only a complex salvage operation conducted over a year later prevented the *Kursk*'s reactors from joining those deliberately dumped into the Arctic Ocean as sources of long-term ecological damage.[23]

The U.S. Navy's use of mid-frequency sonar to detect submarines at long distances has long been suspected of causing the deaths of marine mammals. In 2003, scientists studying the deaths of fourteen whales that beached themselves and died in the Canary Islands during nearby naval exercises reported evidence of depression sickness, likely caused by the whales' response to sonar.[24] In 2004, the Scientific Committee of the International Whaling Commission said that the evidence linking sonar to whale beachings "appears overwhelming."[25]

INDIRECT ENVIRONMENTAL THREATS

Environmental problems unrelated to warfare often constitute serious threats to human welfare and, consequently, raise issues of human security. Deforestation and desertification may deprive people of their livelihoods and even render subsistence farming impossible. Overfishing of the world's oceans to the point of causing the collapse of certain species of fish risks eliminating an important source of nutrition for humankind. Untreated sewage can affect supplies of drinking water, causing widespread illness and even death. Polluted air is a factor in respiratory diseases. Depletion of the ozone layer creates exposure to cancer-causing solar radiation. Global warming, which will be considered in greater detail later in this chapter, threatens many serious effects on humans, including, for some, the inundation of their homes. Without the firing of a single weapon, environmental problems can bring death and destruction.

But there is some evidence that environmental damage may also lead to war in some circumstances. Thomas Homer-Dixon, a leading expert on the relationship between security and the environment, has stated that "scarcities of critical environmental resources—especially of cropland, freshwater, and forests—contribute to violence in many parts of the world."[26] While interstate violence is not a common consequence of environmental strains, violence within countries, especially developing states, can sometimes be attributed to environmental factors. The implications even for more advanced states are significant, since intrastate violence in the developing world can generate refugee flows, provoke humanitarian crises (with attendant pressures for intervention), and, in extreme cases, actually cause the collapse of states. ("Failed states" and the problems they present are discussed in chapters 9 and 11.)

Water is the resource that most commonly causes tensions between states, although oil (which is discussed below) seems to generate more intense conflicts. Many of the world's most important rivers—the Nile, Euphrates, Indus, Ganges, Danube, and Paraná, to note just a few—are shared by two or more states. The construction of dams, such as the Ataturk Dam on the Euphrates River in Turkey and the Gabčíkovo-Nagymaros Project on the Danube in Hungary and Slovakia, have created concerns downstream about environmental consequences of reduced water flows and about potential manipulation of supplies. In parts of the world where fresh water is scarce, access to major rivers and lakes is clearly a matter of national security.[27]

Ultimately, it is human consumption—of water, food, air, and a host of other resources—that, together with the waste such consumption produces, is responsible for virtually all of the environmental problems we face today. That consumption increases with both population growth and with development. Our prehistoric ancestors are thought to have consumed 2,500 calories of energy each per day, all in the form of food. Today the average human uses thirty-one thousand calories of energy per day (Americans consume on average six times that amount), with fossil fuels constituting the majority of that figure.[28] The significance of fossil fuels, and especially petroleum, as a cause of insecurity in the world today merits special attention.

OIL AND SECURITY

For much of the past century oil has been "the prize," the one natural resource capable of empowering backward societies and bringing empires to their knees. It will have the same importance in international politics for years to come, although exactly how many more years is a contentious and crucial question. In the past half-century, some of the poorest states in the world have become some of the world's wealthiest states on the strength of oil revenues alone. Conversely, the world's most advanced states—the industrialized democracies of North America, Western Europe, and Japan—were temporarily crippled by an oil embargo in the 1970s. And Russia, reeling from the effects of its transition from communism to capitalism, has been kept afloat economically by oil exports.

Have there been wars for oil? Some scoff at the idea, while others have taken to the streets with signs demanding, "No blood for oil." What is indisputable is this: Petroleum has been a vital resource for the world's industrialized states and has played a central role in the modern history of warfare. The most destructive war in history, World War II, was propelled in specific directions by the necessity of securing access to oil. As the Japanese military came to exert greater influence on Tokyo's foreign policy in the 1930s, a serious strategic problem presented itself. Japan possessed no petroleum. Although oil at the time met only about 7 percent of Japan's total energy needs, it supplied most of the Japanese military's energy demands. Furthermore, 80 percent of Japan's petroleum came from the United States, at a time when the two Pacific powers appeared to be on a collision course. The thirst for oil ultimately drove Japan across East Asia and into a war with the United States.[29] In the European theater, Germany's decision to push deep into the Soviet Union, however ill fated and unwise it may have appeared in retrospect, was considered necessary by the German military in order to gain control over oil supplies in the Caucasus.

In the six decades since the end of World War II, oil has become more, not less, important to the well-being of states. Economies have become more dependent on oil, as have military establishments. Indeed, it is difficult to overstate the importance of oil to modern societies. As important as the high-tech capabilities associated with command, control, communications, computers, and intelligence (C4I) have become to American military dominance, oil is still the lifeblood of the tanks, trucks, airplanes, and ships that constitute, in turn, the backbone—and the muscle—of modern armed forces. Petroleum is equally significant in the definition of economic power. It may be possible in the Information Age to order virtually any consumer good from virtually anywhere in the world over the Internet, but delivery still requires a FedEx cargo plane or a UPS truck, and neither moves without oil. The configuration of human habitation, with the relentless urbanization that has accompanied industrialization, is dependent on the means of transportation made possible by internal combustion engines, burning petroleum-based fuels. Likewise, the agricultural revolution that has made it possible for fewer and fewer farmers to feed more and more city dwellers from the yield of ever smaller plots of land is based on petrochemical fertilizers and mechanized agricultural machinery.

The extent of American dependence on oil can best be captured in two key numbers. Petroleum accounts for 40 percent of the energy consumed in the United States; in the transportation sector, the figure is 97 percent.[30] In the absence of new technologies, the sudden disappearance of oil would return us to the days of horse-drawn carriages, steam-powered locomotives, and electric trolleys.

Oil is a security concern not only because of its importance to the functioning of advanced industrialized states and the military forces that protect their interests but because of where it is found throughout the world. The vast majority of the world's states have insufficient supplies of petroleum to meet their own needs and, consequently, must rely on imported oil. Net importers must therefore be concerned about the internal stability of petroleum-exporting countries and their continuing willingness to export oil. The security of oil pipelines and tankers is also a matter of considerable concern. On top of everything else, oil prices raise security concerns, since dramatic increases ("price shocks") have the potential for generating economic recessions in oil-dependent economies.

Questions surrounding the dependability of oil-exporting countries (that is, the combination of their internal stability and their willingness to supply particular customers, including the United States, Japan, and the European Union) take on considerable urgency when one looks at who the leading oil exporters are. The top ten net petroleum exporters are Saudi Arabia, Russia, Norway, Iran, the United Arab Emirates, Venezuela, Kuwait, Nigeria, Mexico, and Algeria.[31] Only Norway and Mexico are considered "free," according to the annual assessment of political liberties and civil rights conducted by Freedom House. Saudi Arabia's monarchy, in contrast, is considered one of the world's most repressive regimes.[32] Several countries on the list are also among the world's most corrupt business environments.

The situation is scarcely any better when smaller suppliers and emerging producers, such as the former Soviet republics of the Caspian Sea basin, are considered. The oil-producing states of the region—Azerbaijan, Kazakhstan, Turkmenistan, and Uzbekistan—are expected to export four million barrels of oil per day by 2015,[33] but all are dictatorships with corrupt leaders who are former Communist Party bosses from the period of Soviet rule. The political situation is even worse in certain other oil-producing states. Sudan, for example, has proven petroleum reserves estimated at 563 million barrels of oil, and yet civil war has raged there for over two decades, Al Qaeda operated there during the 1990s, and, more recently, mass killings in the Darfur region have prompted the United States to label the situation there genocide (see chapter 11). To put it simply, petroleum exploration, production, and export often requires oil-importing states to deal with governments that are repressive, corrupt, and unstable.

Geography generates additional problems. In part due to the locations of the world's primary petroleum-exporting countries, much of the world's tanker traffic must pass through one or more maritime chokepoints en route to the oil-importing states. The most critical of these chokepoints is the Strait of Hormuz, separating the Persian Gulf from the Gulf of Oman and the Arabian Sea. Roughly fifteen million barrels of oil per day pass through the Strait of Hormuz on the way to the United States, Japan, or (via the Suez Canal, another significant chokepoint) Western Europe.[34] The other principal means of transporting oil, via pipelines, also raises security questions. Pipelines often traverse the territories of war-torn or otherwise unstable states and present tempting, and generally undefended, targets for saboteurs.

The dilemmas associated with petroleum politics are becoming more, not less, difficult to address, because oil consumption continues to increase worldwide. The U.S. Department of Energy projects global oil consumption to grow an average of 1.9 percent per year between 2003 and 2025.[35] For its part, the United States, which used 19.71 million barrels of oil per day in 2001, will be consuming 28.30 million barrels per day by 2025.[36] The annual rate of growth in petroleum consumption in the United States from 2003 to 2025 is projected to be almost double what it was from 1980 to 2003.[37] Meanwhile, domestic production peaked in 1970 at 9.6 million barrels per day and has been slowly declining ever since.[38]

American consumption may not be the worst aspect of the demand problem in the future (although it appears unlikely that any state will catch the United States in per capita consumption). China and India, both with populations over a billion, are rapidly industrializing. A recent study of global trends undertaken for the CIA concluded that simply in order to maintain steady economic growth rates, by 2020 China will have to increase its energy consumption by 150 percent, while India will require almost twice its current level of energy consumption.[39] An increase in China's per capita consumption of oil to the U.S. level would require eighty-one million barrels per day.[40] (Total world production of oil in 2004 averaged just under eighty-three million barrels of oil per day.)

In spite of the development of new oil fields in the Caspian Sea basin and the South China Sea, there are signs that we may be nearing the upper limit of global oil production. In fact, some scientists have suggested the global "Hubbert peak"—the point at which petroleum production reaches its highest level, after which it declines steadily—could occur within the current decade.[41] Simply put, the world is running out of the oil that has already been discovered and has few places left to look for undiscovered reserves. In the absence of dramatic changes in consumption patterns, the future does not appear to be very secure for petroleum-based economies.

Against this background, it is worth noting the degree to which access to oil has already become a significant part of the U.S. definition of American national security.

In 1991 and again in 2003, the United States went to war against Iraq. On both occasions, most supporters and even some opponents of war were quick to argue that American forces were fighting in Iraq for reasons larger than oil—for Kuwaiti sovereignty or the principle of nonaggression (in 1991) or to defeat global terrorism or promote Iraqi human rights (in 2003). And yet the interest of the industrialized world in oil from the Persian Gulf States was, and is, undeniable. In November 1990, Secretary of State James A. Baker, in fact, was quite forthright about that interest when he explicitly linked the first American military confrontation with Iraq to jobs in the United States.[42]

Baker was not the first to connect Persian Gulf oil to U.S. national security. A decade earlier, a series of dramatic events had prompted President Carter to articulate a new approach to petroleum and national security. In January 1979, the shah of Iran, a faithful ally of the United States, was overthrown in an Islamic revolution. The hostility of the new regime to American interests was demonstrated in November when the American embassy in Tehran was overrun. Then, in December, the Soviet Union invaded neighboring Afghanistan.

Carter responded to these developments in his State of the Union Address on January 23, 1980, with what came to be called the Carter Doctrine. Noting that the Soviet invasion of Afghanistan threatened a region containing "more than two-thirds of the world's exportable oil," Carter said, "Let our position be absolutely clear: An attempt by any outside force to gain control of the Persian Gulf region will be regarded as an assault on the vital interests of the United States of America, and such an assault will be repelled by any means necessary, including military force."[43] To give force to the announcement, a new military command, the Rapid Deployment Joint Task Force, was formed in Tampa, Florida, with responsibility for the Persian Gulf region. Under President Reagan, this Rapid Deployment Force would become the Central Command.[44]

Reagan promoted the securitization of petroleum in other ways as well. In 1983, he signed National Security Decision Directive 114, which declared that "because of the real and psychological impact of a curtailment in the flow of oil from the Persian Gulf on the international economic system, we must assure our readiness to deal promptly with actions aimed at disrupting that traffic."[45] Military action was deemed necessary in 1986 when, as a response to threats to petroleum exports during the Iran-Iraq War, Reagan ordered the U.S. Navy to escort Kuwaiti oil tankers flying the American flag through the Persian Gulf and the Strait of Hormuz. The operation was not without significant costs. In 1987, the frigate USS *Stark* was struck by two Exocet missiles fired by an Iraqi fighter plane while operating in the Persian Gulf. Thirty-seven Americans on board were killed. Just over a year later, another American warship patrolling the Gulf, the cruiser USS *Vincennes*, mistakenly fired on a civilian Iranian airliner, killing 290 people and fueling outrage in the region against the United States.

Fear that the Soviet Union might be advancing toward the vital oil resources of the Persian Gulf region when it invaded Afghanistan in 1979 was a factor in the U.S. government's decision to support Muslim militants—the *mujahidin*—who were to fight against the Soviets in Afghanistan throughout the 1980s. These militants, drawn from all over the Muslim world, included Osama bin Laden, who as a twenty-three-year-old traveled from his home in Saudi Arabia to Afghanistan to support the war in 1980. At the end of the war in 1988, bin Laden decided to transform the anti-Soviet effort into a foundation of future *jihad* by establishing a network called Al Qaeda.[46]

Those who bothered to read the annual White House summaries of national security strategy could not fail to be impressed by their acknowledgment of the continuing importance of Middle Eastern oil during the 1990s. The discussion of American security interests in the Middle East for many years contained the following line: "The United States has enduring interests in pursuing a just, lasting and comprehensive Middle East peace, ensuring the security and well-being of Israel, helping our Arab friends provide for their security, and maintaining the free flow of oil at reasonable prices." (The phrase "at reasonable prices" was dropped after the 1998 edition.)[47]

Among the costs of petroleum production and consumption are those associated with military policies aimed at "maintaining the free flow of oil." Such "externalities" (that is, costs that are not fully allocated by the market) are significant. In addition to the costs of military deployments to protect friendly oil-producing regimes or oil transit routes, there are what may be broadly termed social costs. These include the costs associated with human rights abuses in authoritarian regimes that are propped up by oil revenues, as well as the costs of wars fought for control of oil reserves. On top of these, there are a variety of environmental costs, including those associated with the despoliation of wilderness areas (such as the Arctic National Wildlife Refuge) in the course of oil exploration and production, marine pollution when tankers rupture or offshore oil platforms are damaged, air pollution from the burning of massive quantities of petroleum products, and global warming.

GLOBAL WARMING

As we noted earlier, oil is not the only natural resource to raise security concerns. However, its significance for the economies of the industrialized world puts it in a category by itself. In addition, we have chosen to focus on petroleum because of the key role its use plays in what is perhaps the most important environmental issue of our time—global warming. It is becoming increasingly apparent that the world's dependence on oil (and other fossil fuels) bears primary responsibility for the profound and possibly irreversible climatic changes we are currently witnessing.

How is the consumption of petroleum related to global warming? Let us begin with a gallon of gasoline. When a gallon of gasoline is burned in an internal combustion engine powering a car, a lawnmower, a piece of construction equipment, or some other machine, five pounds of carbon dioxide (CO_2) are released into the atmosphere. Carbon dioxide is not a pollutant in the normal sense of that term. In fact, the release of carbon dioxide into the atmosphere is a necessary feature of our planet's vast carbon cycle; it occurs naturally in the respiration of animals and the decay of dead plants (among other ways). Its presence in the atmosphere makes life possible, by trapping a portion of the sun's radiation and thereby helping to warm the surface of the Earth. The problem is that the use of fossil fuels, together with deforestation on a massive scale, has introduced carbon dioxide into the atmosphere on a scale unprecedented in human history.[48] When the Industrial Age began, the concentration of carbon dioxide in the atmosphere was approximately 280 parts per million; today it is about 370 parts per million.[49] With that increase comes a more pronounced greenhouse effect, as more solar radiation is trapped near the surface of the Earth.

Over the course of the twentieth century, the average global temperature increased by about one degree Fahrenheit. The sea level in that same period rose four to eight inches. The ten hottest years of the century all occurred after 1985, with 1998 being the hottest year ever recorded.[50]

Some impacts of this global warming are obvious. Polar ice is already beginning to melt at alarming rates. The melting of the ice caps, along with icebergs and glaciers, causes sea levels to rise. This, in turn, produces beach erosion, flooding of coastal areas, and, eventually, the complete inundation of low-lying lands, including certain islands. Higher atmospheric temperatures cause evaporation of surface water to occur more rapidly. This means that storms, on average, will become more intense and that rainfall in some parts of the globe will increase. Overall, however, more rapid evaporation will result in a widespread drying of soils and a consequent expansion of deserts. Patterns of vegetation will also be changed across the world, with, in some cases, major impacts on agriculture. In parts of the world where subsistence agriculture is practiced, global warming is likely to produce, and in fact appears already to be producing, large numbers of environmental refugees.

One additional point should be made concerning the impact of global warming: Climate change, like virtually every other environmental threat, will affect the poor much more than it will the rich. The poor are, in many instances, dependent on the very resources and economic activities that are most likely to be affected by climate change. Subsistence agriculture, for example, may be affected in some regions by prolonged drought and in other regions by an increase in the number and severity of violent storms. Either drought or flooding can be devastating to communities living close to the margin of existence. Flooding, of course, is likely to be a particularly acute problem for people living in low-lying coastal areas, among them roughly seventy million Bangladeshis. However problematic and unpalatable many of the solutions will be, wealthy states (and wealthy individuals) will be able to purchase a measure of security against environmental threats, security that will simply be unavailable to many in the world. To put it bluntly but accurately, the rich will be able to buy their way out of many aspects of the problem.[51]

There are, of course, uncertainties inherent in efforts to predict global climate change and its effects, uncertainties that are often exploited by corporations and political leaders who have an interest in deferring remedial measures. The uncertainties are related to causal inferences and predictions, not to existing observations. There is no question concerning the increases in the Earth's average temperature and in the concentration of greenhouse gases in the atmosphere. The range of informed opinion concerning the likely effects of global warming—the area where uncertainty exists—runs from the view that those effects will be serious to the projection that they will be catastrophic.

Examining the areas of uncertainty is unlikely to provide any reassurance about future impacts, but it can make discussions of climate change more intelligible. To begin with, climate-change predictions must deal with uncertainties regarding potential changes in the carbon cycle. For example, it is possible that increases in atmospheric concentrations of carbon dioxide will stimulate the growth of the very vegetation that removes carbon dioxide from the atmosphere. Such an input in the carbon cycle might slow the rate at which greenhouse gases collect in the atmosphere.

There are a number of feedback processes that affect our ability to predict climate change. As snow and ice melt with the progression of global warming, highly reflective materials on the surface of the Earth disappear and reveal darker, more absorbent, materials, such as soil and water. The increased absorption of the sun's radiation has the potential to amplify global warming. Similarly, global warming increases the evaporation of water from the surface of the Earth, causing more clouds to form. The increased cloudiness might result in even more heat being trapped near the Earth's surface or, because clouds also reflect solar energy away from the Earth, the net effect might be the opposite.

Another factor contributing to uncertainty is the potential for abrupt change. Climate changes that have been observed thus far have been incremental; projections typically assume continuing linear change. It is possible, however, that a tipping point might be reached, at which dramatic, and possibly even catastrophic, changes ensue. Among the possibilities are changes in ocean currents (and related impacts) of the type described in the Pentagon study noted below, or the sudden release—due to thawing—of the vast quantities of methane (another greenhouse gas) that are currently frozen in the Arctic tundra.

Finally, it is worth noting the uncertainties associated with computer modeling of climate change. While significant strides have been made in the construction of climate models, the models are both complex and dependent on enormous quantities of data. Minor uncertainties in data inputs can translate into more significant uncertainties when run through large and complex models. We should stress, however, that major climatic impacts are a certainty and, in fact, are already occurring.[52]

With this background in mind, it may be useful to consider what those who are responsible for the national security of the United States have to say about global warming. Two of the best places to look for such assessments are the Pentagon's Office of Net Assessment and the CIA-affiliated National Intelligence Council.

In 1972, Secretary of Defense James Schlesinger brought the Office of Net Assessment to the Pentagon to function as an in-house think tank charged with envisioning the future of warfare. OSD/NA (for Office of the Secretary of Defense/Net Assessment) had been born the previous year as a working group within the National Security Council in an effort to address President Nixon's complaints concerning the quality of the intelligence available to him. From the beginning, OSD/NA has been headed by Andrew Marshall, a man whose career as a professional strategist had begun at the dawn of the Cold War. In fact, as a young economist employed by the RAND Corporation in the 1950s, Marshall was among the first to advocate a counterforce strategy for the use of American nuclear weapons as opposed to the existing counter-city strategy. Now in his eighties, Marshall has been called the "Yoda of the Pentagon."[53]

In 2003, at Marshall's direction, the Office of Net Assessment commissioned a report on the possible impact of global climate change on the security of the United States. The report, entitled *An Abrupt Climate Change Scenario and Its Implications for United States National Security*, considers the implications for national security of a change in the major ocean currents that presently moderate the climate in many of the world's temperate zones.[54] Beginning with the standard assumption of gradual global warming, the report notes the possibility that the increase in fresh water in the oceans due to increased precipitation and the melting of ice in the polar regions might abruptly alter the operation of currents. Without the warmth generated in northern latitudes by ocean currents, average temperatures in parts of the world could drop five to ten degrees Fahrenheit. This, in turn, would change precipitation patterns, sharply reduce growing seasons, and increase the frequency of severe storms.

The report's conclusions concerning the impact of the climate change described on national security are worth noting in detail:

> Violence and disruption stemming from the stresses created by abrupt changes in climate pose a different type of threat to national security than we are accustomed to today. Military confrontation may be triggered by a desperate need for natural resources such as energy, food and water rather than by conflicts over ideology, religion, or national honor. The shifting motivation for confrontation would alter which countries are most vulnerable and the existing warning signs for security threats.
>
> There is a long-standing academic debate over the extent to which resource constraints and environmental challenges lead to interstate conflict. While some believe they alone can lead nations to attack one another, others argue that their primary effect is to act as a trigger of conflict among countries that face preexisting social, economic, and political tension. Regardless, it seems undeniable that severe environmental problems are likely to escalate the degree of global conflict.[55]

The National Intelligence Council's "2020 Project" acknowledges the scientific consensus that "the greenhouse effect is real." It takes a more circumspect view of the effects of global warming; nonetheless, the report concludes that the United States "is likely to face significant bilateral pressure to change its domestic environmental policies and to be a leader in global environmental efforts."[56]

INCREASING SECURITY BY REDUCING CONSUMPTION

Environmental threats and resource issues are, as we have seen, connected in many different ways. Not surprisingly, many of the policies that can improve environmental security promise at the same time to ameliorate resource scarcities. Because petroleum consumption is central to much of the world's environmental security dilemmas, we begin our discussion of solutions there.

By now, it is widely understood that increasing petroleum production in the United States is simply not a possibility. During the summer of 2005, the rotary-rig count in the United States reached an all-time high. At the same time, the nominal price of a barrel of oil reached one record high after another. In other words, never before had there been as many oil wells being drilled, with so little possibility of affecting the world price of oil. The United States, once the world's leading oil producer, is well past its Hubbert peak. Much of the oil exploration occurring in the United States today involves drilling in fields that were formerly too marginal to be profitable. But even Saudi Arabia, with the largest proven oil reserves in the world, may be in essentially the same position.

Michael Klare has argued that the United States needs to separate oil imports from security commitments, reduce its "addiction" to imported oil, and move toward a "postpetroleum economy."[57] Undemocratic and even aggressive regimes have too often turned oil exports into American military hardware or even security guarantees from the U.S. government. This has been the pattern in the Middle East for over half a century; it is currently being duplicated in the Caspian Sea basin, a development that could have profound implications for future U.S. national security.

Reducing oil consumption in general (and the consumption of imported oil in particular) means conservation in the near term and a shift to new technologies in the longer term. So-called light-duty vehicles—the cars, trucks, and SUVs that most Americans drive—account for roughly 60 percent of America's transportation-sector oil consumption. In spite of Congress's introduction of fuel economy requirements in 1975 and a gradual toughening of the requirements since then, fuel efficiency has actually been declining recently. "Light trucks" (including SUVs), which have fuel economy standards that are lower than those for cars, have made up an ever-increasing share of the vehicles on the road in the United States. In fact, the three top-selling vehicles in the United States year after year are pickup trucks. America's addiction to imported oil is, in large measure, an addiction to gas-guzzling vehicles.

A shift to alternative sources of energy holds some promise for reducing oil dependency and greenhouse gas emissions. Natural gas has the advantage of being a close substitute for oil in many applications while producing less CO_2 than oil. The problem with natural gas is that it is no less finite a resource than oil. It also happens to be most abundant in those same troubled parts of the world from which much of our oil comes.[58]

Some alternative sources of energy impose different costs. The construction of dams for hydroelectric power produces environmental impacts that we are only beginning to comprehend. It also carries the possibility of creating interstate tensions, as we noted earlier. Nuclear energy raises other security issues. Consider the prediction of the Defense Department's *Abrupt Climate Change* report: "As cooling drives up demand, existing hydrocarbon supplies are stretched thin. With a scarcity of energy supply—and a growing need for access—nuclear energy will become a critical source of power, and this will accelerate nuclear proliferation as countries develop enrichment and reprocessing capabilities to ensure their national security."[59]

It is, ultimately, conservation that is the key to addressing environmental threats, and not only the conservation of petroleum. The first step toward environmental security is simply to understand the true costs—in dollars and cents, certainly, but also in military commitments, in climate change, in polluted air and water, in lost wilderness, and in many other forms—of the choices we make as consumers. To ignore these costs is to put at risk both our quality of life and our security.

RECOMMENDED READING

Printed Sources

Diamond, Jared. *Collapse: How Societies Choose to Fail or Succeed*. New York: Viking, 2005.
Homer-Dixon, Thomas F. *Environment, Scarcity, and Violence*. Princeton, N.J.: Princeton University Press, 1999.

Klare, Michael T. *Blood and Oil: The Dangers and Consequences of America's Growing Dependency on Imported Petroleum.* New York: Metropolitan Books, 2004.

Pirages, Dennis Clark, and Theresa Manley DeGeest. *Ecological Security: An Evolutionary Perspective on Globalization.* Lanham, Md.: Rowman & Littlefield, 2004.

Victor, David G. *Climate Change: Debating America's Policy Options.* New York: Council on Foreign Relations, 2004.

Websites

Energy Information Administration: www.eia.doe.gov
Greenpeace International: www.greenpeace.org/international_en/
Natural Resources Defense Council: www.nrdc.org/.

13

Living in the Shadow of the World Trade Center: Coping with the Threat of Terrorism

When the three airplanes crashed into the Pentagon and the World Trade Center on September 11, 2001, a new era began, making an indelible distinction between the world before and after September 11. As former secretary of state Colin Powell put it, "This marks the end of the cold war and the post–cold war periods." Uncertainty and fear were to characterize this new era.

People were initially astonished by the images of the two commercial airliners crashing into the twin towers, but soon astonishment was replaced by anger, fear, and eventually resolve. The world and how people thought about it had been changed before in such a way, following the first use of nuclear weapons in August 1945. One need only recall Bernard Brodie's reaction to the bombing of Hiroshima, described in chapter 3, and his lament that "everything that I have written is obsolete."[1]

Many assumed that surely experts on terrorism would have some answers. Dr. Bruce Hoffman at the RAND Corporation, one of the world's leading experts on terrorism, met with his colleagues several days after the attacks. He was asked what his views of the attacks were, in light of his more than twenty years' study of terrorism. He thought a moment and replied, "Nothing in my years of study prepared me for this kind of attack, and I really do not know what is going to happen."

Michael Krepon, a perceptive observer of the international scene, asserted succinctly in the days after the attacks that we had lived in a "fool's paradise" prior to September 11 and that things would never be the same. Of course, he was right—for better or worse.

The September 11 attacks killed more Americans than were killed at Pearl Harbor, and unlike Pearl Harbor, almost all of those killed on September 11 were civilians. In ten years of fighting in Vietnam, the United States lost 58,209 citizens; on the single day of September 11, the United States lost more than 5 percent of that number. It was the greatest loss of American life resulting from hostilities in a single day since the Civil War.

There is little doubt that September 11 has displaced the Cuban missile crisis as the focal point of study and analysis in political science and international relations for decades to come. In addition, the attacks have profoundly influenced the way in which Americans—citizens and analysts alike—think about foreign and defense policy, just as Pearl Harbor cast its shadow over the decades of the Cold War. On the night of the 9/11 attacks, President George W. Bush noted in his diary, "The Pearl Harbor of the 21st century took place today."[2] In a similar way, Japan's surprise attack on Port Arthur in the Russo-Japanese War caused Russians to fixate on the problem of surprise attack for generations.[3]

The importance of the attacks is undeniable, but how should the attacks influence our thinking about security? This chapter explores the significance of terrorism and means of coping with the threat that it poses.

THE "NEW TERRORISM"

Terrorism is as old as recorded history. Numerous examples of terrorism can be found in the Old Testament, the common sacred text of Judaism and Christianity. However, recent manifestations of terrorism are characterized by some new elements. This section of the chapter will focus on definitions of terrorism, recent terrorist acts, and the characteristics of what some have called "the new terrorism."[4]

A longtime student of terrorism and former RAND analyst, Brian Jenkins, has defined terrorism as "the use or threatened use of force designed to bring about a political change."[5] Walter Laqueur defines it as "the illegitimate use of force to achieve a political objective when innocent people are targeted."[6] More recently, Jessica Stern has defined terrorism as "an act or threat of violence against noncombatants with the objective of exacting revenge, intimidating or otherwise influencing an audience."[7] The U.S. government has defined terrorism as "premeditated, politically motivated violence perpetrated against noncombatant targets by sub-national groups or clandestine agents, usually intended to influence an audience."[8] In his definition, Bruce Hoffman calls attention to the psychological dimension: "Terrorism is fundamentally the use (or threatened use) of violence in order to achieve psychological effects in a particular target audience, fomenting widespread fear and intimidation."[9] (We will return to the psychological dimension later in this chapter.) Note that these analysts as well as most others who study terrorism exclude from their definitions large-scale massacres carried out by guerrilla groups or militaries employing guns, machetes, or other small arms. In addition, killings carried out by paramilitary groups motivated by ethnic hatred—for example, Bosnian Serbs, Islamic radicals in Algeria, Rwandan militias, or the Vietcong—are not defined as terrorism.[10]

From 1925 through 2004, there were thirteen cases of terrorism in which more than a hundred people were killed. Aggregate statistics on terrorism compiled by the RAND Corporation and St. Andrew's University reveal that terrorist acts have declined in recent years: 484 (1991), 343 (1992), 360 (1993), 353 (1994), 278 (1995), and 250 (1996).[11] The total for 1996 was the lowest in twenty-three years. That is the good news. The bad news is that terrorism has increased since then, and the "new terrorism" has become more lethal. In the 1970s, 17 percent of terrorist attacks killed someone; in the 1980s this increased to 19 percent, in the 1990s to 22 percent. As table 13.1 shows, the worst loss of life in a single terrorist event from 1983 to 2000 was the bombing in January 1985 of an Air India airliner over the Irish Sea, killing 329 people. To place the September 11 attacks in context, they killed more than nine times that number. Further, as British prime minister Tony Blair has noted, more British citizens died in the World Trade Center than in any other terrorist act in British history, including the attacks from the Irish Republican Army over the course of many decades.

Terrorist acts are also increasingly aimed against either Americans or the United States itself. Of the sixteen most serious terrorist attacks from 1983 to 2001, *The Economist* calculates, 50 percent targeted Americans or the United States.[12] Table 13.1 lists twenty-eight acts of terrorism from 1983 to 2005, of which twelve were directed at American targets. Osama bin Laden, in his widely distributed threats, has focused primarily on the United States and Americans. Bin Laden told one interviewer: "You say I am fighting against the American civilians. My enemy is every American who is fighting against me even by paying taxes."[13]

Other aspects that distinguish the "new terrorism" from "conventional terrorism" (if that is not an oxymoron) are the characteristics of the terrorists themselves. Traditionally, most Islamic terrorists were young, single, uneducated, and recent arrivals in the United States. The nineteen perpetrators of the September 11 attacks were for the most part older and more mature; several were married and had children; some were educated; and most had lived in the United States for several years prior to 9/11. Mohamed Atta, the suspected leader, was thirty-two years old, had studied urban planning in Germany for seven years, lived in the United States for several years, and clearly intended to kill as many Americans as possible. He was very different than the traditional terrorist.

The new terrorism had profound implications for both the practice and study of international relations. One of the central topics in the field for both academic analysts and practitioners concerns the identity of the world's political "actors." States, as we know them, began to emerge in the aftermath of the Thirty Years' War; they have been the central actors in world politics for the three and a half centuries since then. Terrorism questions the assumption that states are the central actors, as former Secretary of State Warren Christopher noted in his memoirs:

> What had happened at Khobar Towers [in 1996] was different in ways I had understood as an intellectual matter before my visit to Dhahran, but which I now felt viscerally, as if I had been an intended target. The enemy was not a state but a person or collection of people without an identifiable face. We had no knowledge of what they stood for or where they made their home. While we surmised that their motive derived from some

Table 13.1. Chronology of Major Terrorist Acts, 1983–2005

Date	Event	Suspect(s)	U.S. as Target?	Number Killed	Number Wounded
April 1983	U.S. Embassy, Beirut		Yes	63	
October 1983	U.S. Marine Barracks, Beirut	Hezbollah	Yes	299	
January 1985	Air India over Irish Sea			329	
1986	Attack on German disco	Libya	Yes	2	200
1987	Bombing of South Korean plane			117	
1987	Car bomb in Sri Lanka			113	
October 1988	Pan Am flight 103/Lockerbie	Libya	Yes	270	
1989	Bombing of Avianca plane			107	
September 1989	UTA flight over Chad			170	
February 1993	World Trade Center bomb	Al Qaeda	Yes	6	1,000
1993	Bombings in Bombay			235	
July 1994	Jewish Center, Argentina			96	
October 1994	Suicide bus bomb, Tel Aviv	Iran		23	
March 1995	Tokyo subway Sarin attack	Aum Shinrikyo		12	4,000
April 1995	Federal building, Oklahoma City	Timothy McVeigh	Yes	168	
June 1996	Al-Khobar towers	Iran & Al Qaeda?	Yes	19	372
1996	Truck bomb, Colombo, Sri Lanka	Tamil Tigers			1,400
November 1997	Tourists in Luxor, Egypt			62	
August 7, 1998	U.S. Embassies in Kenya and Tanzania	Al Qaeda	Yes	224	5,500
August 1998	Omagh town bomb, Northern Ireland			29	
September 1999	Moscow apartment			118	
October 2000	USS Cole	Al Qaeda	Yes	17	30
September 11, 2001	Pentagon and airliner	Al Qaeda	Yes	189	106
September 11, 2001	World Trade Center	Al Qaeda	Yes	3,065	
September 11, 2001	United Airlines	Al Qaeda	Yes	92	
October 12, 2002	Bali, Indonesia	Al Qaeda	No	202	1,500
March 11, 2004	Madrid trains	Moroccan Islamic Combatant group	No	191	1,400
July 7, 2005	London		No	55	300

extreme form of Islamic ideology and that they might be the willing tools of a rogue state, that suspicion, even if confirmed, led to no obvious conclusion as to how to anticipate or prevent such attacks in the future.[14]

A world in which states were not the central actors was a very different one. Consider one of the most important concepts of international relations, deterrence.[15] As we pointed out in chapter 3, deterrence is as old as humanity. Parents have practiced deterrence for millennia, telling their children, "Do not do x, because if you do, we will do y." In a like manner, leaders of one country would tell the leaders of another, "Do not attack my country, because if you do, my country will attack yours." With the advent of nuclear weapons, deterrent threats became more frightening; the leaders of the United States and the Soviet Union told one another, "Do not attack my country, or my country will destroy your country." Some argue that the existence of nuclear weapons and the two superpowers' deterrent threats resulted in the "long peace" of the Cold War.[16]

It is important to note that deterrence was effective even against rogue states, such as Iraq under Saddam Hussein. At the time of the first Gulf War (1990–91), the United States was concerned that Iraq might use weapons of mass destruction against the American-led coalition forces. In his memoirs, former Secretary of State James Baker recalled:

> In hopes of persuading them [the Iraqis] to consider more soberly the folly of war, I purposefully left the impression that the use of chemical or biological agents by Iraq could invite tactical nuclear retaliation. (We do not really know whether this was the reason there appears to have been no confirmed use by Iraq of chemical weapons during the war. My own view is that the calculated ambiguity regarding how we might respond has to be part of the reason.)[17]

There are, of course, states that support terrorism. The United States has formally identified seven: Iraq (before March 2003), Iran, Sudan, Syria, Libya, North Korea, and Cuba. To the degree that states can be linked to terrorist acts, they can be held responsible for those acts; however, it is increasingly difficult to establish such a link. In fact, one of the discontinuities that terrorism introduces into contemporary international relations is the difficulty of identifying who can be held responsible for acts of terrorism. In the case of the Pan American airplane that was bombed in 1988 over Lockerbie, Scotland, two Libyan intelligence officers were charged and tried, rather than Libya itself (although the government of Libya did eventually agree to pay the victims' families 2.7 billion dollars in compensation). This characterized the way in which the United States attempted to deal with terrorism prior to September 11. The United States sought to treat terrorist acts as violations of laws, and its response employed a law-enforcement approach.

If states are not the perpetrators of terrorism (as is increasingly the case), profound problems arise for some of the central concepts of security; consider again, for example, the theory and practice of deterrence. One of the most important assumptions of deterrence is that "wars are generated by a process of reasoned calculations and can be prevented by the same means."[18] Terrorists who are not sponsored by a state may not think in the same ways that state-based actors reason and calculate. Retribution cannot be inflicted upon opponents who cannot be identified and located. In addition, as John Steinbruner has noted, "deterrence has proved to be more credible among opponents of comparable capability than between unbalanced adversaries."[19] Terrorists have no state to lose and, therefore, cannot be effectively deterred by the threat of retaliation.

Members of the George W. Bush administration have noted the significance of nonstate actors on the concept of deterrence. In the 2002 edition of its congressionally mandated *National Security Strategy*, the administration argued, "The nature of the Cold War threat required the United States—with our allies and friends—to emphasize deterrence of the enemy's use of force, producing a grim strategy of mutual assured destruction. With the collapse of the Soviet Union and the end of the Cold War, our security environment has undergone profound transformation."[20] The report goes on: "Traditional concepts of deterrence will not work against a terrorist enemy whose avowed tactics are wanton destruction and the targeting of innocents. The overlap between states that sponsor terror and those that pursue WMD [weapons of mass destruction] compels us to action."[21]

The stability of deterrence rested, essentially, on a foundation of fear. Terrorism, like deterrence, is dependent on fear. Osama bin Laden and his followers sought in the September 11 attacks to inculcate a sense of fear among the American public, ultimately to create mass panic, leading in turn to economic, political, and social dislocations. The significant decline of the stock market following the attacks showed both the degree to which the American and international economies are interdependent and the way in which mass panic could cripple the U.S. economy. It appears that the economic consequences of the September 11 attacks were unanticipated by the terrorists. Two economists at the University of California at Irvine have calculated the economic costs of the September 11 attacks: in property damage, ten to thirteen billion dollars; in lost economic output in the immediate aftermath, forty-seven billion dollars; in microeconomic costs of responses to terrorism (airport security, sky marshals, etc.), up to forty-one billion. The United States suffered losses exceeding a hundred billion dollars.[22] The loss of stock market wealth was even more striking. Stock market indices dropped as indicated in table 13.2.

The cost of terrorism should not be limited solely in terms of the direct costs of the 9/11 attacks. Steven Kosiak, a researcher at the Center for Strategic and Budgetary

Table 13.2.   Loss of Stock Market Wealth

	Drop in Index (As of 9/21/01)	Loss in Market Capitalization
NYSE	−11.24%	−$1.3 trillion
Nasdaq	−16.05%	−$407 billion
Amex	−8.01%	−$8.5 billion

Assessments, has estimated that since September 11, 2001, approximately twenty-six billion dollars has been spent in the United States to improve critical infrastructures. He also notes that the fiscal year 2004 federal budget requested a total of $41.3 billion for domestic security, and that for fiscal year 2005, $47.5 billion. Kosiak further estimates that $407 billion has been spent in the wake of 9/11, a figure that includes the cost of military operations in Afghanistan and Iraq through mid-2004. If these estimates are accurate, more than 1 percent of the U.S. gross domestic product since 9/11 has been spent to increase security and fight the wars in Afghanistan and Iraq.[23]

If fear played a central role in both the Cold War–era and the new post–September 11 international systems, it had very different results. In the Cold War deterrent system, fear essentially promoted stability; it was essential if deterrence was to operate successfully. Traditional national security was therefore dependent upon a feeling of insecurity; indeed, during the Cold War security was increased to some extent by insecurity. That is no longer the case.

In 1933, Franklin Delano Roosevelt declared, "The only thing we have to fear is fear itself." During the Cold War, proponents of the assured-destruction variant of deterrence argued, in essence, "The only thing we have to fear is the absence of fear itself." Today, in the context of the war on terrorism, fear leading to mass panic is a threat to stability and order. A central question, if not *the* central question, at present is how to deal with the fear that most Americans feel, to a greater or lesser degree.

PREEMPTION, PREVENTIVE WAR, AND COOPERATIVE SECURITY

There are many different ways in which states can attempt to deal with terrorism, ranging from preemption and preventive war, at one extreme, to cooperative security at the other. These extremes may be considered, following Max Weber, "ideal types."

George W. Bush entered office emphasizing the need for the United States to act unilaterally in international affairs. Within six months of taking office, Bush had withdrawn from the Kyoto Protocol on Climate Change, indicated his desire to withdraw from the Anti-Ballistic Missile (ABM) Treaty, opposed the Comprehensive Test Ban Treaty prohibiting all nuclear weapons test, opposed the participation of the United States in the International Criminal Court, refused to participate in a conference to provide verification measures for the 1972 Biological Weapons Convention, and undermined a United Nations conference designed to control the spread of small arms and light weapons.[24]

Following the attacks of 9/11, however, the administration found that it was impossible to fight terrorism effectively without the cooperation of the other states. The logic of counterterrorism was fundamentally multilateral. The administration actively cooperated with both longtime allies like Britain, France, and Germany, former competitors (Russia), and even several hostile states, such as Syria.

The American military response to the 9/11 attacks came one month after the attacks, when several hundred Special Forces soldiers working in tandem with American airpower and Northern Alliance forces overthrew the Taliban government and attacked Al Qaeda training camps in Afghanistan. Rarely in military history had so few done so much. The United States was supported in these efforts by most other countries.

Having succeeded in Afghanistan, members of the Bush administration sought to develop a strategy for dealing with terrorism. In June 2002, President Bush argued in his commencement address at the U.S. Military Academy, "The gravest threat to freedom lies at the perilous crossroads of radicalism and technology." He argued that the policies of containment and deterrence were not applicable against nonstate actors, such as terrorist groups.[25] Several months later, the White House released *The National Security Strategy.* This annual report typically received little or no public attention;[26] the eminent Yale historian John Lewis Gaddis contended that this one, however, was the most significant reconceptualization of American foreign policy since George Kennan laid out the doctrine of containment.[27] In the place of that foundation of U.S. post–World War II foreign policy, President Bush proposed that the United States be proactive, postulating that the traditional concept of state sovereignty need not be honored, given the threat posed by terrorists to the United States.

Preemption of threats, then, was proposed as necessary and proper. As a whole, the president's new approach came to be known as the Bush Doctrine. According to political scientist Robert Jervis, it had four elements:

> A strong belief in the importance of a state's domestic regime in determining its foreign policy and the related judgment that this is an opportune time to transform international politics; the perception of great threats that can be defeated only by new and vigorous policies, most notably preventive war; a willingness to act unilaterally when necessary; and, as both a cause and a summary of these beliefs, an overriding sense that peace and stability require the United States to assert its primacy in world politics.[28]

Although members of the Bush administration tried to present the central pillar of the Bush doctrine as "preemptive war," most international relations scholars believed that the policy could more accurately be described as one of "preventive" war. This is an important difference. A preemptive war entails military action against an imminent threat, whereas a preventive war, according to political theorist Michael Walzer, "is designed to respond to a more distant threat."[29]

As for Iraq, members of the Bush administration contended that there were three principal reasons to wage a preventive war: (1) that it possessed weapons of mass destruction, (2) that Iraq was directly linked to Al Qaeda and the 9/11 attacks, and (3) that the overthrow of Saddam Hussein would usher in a new democratic movement in Iraq and the rest of the Middle East.

Two years after President Bush announced the end of "major combat operations" in Iraq, no weapons of mass destruction had been found, no evidence directly linking Iraq and Al Qaeda had been discovered, and democracy in Iraq, let alone the rest of the Middle East, was a distant goal and problematic at best.[30]

Although the Bush administration continued after the invasion of Iraq to portray it as part of the war on terrorism, many wondered whether the invasion had had a positive or negative effect on the incidence of terrorism. The Department of State's annual report on terrorism for 2003 indicated that the number of significant international terrorist episodes had increased from 205 in 2002 to 208 in 2003.[31] It also indicated that the number of people killed and injured in international terrorist events had grown from 2,013 in 2002 to 3,646 in 2003.[32]

What alternative is there to combating terrorism through preventive war? Human beings have always sought greater security through cooperation. From the earliest human family- and tribal-based communities, people have banded together to reduce fear and to increase safety. The classic political philosophers noted this fact. For example, in *The Leviathan* Thomas Hobbes argued that life in the state of nature (which generations of political realists since Hobbes have compared to the international system) was "nasty, brutish and short," and that to escape its dangerous anarchy people formed political communities that could not function without cooperation. In this sense, cooperation was essential for security.

Villages and eventually cities were developed in part to provide security for their residents.[33] Initially, walls around cities performed that function, but around the third millennium BC, wall-less cities arose in Mesopotamia.[34] The great cities of antiquity, Rome and Alexandria, flourished in periods when walls were not needed to provide security; commerce and trade flourished in such environments. However, when the barbarians threatened, security declined, along with the great cities. Mohamed Atta, during his study of urban planning in Germany, may have realized the importance of cities in the evolution of the communal sense of security; perhaps (unless he was simply following Osama bin Laden's orders) he sought to attack one of the world's greatest cities specifically in order to shake that sense of security.

How can Americans regain that sense in the face of the new (at least to Americans) fear-inducing threat of terrorism? One way is greater cooperation with one another. Since the disintegration of the Soviet Union and the end of the Cold War, a number of security analysts have focused on the need for and advantages of "cooperative security." They have produced both a significant body of literature on this subject and gained some experience in translating theory into actual diplomatic practice.[35]

Cooperative security represents an alternative to preventive war for dealing with terrorism. Proponents of cooperative security define it as "in essence, a commitment to regulate the size, technical composition, investment patterns, and operational practices of all military forces by mutual consent for mutual benefit."[36] A number of the central elements of cooperative security are relevant to the war on terrorism.

First, proponents of cooperative security believe that strict controls and security measures for nuclear weapons, particularly those in the former Soviet Union, should be established.[37] The successes in de-nuclearizing the former Soviet Union were some of the most significant accomplishments of the Clinton administration. The world would be a far more dangerous place if Belarus, Ukraine, and Kazakhstan still possessed nuclear weapons. Due to the foresight of the executive and congressional branches of government, the United States assisted with the removal or dismantling of nuclear weapons and fissile materials from those three non-Russian former Soviet republics. In addition, the United States assisted Russia itself with the dismantling and safekeeping of its own nuclear weapons.

Despite this progress, much remains to be done, however. There are an estimated ten thousand scientists in the former Soviet Union who know how to create a nuclear weapon. A number of those are currently gainfully and legally employed, thanks to a cooperative program in de-nuclearization funded by the United States. There are another estimated five thousand scientists in the former USSR with the knowledge to create biological and chemical weapons. While some of these are employed with U.S. funds, many are not, and these may be tempted to work for Iran, North Korea, or other states with goals opposed to those of the United States. More could be done to address the employment of former Soviet scientists in the CBW field.

The proponents of the cooperative security field focus primarily on Russia and its nuclear weapons as the single most important threat facing the United States. This was certainly true during and immediately after the Cold War, but it may not be true today. More effort should be devoted to making non-Russian nuclear weapons safe. For example, experts believe that Pakistan has between twenty and fifty nuclear weapons, without the safety mechanisms called "permissive action links" (PALs). On the assumption that centralized governmental control of nuclear weapons is desirable, the United States could provide Pakistan, India, and other countries that request them rudimentary PALs in order to make stolen nuclear weapons unusable.[38]

The second element of cooperative security is support for an internationally supported concept of effective and legitimate intervention, in which the use of force is usually multilateral and a last resort. Cooperative security calls for the integration of the planning and implementation of security policies by allied states. As we have suggested throughout this book, contemporary security threats broadly conceived—such as population growth and migration, environmental degradation, cyberwar, and terrorism—can be effectively dealt with only on a multilateral basis.

As we have seen, the unilateral approach favored by George W. Bush during his first eight months in office was buried under the debris of the World Trade Center. Intelligence agencies estimated that Al Qaeda had established terrorist cells in sixty countries and that in Afghanistan eighty to a hundred thousand people had been trained as terrorists. Even if all of the twenty thousand Al Qaeda-trained terrorists then estimated to be in Afghanistan had been captured or killed, there would still be sixty to eight thousand more spread throughout sixty countries. Clearly, even the world's sole superpower cannot "go it alone" if it is to combat terrorism effectively; the cooperation of many states is absolutely essential.

The international cooperation that was forged in the days following 9/11 was fractured by the invasion of Iraq. A central point of contention between the United States and its critics was whether war in Iraq was truly a "last resort." Traditional just-war theory posits that war is to be waged only when all other alternatives have been tried and found wanting. Just-war theorist Michael Walzer questions the feasibility of this criterion, in connection with a third element of cooperative security—that it seeks to be just as well as militarily effective. Fundamentally, the war on terrorism is a contest to enlist support against terrorism. As Walzer has noted, "In a war for 'hearts and minds,' rather than for land and resources, justice turns out to be a key to victory . . . there are now reasons of state for fighting justly. One might almost say that justice has become a military necessity."[39]

Fourth, cooperative security calls for new security partnerships. Writing in the 1990s, proponents of cooperative security did not envision new partnerships with repressive regimes or nefarious individuals or organizations. The war on terrorism and the threats posed by terrorists have caused the United States to establish relationships that it would not have even considered prior to September 11, 2001. Thus, the United States has cooperated with Syria, a sponsor of terrorism, and with Uzbekistan, with one of the most repressive governments in the world. Critics would argue that in its simultaneous pursuit of justice and counterterrorism effectiveness, cooperative security is contradictory; however, the approach allows for a certain level of elasticity in order to achieve central objectives.

Fifth, advocates of cooperative security call for new initiatives promoting non-proliferation and security cooperation. Gone are the days when a president of the United States, Ronald Reagan, could say that the proliferation of nuclear weapons is "other states' business." In a world in which terrorists are actively seeking control of nuclear weapons, the United States, as the "world's last remaining superpower" and the biggest target of international terrorism, has a vital interest in nonproliferation. The future challenge will be to continue to shape American security policies so that they are responsive to the changing conditions and realities of the future.

Some principles of the cooperative security approach do not appear nearly as important after September 11 as they did before. For example, cooperative security advocates in the 1990s called for further reductions in conventional forces in Europe. Ironically, terrorism could contribute to this objective; there is substantial pressure on American and European military forces, and some have had to be moved from Europe to the Middle East and Southwest and Central Asia. Cooperative security proponents also called for the conversion of excess defense capacity to civilian uses. This is not likely to be important for some time.

As we have seen, cooperative security proponents focus primarily on Russia. Steinbruner, for example, argues in the conclusion of his book *Principles of Global Security*, published in 2000, "A dedicated U.S. policy to achieve transformation would necessarily focus on Russia as the most urgent and most consequential application."[40] In their call for a new security policy for the United States, Ashton Carter and William Perry built their proposals on the foundation of cooperative security, focusing primarily on the American-Russian relationship. These analysts would likely no longer claim the preeminence of this relationship. Indeed, the relationship has changed significantly, with Russia now cooperating with the United States in allowing over-flights of Russia to American bases in Uzbekistan. Who would have thought such cooperation possible?

Cooperative security was developed as a new way of thinking about the threats and opportunities facing the United States in the future. It emphasized different elements than did the traditional approach to the study and implementation of security. The events of September 11 have changed the security priorities of the United States, and it is tempting to go back to the traditional security approach; however, that is not viable, because threats that existed on September 10—including environmental degradation, demographic pressure, and cyber-threats—still exist today. To be sure, they are given different priority, but they remain and must be dealt with in the future. The cooperative security framework provides one means to think about how the United States might deal with the vastly complicated and threatening world of the twenty-first century. To quote John Steinbruner once again, "As Soren Kierkegaard once observed, life is understood backward but lived forward. Thinking forward under uncharted circumstances is risky, confusing, and contentious but must nonetheless be attempted."[41]

RECOMMENDED READING

Printed Sources

Allison, Graham. *Nuclear Terrorism: The Ultimate Preventable Catastrophe.* New York: Times Books, 2004.

Benjamin, Daniel, and Steven Simon. *The Age of Sacred Terror.* New York: Random House, 2002.

Hoffman, Bruce. *Inside Terrorism.* New York: Columbia University Press, 1999.

Hoge, James F., Jr., and Gideon Rose, eds. *Understanding the War on Terror.* New York: Council on Foreign Relations and W. W. Norton, 2005.

Lesser, Ian O., Bruce Hoffman, John Arquilla, David Ronfeldt, and Michele Zanini. *Countering the New Terrorism.* Santa Monica, Calif.: RAND, 1999.

National Commission on Terrorist Attacks on the United States. *The 9/11 Commission Report.* New York: W. W. Norton, 2004.

Stern, Jessica. *The Ultimate Terrorists.* Cambridge, Mass.: Harvard University Press, 1999.

Websites

Council on Foreign Relations website on terrorism: www.terrorismanswers.org

Department of State terrorism report: www.state.gov

Federal Bureau of Investigation: www.fbi.gov

International Relations and Security Network (Switzerland): www.isn.ethz.ch

National Defense University: www.ndu.gov

RAND Corporation: www.rand.org.

14

Seeking Security in an Insecure World: The Way Forward

Twenty years ago, the United States and the Soviet Union were nearing the end of a long military and political struggle that had dominated international politics for a generation. Reflecting that struggle (and unaware that it was nearing an end), security studies focused heavily on deterrence and the threat of nuclear war. The journal *International Security* in the mid-1980s was publishing articles with titles like "The Consequences of 'Limited' Nuclear Attacks on the United States," "Controlling Nuclear War," and "Extending Deterrence with German Nuclear Weapons." Policy debates in the United States centered on the feasibility (and advisability) of the "Star Wars" space-based missile defense system and the prospects for bilateral nuclear arms control with the Soviet Union. Defense planners worried about the vulnerability of America's intercontinental ballistic missiles (ICBMs) to preemptive strikes by Soviet submarine-launched ballistic missiles (SLBMs). As had been the case since shortly after World War II, the world lived under the threat of nuclear annihilation.

On November 9, 1989, having forced the resignation of their communist leaders just two days earlier, crowds of East Germans began tearing down the Berlin Wall, the long-standing symbol of the rigid division of the world into two implacably hostile camps armed with the most destructive weapons ever devised. The dominoes began falling—in reverse—and in a remarkably short span of time the Soviet Union collapsed and the Cold War, the central political reality of the post–World War II period, was over.

It is instructive for several reasons to look back at the tensions of the mid-1980s and the euphoria of the early 1990s. First, it cannot help but produce humility among those of us who wish to make predictions about the prospects for security in the international system. Second, that period stands as an important signpost against which to measure the distance, and perhaps more importantly the direction, in which the world has traveled in the past decade or so.

It is, of course, not enough to note that change has occurred. While there is much about the quest for security that does not change (so that Sun Tzu, Thucydides, and Clausewitz continue to reward those who read their observations on security), at another level change is a constant. Indeed, it would be a betrayal of the reader's trust to have brought him or her to this point only to conclude that what was written during the Cold War remains sufficient for a clear understanding of international security. While the evidence presented to this point concerning the spread of weapons of mass destruction, the threatening confluence of globalization and disease, or the rise of new forms of terrorism may well be enough to make the point about the significance of changes in the security environment, part of our purpose here is to highlight the specific changes we believe to be most significant.

Surveying the problems of an insecure world, it is apparent that, first, nonstate actors—including ideologically driven individuals, terrorist networks, and transnational criminal organizations—have become significant threats to both states and individuals since the end of the Cold War. Second, the threats we confront are increasingly transnational in character. Third, in large part due to the increasing significance of nonstate actors and transnational threats, security, now more than ever, is indivisible; we are all connected. Security is, fourth, increasingly subject to the law of unintended consequences—that is, actions taken to address specific threats often create insecurities in different areas. Finally, when we return to the traditional geopolitical focus of the traditional approach to international security, we find that the geographical center of concern has shifted dramatically.

THE RISE OF NONSTATE ACTORS

During the Cold War and (with various local and temporary exceptions) for centuries before that, back to the 1648 Peace of Westphalia, seeking security meant taking actions to counter the threats posed by states. The Anglo-German naval arms race that preceded World War I, the French development of the Maginot Line after World War I, the establishment after World War II of the North Atlantic Treaty Organization (NATO) in the West and the Warsaw Pact in the East were all manifestations of states' determination to protect themselves from other states.

Within the discipline of international relations, considerable attention has always been given to strategies for restraining the aggressive behavior of states. Balance-of-power theory and its Wilsonian rival, the theory of collective security, reflect this emphasis on restraining states. International law, international organizations, alliances, and many other features of modern international politics place the security of states front and center.

There are certainly good reasons for worrying about the security of states. When functioning properly, the state structures the political, economic, and social life of the community in such a way that freedom, commerce, and culture can flourish. But, looking outward from within the state, other states may appear threatening. In fact, few social institutions can pose a greater threat to the state than other states.

Because states have, for a very long time, been central to the way we understand international security, it is difficult to shift the focus to threats posed by nonstate actors. As Ralph Waldo Emerson said, "People only see what they are prepared to see." There is, however, much to see beyond the state.

Following the attacks in the United States on 9/11, in Bali on October 12, 2002, in Spain on March 11, 2004, and in London on July 7, 2005, the true scope of the threat to security posed by terrorist groups was, at last, universally recognized. But terrorists are not the only nonstate actors to raise serious security concerns in recent years. The potential for individuals like A. Q. Khan, the Pakistani nuclear scientist who sold nuclear secrets and technology for personal gain, to threaten global security is becoming more evident. The negative impact that transnational criminal organizations have on security through the sale of weapons in conflict-prone regions, through the financing of revolutionary violence and terrorism via drug trafficking, and through their own efforts to subvert states is also more apparent now than ever before. These and other examples of the problems caused by nonstate actors make it plain that states and the international system itself are no longer threatened solely, or even primarily, by other states.

Shifting the focus, even partially, from states to nonstate actors will have a significant effect on the way we view security. This is true first and foremost for this reason: In a system in which states are considered both the primary objects of and threats to security, interstate war must be the primary concern of those who think about security. And if war is the primary concern, the military will be the primary means of addressing that concern. The response to major threats involving nonstate actors bears this out. The threat posed by drug trafficking has, at least in the United States, elicited a "war on drugs," with a major role for the Department of Defense. The 9/11 attacks, perpetrated by a terrorist network, brought on a "war on terror." Whether war is the appropriate form of response or not, it appears to be what our state-centered mode of thinking leads us to whenever we identify a security threat.

The rise of homeland security, as a subject of both academic concern and government policy, is worth noting in this context. Homeland security is a concept that is clearly a product of a state-centered perspective, even though it arose as a response to threats posed by nonstate actors. To speak of homeland security is, on the positive side, to acknowledge that security concerns do not stop at the borders of the state. This point was brought home (quite literally) by the fact that the hijackers of the four airplanes that were brought down on 9/11 had lived and trained themselves to fly in the United States. On the other hand, the concept of homeland security is based on the idea that normal means of law enforcement are inadequate to deal with the new threats to security inside the state. It suggests that in the "war on terror" there is a need for an internal security agency (the Department of Homeland Security) and an external security agency (the Department of Defense). Having a Department of Homeland Security, in other words, brings the "war on terror" home, though war may not be the most appropriate response even beyond the borders of the United States.

States continue to be the primary providers of security, but even in this realm nonstate actors are making inroads. Increasingly, we are being forced to think of security as a commodity that can be treated as either a public good or a private good. Like the nobles of the medieval period in Europe who built castles as private investments in security, more and more people worldwide who can afford to do so are retreating into gated communities or hiring private security firms for protection. But the privatization of security (and with it the legitimation of nonstate actors with security functions) is not limited to the individual level. States too appear to be privatizing more and more aspects of security, as we have seen in the widespread use of private security firms by the United States in Iraq since the March 2003 invasion.

THE RECOGNITION OF TRANSNATIONAL THREATS

One of the most obvious and, we believe, most significant changes in the post–Cold War security environment is the rise of transnational, as opposed to international, threats. Such threats are not new (as the post–World War I Spanish flu pandemic, to take but a single example, illustrates), but a number of factors have dramatically increased their significance in recent years. First, it must be acknowledged that one of the effects of the ending of the Cold War was to create a space in which it was possible for states in the developed world at least to begin giving serious attention to nontraditional threats. The demise of the Warsaw Pact created a "zone of peace,"[1] or a "unipolar moment,"[2] in which security against traditional threats of the vast majority of the developed world seemed assured. It seems reasonable to suggest that the dramatic reduction in the traditional state-centered threats that accompanied the end of the Cold War might explain the sudden interest of security analysts in nontraditional concerns.

Whether or not students of international security turned from nuclear deterrence to, say, epidemic disease as a self-interested means of preserving their policy relevance in the aftermath of the Cold War, one thing is certain: In the competition for scholarly attention and defense spending (two matters that are often connected), big threats trump small threats. To say that the end of the Cold War permitted academics and policy makers to pay more attention to small threats ("small" in relation to the threat of nuclear annihilation, that is) is by no means equivalent to saying that they invented these smaller, nontraditional threats. Most of those threats were always with us but had to be put on the back burner when Berlin was being blockaded, hydrogen bombs were being tested, Cuba was becoming a Soviet ally, and proxy wars were being fought in Asia and Africa.

Military threats to security have been and are likely to continue to be around for a long time to come; however, there are other problems that have not received adequate attention. Some should be (and in some cases now are) recognized as security threats. For example, smallpox, although now eradicated in nature, killed an estimated three to five hundred million people in the twentieth century alone. During the same period, an estimated hundred million people died as a consequence of war. Clearly, smallpox posed a greater threat to humans during the twentieth century than warfare, yet throughout the century students of international security focused on the threat of war rather than that of smallpox.

Transnational threats take a variety of forms, including those associated with non-state actors, but what defines that category is the irrelevance of borders as devices for stopping the threats. Just as the humanitarian organization called Doctors Without Borders (Médicins sans Frontières) aspires to do good in the world without regard to the artificial barriers thrown up by the borders of sovereign states, so malevolence (in the form of disease, nihilistic ideologies, drugs, child prostitution, and many other problems) spreads widely across the globe with few obstacles. The problem, at one level, is globalization. Globalization in its many guises creates a world increasingly vulnerable to computer- and communications-network disruptions, the spread of disease, financial instability, and many other problems. At another level, however, freedom is responsible. The freedom to travel to virtually any spot on the globe carries with it the possibility of transporting disease in the process. The freedom to communicate via the Internet offers a medium through which both scholars can plan a conference and terrorists can plan an attack. The freedom to purchase goods manufactured abroad presents the frightening prospect that, some day, a container ship bringing cars or computers or clothing from Asia may also carry a nuclear device. As Kenneth Waltz noted, "States, like people, are insecure in proportion to the extent of their freedom. If freedom is wanted, insecurity must be accepted."[3]

As we noted in chapter 9, the significance of transnational threats is now being acknowledged to some degree. The 9/11 Commission stated that "threats are defined more by the fault lines within societies than by the territorial boundaries between them. From terrorism to global disease or environmental degradation, the challenges have become transnational rather than international."[4] Similarly, President Clinton noted in a May 2000 commencement address at the Coast Guard Academy that globalization and technological developments are "making us more vulnerable to problems that arise half a world away: to terror; to ethnic, racial and religious conflicts; to weapons of mass destruction, drug trafficking and other organized crime."[5] These, indeed, are the very issues that we have examined in this book.

THE INDIVISIBILITY OF SECURITY

Security today is indivisible. As we noted earlier, a narrowly self-interested security policy cannot be narrowly self-interested. John Muir, the eminent environmentalist and founder of the Sierra Club, could have been talking about international security rather than nature when he wrote, "When we try to pick out anything by itself, we find it hitched to everything else in the Universe."[6]

Everywhere we look, we see connections between various sources of insecurity. Economic insecurity may lead to slash-and-burn agriculture, with deforestation (and environmental insecurity) as a result. The devastation of an ecosystem may, in turn, create a refugee crisis that leads to ethnic conflict. An intrastate war may generate a market for arms traffickers. Trafficking in small arms and light weapons may then open up a network through which chemical, biological, or even nuclear materials are traded. The proliferation of weapons of mass destruction may make it possible for terrorists to acquire a nuclear device. And so on.

Consider the beginning of the chain above. Poverty, it should be clear, contributes to many other forms of insecurity. Former World Bank president James D. Wolfensohn put it this way:

> Poverty in itself does not immediately and directly lead to conflict, let alone to terrorism. Rather than responding to deprivation by lashing out at others, the vast majority of poor people worldwide devote their energy to the day-in, day-out struggle to secure income, food, and opportunities for their children. And yet we know that exclusion can breed violent conflict. Careful research tells us that civil wars have often resulted not so much from ethnic diversity—the usual scapegoat—as from a mix of factors, of which, it must be recognized, poverty is a central ingredient.[7]

Addressing the issue of global poverty requires, more than anything else, a simple recognition on the part of wealthy states that security is indivisible and that their willingness to take action is, in fact, an investment in their own security. To act on this recognition, Wolfensohn recommends increasing foreign aid, reducing trade barriers, "focus[ing] development assistance to ensure good results," and acting internationally on global issues.

In September 2000, the United Nations General Assembly unanimously adopted the Millennium Development Goals, an ambitious set of plans that calls on the international community to eradicate extreme poverty and hunger, achieve universal primary education, promote gender equality and empower women, reduce child mortality, improve maternal health, combat HIV/AIDS, malaria, and other diseases, ensure environmental sustainability, and develop a global partnership for development. The achievement of these goals would go a long way toward making both the United States and the world more secure, by addressing a number of the interdependent sources of insecurity. Unfortunately, progress toward the achievement of the Millennium Development Goals has been slow, in part because of the rapid reversion to traditional modes of addressing national security in the wake of 9/11. To meet the Millennium Goals, the world's developed states have pledged to devote 0.7 percent of their national incomes for aid to developing states. Only five states have met this goal so far: Denmark, Luxembourg, the Netherlands, Norway, and Sweden. The United States will have to significantly increase its share of gross national product devoted to aid in order to meet the 0.7 percent target.

We have examined many different threats to the well-being—the security—of individuals, states, and the international system. These have included traditional military threats posed by states, new threats (including the "new terrorism") presented by nonstate actors, and threats posed by infectious disease, poverty, the proliferation of weapons of mass destruction, cyberwar, transnational crime, ethnic conflict, and environmental degradation. Even the controversial White House document that outlined the Bush administration's strategy of preemptive war in September 2002 noted that "poverty, weak institutions, and corruption can make weak states vulnerable to terrorist networks and drug cartels within their borders."[8] The interconnectedness of these threats offers a compelling case, we believe, for the conclusion that security is, now more than ever, indivisible.

THE PROBLEM OF UNINTENDED CONSEQUENCES

We have noted that often the attempt to achieve greater security has the unintentional result of threatening security. For example, in chapter 7 we pointed out that the U.S. Department of Defense originally developed the precursor to the Internet to provide for assured, redundant communications among military bases and installations; if one communications node was destroyed in an attack, the Internet provided an alternate means of communication. Over time, the Internet became a means by which the security of individuals, organizations, and states could be threatened. Or consider infectious diseases. The World Health Organization worked diligently to eradicate smallpox as a threat to the world's peoples. In order to develop defenses against an enemy employing smallpox as a weapon, the defense establishments of both Russia and the United States retained strains of smallpox. Now there is concern that these strains could become available to terrorists and be used to unleash the deadly disease on an unprotected world.

Unintended consequences—or "blowback," in the phrase used by the CIA[9]—may be most apparent in the "war on terrorism." The 2003 Iraq war has generated mistrust and animosity toward the United States and has provided a training ground for Islamist militants. It risks duplicating the effects of the Soviet Union's war in Afghanistan during the 1980s, in terms of providing a stimulus to global terrorism. In fact, the well-respected International Institute for Strategic Studies issued a report in October 2004 that indicated that the Iraq war had aided Al Qaeda's recruitment efforts.[10]

Even American "successes" against Al Qaeda may be making terrorism more difficult to address. Many intelligence analysts believe that in response to attacks on its leadership and its financing, Al Qaeda has transformed itself into an ideology and a decentralized movement of jihadists. The loss of its base in Afghanistan is thought to have prompted the dispersal of militants all over the world and the spread of its ideology.[11]

While it may be objected that more carefully constructed policies can avoid unintended consequences, history offers little encouragement. Providing Stinger missiles to the *mujahidin* in Afghanistan accomplished its primary purpose of inflicting serious losses on the Soviet Union, but "loose" Stingers now pose a significant threat to civil aviation. The military containment of Iraq during the 1990s was a policy success and, it seems, necessary, but the required stationing of U.S. forces in the Persian Gulf region thereafter was a factor in the decision of Muslim fundamentalists to attack American interests both in the region and in the United States itself.

GEOGRAPHICAL SHIFTS

Even if we were not adopting an expanded view of security, we would be forced to note that the geographical focus of security studies has shifted dramatically in recent years. The broader view of security, however, provides even more reason for looking closely at different parts of the world.

Many of the threats that we have described in this book come together in Africa. It is the area hardest hit by HIV/AIDS; it contains many of the world's poorest countries; it has both harbored terrorists and suffered from terrorist attacks; it is an important focus of trafficking of all types; and it has suffered more than any other continent from the effects of ethnic conflict. East Africa and the Horn, including Djibouti, Ethiopia, Eritrea, Kenya, Somalia, Tanzania, and Uganda, is an area of particular concern, given the conflicts in the region, the poverty, corruption, and high incidence of HIV/AIDS. Not surprisingly, Al Qaeda was active in Somalia and, according to reports, advised members of Mohammed Aideed's militia on how to use rocket-propelled grenades to shoot down U.S. Black Hawk helicopters. In addition, Al Qaeda operated out of Sudan and perpetrated the 1998 attacks on the American embassies in Nairobi, Kenya, and Dar es Salaam, Tanzania.

Other areas of Africa are also of concern and importance to American security. Africa's most populous country is Nigeria, with 137 million people (almost half the population of the United States); about half of these are Muslims.[12] Currently, Nigeria provides approximately 7 percent of the oil of the United States. It is estimated that West Africa may provide 25 percent of U.S. oil supplies by 2015.[13] A number of African countries have majority populations of Muslims, and there is the possibility that Islamic radicalism will grow among them. To address, then, the threats of HIV/AIDS, poverty, ethnic conflict, and illegal trafficking of drugs, humans, and diamonds is a matter of security. The United States and other wealthy, industrial states ignore these threats at their peril. As the previously cited study jointly sponsored by the Milbank Memorial Fund and the Council on Foreign Relations noted, "With reduced ability to deal with either economic development or security, Africa will become increasingly susceptible to conflict and increasingly attractive as a haven for terrorists and transnational criminal elements hostile to the United States."[14]

Other important developments with security implications are occurring in Asia. In the next fifteen years, India and China are likely to grow more powerful both politically and economically. In its report on global trends to the year 2020, the National Intelligence Council predicted that "the likely emergence of China and India, as well as others, as new major global players—similar to the advent of a united Germany in the nineteenth century and a powerful United States in the early twentieth century—will transform the geopolitical landscape, with impacts potentially as dramatic as those in the previous two centuries."[15] The U.S. Census Bureau estimates that the population of China in 2020 will be 1.4 billion; India's population will be 1.3 billion. Due to China's one-child policy, its population will age more rapidly than others; by 2020 an estimated four hundred million Chinese will be over sixty-five. This will put increased demands on the younger members of Chinese society. From a more traditional security perspective, the greatest military threats to stability and peace in Asia during the next decade and a half will concern relations between China and Taiwan on the one hand and China and North Korea on the other. Conflicts involving either of these pairings could rapidly escalate and draw in the United States.

TWO VIEWS OF SECURITY FOR A NEW ERA

As we have noted throughout this book, the traditional view of security centers on the state. The perspective that puts *national security* front and center considers the central threats in the international system (and therefore the principal concerns of security studies) to be threats to the sovereignty, the territorial integrity, and the political and economic systems of *the state*. It is also state-centered in that it views states as the primary sources of threats.

Seeking security in the twenty-first century requires attending to national security, because state-based threats to states still exist. We have just noted the concerns raised by the People's Republic of China. North Korea poses a serious threat to the stability of East Asia due to its economic instability coupled with its ongoing nuclear program. Failed states, as we noted in chapters 9 and 11, pose a different kind of state-based problem, but one that is nonetheless very serious.

Because the traditional paradigm does not adequately address the various security threats that we have examined, it is important to go beyond national security. Our conclusions lead us to suggest that *human security* and *cooperative security* must be part of any comprehensive approach to security in the century ahead.

The concept of human security emerged in the early 1990s to bring together several distinct efforts to widen the traditional security agenda. Unlike national security, human security focuses on the individual human being rather than the state. It also includes a range of threats to human welfare that go well beyond the traditional focus on defense against aggression. UN Secretary General Kofi Annan has described human security in these terms:

> Human security in its broadest sense, embraces far more than the absence of violent conflict. It encompasses human rights, good governance, access to education and health care and ensuring that each individual has opportunities and choices to fulfill his or her potential. Every step in this direction is also a step towards reducing poverty, achieving

economic growth and preventing conflict. Freedom from want, freedom from fear, and the freedom of future generations to inherit a healthy natural environment—these are the interrelated building blocks of human—and therefore national security.[16]

Human security has its conceptual roots in international humanitarian law, international human rights, the concept of humanitarian intervention, and the dual concepts of economic development and human development. As with human rights, the adjective "human" signals a move not only toward thinking about the individual but toward concern for humankind as well. Human security, in other words, is simultaneously individual security and universal security.

The structure of the international system complicates efforts to address many of the most serious problems we have discussed in this book. Sovereignty means that each of the two hundred states in the system is free to address (or to ignore) global warming or human trafficking or terrorism, as it sees fit. This feature of the international system makes transnational threats particularly difficult to address. The failure of one state to reduce HIV/AIDS infection rates poses a threat to other states. The failure of one state to curb greenhouse gas emissions or to stop the destruction of rainforests has a negative impact on all states that are attempting to address global warming. Furthermore, nonstate actors—terrorists, arms traffickers, nuclear scientists willing to sell their services to the highest bidder—exploit differences among states and operate in the gaps of the international system.

These facts argue strongly for seeking security through the methods presented in the cooperative security paradigm. Cooperative security, as we noted in the previous chapter, seeks to bring states together in ways that address the weaknesses of the international system as it is currently constituted. It approaches security as something to which all states are entitled and that can only be gained by mutual efforts. By treating security as a public good, it establishes the understanding that all states have a common interest in promoting a shared system of security and that "free riders" must be brought into a cooperative framework.

Cooperative security requires a degree of multilateralism that has been absent from U.S. foreign policy since the decision to go to war in Iraq. It is difficult to know at present whether the United States will be willing to shift its mode of operation sufficiently to move toward cooperative security in the near future.

THE WAY FORWARD

In 1979, Ken Booth published a book entitled *Strategy and Ethnocentrism* in which he noted the failure of most security analysts to take adequate account of differences among cultures.[17] In the Cold War context in which Booth was writing, the Western emphasis on rationality as the foundation of nuclear deterrence theory was an especially striking example of this problem. Almost a decade later, however, scholars were still noting "the pitfalls of ethnocentrism due to American dominance of the field."[18]

However much Western policy makers and scholars may have become sensitive to the problems posed by the difficulty of seeing beyond their own cultural constructs, we suspect that ethnocentrism may be an even greater problem today, in the middle of an ill-defined "war on terror," than it was during the Cold War. If our conclusions to this point have been correct—that seeking security today requires countering threats from nonstate actors, recognizing threats that are transnational and, consequently, indivisible in character, dealing with the problems of unintended consequences, and operating in parts of the world that are especially unfamiliar to most of us in the West—then the ability to understand and even to empathize with those in other cultures is more important than ever before.

What policy makers, analysts, and even entire societies understand by "security" varies more than we ordinarily acknowledge, with the variations relating to political, social, technological, and other circumstances. The meaning of security differs across cultures, but within a culture it is also subject to change over time. This is so because political and social differences affect what societies desire to protect, because technological advances alter the types of threats that must be protected against, and, most importantly, because the very subjectivity of the concept of security ensures that individuals in different situations will value social goods and assess threats differently. The concept of security, to put it simply, is socially constructed.

To the extent that "security studies" has some common content that transcends political and cultural differences in the world, the influence of the privileged elites in the world must be credited. Certainly, the fears of male defense intellectuals discussing security at an arms control seminar in Cambridge, Massachusetts, in the early 1960s were quite different from the fears of Congolese women living through revolution and ethnic conflict in that same period. Not surprisingly, security studies in that era paid little attention to threats facing women in Africa.

Circumstances, in large measure (but with some input from psychological factors), determine what we fear. Many feminists, noting the greater vulnerability of women to acts of sexual violence and physical abuse, have suggested that feminine conceptions of security differ from masculine conceptions as a consequence.[19] Because men are generally free from the fear of sexual violence and physical abuse, male-formulated notions of security manifest no concern for security as freedom from fear of sexual assault.[20] Similarly, security as defined by academics and strategists living and working in liberal democracies has tended to ignore the possibility that the state may generate fear among its own citizens.

As we noted in chapter 10, since World War II, developing states have been the scenes of most of the world's violent conflict. Much of that conflict has been intrastate and interethnic. This in itself should alert us to the divergence between our ethnocentric concern with insecurity defined in terms of external threats and the form of insecurity that most of the world actually experiences. As Mohammed Ayoob has observed, the primary security concerns of weak states are "internal in character" and are characteristic of "the early stages of state making."[21] A sophisticated understanding of security must take such considerations into account, particularly if concern for human welfare characteristic of human security or concern for complementary strategies characteristic of cooperative security is part of the mix.

Seeking security in an insecure world has always been an extraordinary challenge. It is perhaps an even greater challenge in a world that is also interdependent. More than ever, creating a more secure world requires understanding and even empathy. Where threats are so numerous, so interconnected, and so complex, it is unwise to rely solely on the approaches of the past.

RECOMMENDED READING

Printed Sources

Buzan, Barry. *People, States and Fear: An Agenda for International Security Studies in the Post–Cold War Era.* Rev. ed. Boulder, Colo.: Lynne Rienner, 1992.

Carnegie Commission on Preventing Deadly Conflict. *Final Report.* Washington, D.C.: Carnegie Commission on Preventing Deadly Conflict, 1997.

Haass, Richard N. *The Opportunity: America's Moment to Alter History's Course.* New York: PublicAffairs, 2005.

Lipshutz, Ronnie D., ed. *On Security.* New York: Columbia University Press, 1995.

Lyman, Princeton N., and J. Stephen Morrison. "The Terrorist Threat in Africa." *Foreign Affairs* 83 (January/February 2004): 75–86.

Steinbruner, John D. *Principles of Global Security.* Washington, D.C.: Brookings Institution, 2000.

U.S. National Intelligence Council. *Mapping the Global Future.* Report on the 2020 Project. Washington, D.C.: Government Printing Office, December 2004.

Websites

Human Security Network: www.humansecuritynetwork.org

United Nations Foundation, United Nations and Global Security: www.un-globalsecurity.org/index.asp

U.S. Department of Homeland Security: www.dhs.gov/dhspublic/index.asp.

Notes

CHAPTER 1: THE MEANING OF SECURITY TODAY

1. All figures are from the *CIA World Factbook,* available at www.cia.gov/cia/publications/factbook/rankorder/2034rank.html.

2. Arnold Wolfers, "National Security as an Ambiguous Symbol," in *Discord and Collaboration: Essays on International Politics* (Baltimore: Johns Hopkins University Press, 1962), 147–65. This chapter originally appeared in *Political Science Quarterly* in 1952.

3. John Baylis, "International Security in the Post–Cold War Era," in *The Globalization of World Politics: An Introduction to International Relations,* ed. John Baylis and Steve Smith (Oxford: Oxford University Press, 1997), 194. K. J. Holsti has written, "Probably few concepts employed in statecraft and in the study of international politics have as vague referents as do *security* or *national security.*" *International Politics: A Framework for Analysis,* 7th ed. (Englewood Cliffs, N.J.: Prentice Hall, 1995), 84 (italics original).

4. The billions of dollars spent to address potential problems that, it was feared, would result from the Y2K bug could easily be regarded as expenditures designed to address national security concerns, at least according to most current definitions of security.

5. The shift in emphasis concerning the meaning of security was articulated early on in the following works (among others): Richard H. Ullman, "Redefining Security," *International Security* 8 (Summer 1983): 129–53; and Jessica Tuchman Mathews, "Redefining Security," *Foreign Affairs* 68 (Spring 1989): 162–77.

6. James N. Rosenau, "New Dimensions of Security: The Interaction of Globalizing and Localizing Dynamics," *Security Dialogue* 25 (September 1994): 255.

7. See Hedley Bull, *The Anarchical Society: A Study of Order in World Politics* (New York: Columbia University Press, 1977), 16–20. Bull defined international order as "a pattern or disposition of international activity that sustains those goals of the society of states that are elementary, primary, or universal." These goals, according to Bull, include preservation of the system itself, preservation of individual parts of the system (states), peace, and the limitation of violence.

8. See Lars Schoultz, *National Security and United States Policy toward Latin America* (Princeton, N.J.: Princeton University Press, 1987).

9. It may be objected that the transnational spread of disease, as with the Black Death that claimed roughly one-third of Europe's population in the 1300s, was an even greater threat to the security of states (or their medieval precursors) in the Middle Ages than it is today. However, the inability to understand pathogenesis in a prescientific era prevented any serious efforts—efforts beyond closing city gates to strangers—to securitize the problem of contagion.

See Barbara W. Tuchman, *A Distant Mirror: The Calamitous 14th Century* (New York: Alfred A. Knopf, 1978).

10. Richard Rosecrance provides a particularly perceptive discussion of the declining significance of land for the modern state in *The Rise of the Virtual State: Wealth and Power in the Coming Century* (New York: Basic Books, 1999), 3–25.

11. See, for example, Barry Buzan, Ole Waever, and Jaap de Wilde, *Security: A New Framework for Analysis* (Boulder, Colo.: Lynne Rienner, 1998); and Richard Wyn Jones, *Security, Strategy, and Critical Theory* (Boulder, Colo.: Lynne Rienner, 1999).

12. Wyn Jones, *Security, Strategy, and Critical Theory*, 103. Buzan, Waever, and de Wilde use the term "widening" in *Security*.

13. See Buzan, Waever, and de Wilde, *Security*, 2–5.

14. See Gareth Evans, *Cooperating for Peace: The Global Agenda for the 1990s* (London: Allen and Unwin, 1993); and Gareth Evans, "Cooperative Security and Intrastate Conflict," *Foreign Policy* 96 (Fall 1994): 3–20.

15. See *Human Development Report 1994* (New York: United Nations Development Program, 1994). The concept of human security has been promoted at the UN more recently by the joint action of Canada and Norway. See Astri Suhrke, "Human Security and the Interests of States," *Security Dialogue* 30 (September 1999): 265–76.

16. R. B. J Walker, "The Subject of Security," in *Critical Security Studies: Concepts and Cases*, ed. Keith Krause and Michael C. Williams (Minneapolis: University of Minnesota Press, 1997), 63.

17. UN Department of Public Information, "Opening Session of Millennium Summit Hears Statements by 19 Heads of State, 10 Heads of Government, Two Vice-Presidents," UN Press Release GA/9750, September 6, 2000.

18. See, for one of the classic discussions of the security dilemma, Robert Jervis, *Perception and Misperception in International Politics* (Princeton, N.J.: Princeton University Press, 1976).

19. The first statement of the idea of the security community was Karl Deutsch et al., *Political Community in the North Atlantic Area* (Princeton, N.J.: Princeton University Press, 1957).

20. For a British astronomer's discussion of this and many other dramatic threats to the survival of our planet, see Martin Rees, *Our Final Hour* (New York: Basic Books, 2003).

21. See Scott D. Sagan, *The Limits of Safety: Organizations, Accidents, and Nuclear Weapons* (Princeton, N.J.: Princeton University Press, 1995).

22. Barry Buzan, *People, States and Fear: An Agenda for International Security Studies in the Post–Cold War Era*, 2nd ed. (Boulder, Colo.: Lynne Rienner, 1991), 146.

23. Wyn Jones, *Security, Strategy, and Critical Theory*, 99.

24. Robert Kaplan, *The Coming Anarchy: Shattering the Dreams of the Post–Cold War* (New York: Random House, 2000), 175–76.

25. For a noteworthy example of this, see Ken Booth, "Security and Self: Reflections of a Fallen Realist," in *Critical Security Studies*, ed. Krause and Williams, 83–119.

CHAPTER 2: CONVENTIONAL WEAPONS AND WAR

1. International Rescue Committee, "IRC Study Reveals 31,000 Die Monthly in Congo Conflict and 3.8 Million Died in Past Six Years," December 9, 2004, available at www.theirc .org/index.cfm/wwwID/2132.

2. Spencer C. Tucker, "Casualties," *Encyclopedia of the Vietnam War: A Political, Social, and Military History,* 3 vols. (Santa Barbara, Calif.: ABC-CLIO, 1998), I:106.

3. Washington Headquarters Services, Directorate for Information Operations and Reports, "Vietnam Conflict: Casualty Summary (As of June 15, 2004)," web1.whs.osd.mil/mmid/CASUALTY/vietnam.pdf.

4. Thomas C. Schelling, *Arms and Influence* (New Haven, Conn.: Yale University Press, 1966), 19.

5. Schelling, *Arms and Influence,* 1–2.

6. Schelling, *Arms and Influence,* 12–34.

7. The British decision to wage war in this fashion is extensively analyzed in Stephen A. Garrett, *Ethics and Airpower in World War II: The British Bombing of German Cities* (New York: St. Martin's, 1993).

8. Michael Walzer, *Just and Unjust Wars: A Moral Argument with Historical Illustrations,* 3rd ed. (New York: Basic Books, 2000), 255.

9. Washington Headquarters Services, Directorate for Information Operations and Reports, "Persian Gulf War: Casualty Summary (Desert Shield/Storm as of June 15, 2004)," web1.whs.osd.mil/mmid/casualty/GWSUM.pdf.

10. Washington Headquarters Services, Directorate for Information Operations and Reports, "Operation Iraqi Freedom: Military Deaths (Through April 30, 2003)," web1.whs.osd.mil/mmid/casualty/OIF-Deaths-Before.pdf.

11. "NATO's Role in Kosovo," NATO, available at www.nato.int/kosovo/kosovo.htm.

12. *Sun-tzu on the Art of War: The Oldest Military Treatise in the World,* trans. Lionel Giles (Mountainview, Calif.: Wiretap, n.d.), 45 [e-book].

13. Washington Headquarters Services, Directorate for Information Operations and Reports, "Operation Iraqi Freedom: Military Deaths (Since May 1, 2003)," available at web1.whs.osd.mil/mmid/casualty/OIF-Deaths-After.pdf.

14. Stockholm International Peace Research Institute (SIPRI), *SIPRI Yearbook 2004–Armaments, Disarmament and International Security* (Oxford: Oxford University Press, 2004), appendix 10A. SIPRI figures for U.S. military expenditures are based on year 2000 market exchange rate and dollars.

15. Linda Fasulo, *An Insider's Guide to the UN* (New Haven, Conn.: Yale University Press, 2004), 116.

16. Dwight D. Eisenhower, *The White House Years: Mandate for Change, 1953–1956* (Garden City, N.Y.: Doubleday, 1963), 145.

17. Tim Weiner, "A Fighter in Search of an Adversary (Other than the Bottom Line)," *New York Times,* October 27, 2004, C1.

18. Robert L. Paarlberg, "Knowledge as Power: Science, Military Dominance, and U.S. Security," *International Security* 29 (Summer 2004): 122–51.

19. SIPRI, "Burden Comparison," available at www.sipri.org/contents/milap/milex/mex_burden.html.

20. Quoted in Charles W. Kegley, Jr. and Eugene R. Wittkopf, *World Politics: Trend & Transformation,* 9th ed. (Belmont, Calif.: Wadsworth/Thomson Learning, 2004), 450.

21. Quoted in Kegley and Wittkopf, *World Politics,* 450.

22. *Small Arms Survey 2002: Counting the Human Cost* (New York: Oxford University Press, 2002), 156–57.

23. "Speech by Lloyd Axworthy, Canadian Minister of Foreign Affairs, to U.N. Security Council Ministerial on Small Arms, September 24, 1999," International Action Network on

Small Arms (IANSA), available at www.iansa.org/documents/un/un_pub/statements/axworthy .htm.

24. See, among a wide variety of sources on the origins and distinctive characteristics of the SALW issue, Edward J. Laurance, *Light Weapons and Intrastate Conflict: Early Warning Factors and Preventive Action,* A Report to the Carnegie Commission on Preventing Deadly Conflict (New York: Carnegie Commission on Preventing Deadly Conflict, July 1998), 13–19; and Jeffrey Boutwell and Michael T. Klare, eds., *Light Weapons and Civil Conflict: Controlling the Tools of Violence* (Lanham, Md.: Rowman & Littlefield for the Carnegie Commission on Preventing Deadly Conflict, 1999), 1–5.

25. Aaron Karp, "Laudable Failure," *SAIS Review* 22 (Winter–Spring 2002): 179.

26. "Notes for an Address by the Honourable Lloyd Axworthy, Minister of Foreign Affairs, to the 52nd Session of the United Nations General Assembly," September 25, 1997, International Action Network on Small Arms (IANSA), available at www.iansa.org/documents/un/ un_pub/statements/axworthy.htm.

27. Statement by John R. Bolton, U.S. Under-Secretary of State for Arms Control and International Security Affairs, UN Conference on the Illicit Trade in Small Arms and Light Weapons in All Its Aspects, July 9, 2001, available at disarmament.un.org/cab/smallarms/statements/usE .html.

28. Human Rights Watch, *Landmines: A Deadly Legacy* (Washington, D.C.: Human Rights Watch, 1993), 148–56.

29. *Breaking the Conflict Trap: Civil War and Development Policy* (Herndon, Va.: World Bank, 2003), 31.

30. "A World War II Mine Forces Mass Evacuation," *International Herald Tribune,* February 9, 2004, available at www.iht.com/articles/128605.html.

31. Paul Watson and Lisa Getter, "Silent Peril Lies in Wait for Afghanistan's People," *Los Angeles Times,* December 1, 2001, A1.

32. Watson and Getter, "Silent Peril," A1.

33. John Donnelly, "Cluster Bombs Found to Spare Civilian Areas," *Boston Globe,* February 23, 2002, A1.

34. Carmen Sorger and Eric Hoskins, "Protecting the Most Vulnerable: War-Affected Children," in *Human Security and the New Diplomacy: Protecting People, Promoting Peace,* ed. Rob McRae and Don Humbert (Montreal: McGill-Queen's University Press, 2001), 134.

35. Graça Machel, *Impact of Armed Conflict on Children,* A/51/306 (New York: United Nations, August 26, 1996).

36. Coalition to Stop the Use of Child Soldiers, *Child Soldiers Global Report 2004* (London: 2004), 13.

37. Coalition to Stop the Use of Child Soldiers, *Child Soldiers Global Report 2004,* 17, 21.

38. See Machel, *Impact of Armed Conflict on Children,* 11–13; Coalition to Stop the Use of Child Soldiers, *Child Soldiers Global Report 2004,* 20–21.

39. Dana Priest and Mary Pat Flaherty, "Under Fire, Security Firms Form an Alliance," *Washington Post,* April 8, 2004, 1.

40. P. W. Singer, *Corporate Warriors: The Rise of the Privatized Military Industry* (Ithaca, N.Y.: Cornell University Press, 2003), 3–4.

41. Thom Shanker, "Pentagon Sets Bonuses to Retain Members of Special Operations," *New York Times,* February 6, 2005, 4.

CHAPTER 3: NUCLEAR WEAPONS

1. Richard Rhodes, *The Making of the Atomic Bomb* (New York: Simon and Schuster, 1986), 711.

2. Quoted by Rhodes, *The Making of the Atomic Bomb,* 725.

3. Quoted by Rhodes, *The Making of the Atomic Bomb,* 711.

4. "The Peace: The Bomb," *Time,* August 20, 1945, 19.

5. Quoted by Fred Kaplan, *Wizards of Armageddon* (New York: Simon and Schuster, 1983), 9–10.

6. Frederick S. Dunn, "The Common Problem," in *The Absolute Weapon: Atomic Power and World Order,* ed. Bernard Brodie (New York: Harcourt, Brace, 1946), 4.

7. Carl von Clausewitz, *On War,* ed. and trans. Michael Howard and Peter Paret (Princeton, N.J.: Princeton University Press, 1976).

8. Quoted in Kaplan, *Wizards of Armageddon,* 31.

9. Herman Kahn, *On Thermonuclear War* (Princeton, N.J.: Princeton University Press, 1960).

10. Jeffrey Porro, "The Policy War: Brodie vs. Kahn," *Bulletin of the Atomic Scientists* (June 1982): 16–20.

11. George Kennan, "On Nuclear War," *New York Review of Books,* January 21, 1982, 8.

12. George Kennan, "The Atomic Bomb and the Choices for American Policy" (1950), in *The Nuclear Delusion: Soviet-American Relations in the Atomic Age* (New York: Pantheon Books, 1982), 3–6.

13. Winston S. Churchill, *The Second World War: The Grand Alliance* (Boston: Houghton Mifflin, 1951), 370.

14. Henry L. Stimson and McGeorge Bundy, *On Active Service in Peace and War* (New York: Harper and Brothers, 1948), 642–46.

15. Stimson quoted by Godfrey Hodgson, *The Colonel: The Life and Wars of Henry Stimson 1867–1950* (New York: Alfred A. Knopf, 1990), 357.

16. Stimson quoted by McGeorge Bundy, *Danger and Survival: Choices about the Bomb in the First Fifty Years* (New York: Random House, 1988), 136.

17. "Transcript of Press Interview with President at White House," *New York Times,* March 30, 1983, 14.

18. George Quester, *Deterrence before Hiroshima: The Airpower Background of Modern Strategy* (New Brunswick, N.J.: Transaction, 1986).

19. See B. H. Liddell Hart, *Deterrence or Defense* (New York: Praeger, 1960); William W. Kaufman, *The McNamara Strategy* (New York: Harper and Row, 1964); Henry Kissinger, *Nuclear Weapons and Foreign Policy* (New York: Harper, 1957); Maxwell Taylor, *The Uncertain Trumpet* (Harper and Brothers, 1960).

20. John F. Kennedy in Allan Nevins, ed., *The Strategy of Peace* (New York: Harper, 1960), 184.

21. Gregg Herken, *Counsels of War* (New York: Alfred A. Knopf, 1985), 155.

22. *National Security Strategy of the United States* (Washington, D.C.: White House, September 2002), available at www.whitehouse.gov.

23. Albert Wohlstetter, "The Delicate Balance of Power," *Foreign Affairs* 39 (January 1961): 211–34.

24. Donald Brennan, ed., *Arms Control, Disarmament and National Security* (New York: George Braziller, 1961); Hedley Bull, *The Control of the Arms Race* (London: Weidenfeld and

Nicholson, 1961); and Thomas Schelling and Morton Halperin, *Strategy and Arms Control* (New York: Twentieth Century Fund, 1961).

25. Schelling and Halperin, *Strategy and Arms Control*, 2.

26. Elizabeth Young, *A Farewell to Arms Control* (Baltimore: Penguin Books, 1972), 86.

27. Dan Caldwell, *The Dynamics of Domestic Politics and Arms Control: The SALT II Treaty Ratification Debate* (Columbia: University of South Carolina Press, 1991).

28. Schelling and Halperin, *Strategy and Arms Control*.

29. For a description of these types of weapons, see www.physicstoday.org/vol-56/iss-11/p32.html.

30. John D. Steinbruner, *Principles of Global Security* (Washington, D.C.: Brookings Institution Press, 2000), 23.

31. Ivo Daalder, "The Future of Arms Control," *Survival* 34 (Spring 1992): 51–52.

CHAPTER 4: BUGS AND GAS

1. Andrew C. Revkin, "A Nation Challenged: Tracing the Spores—Testing Links Anthrax in Florida and at NBC," *New York Times,* October 18, 2001, 5.

2. Barbara Hatch Rosenberg, "Bioterrorism: Anthrax Attacks Pushed Open and Ominous Door," *Los Angeles Times,* September 22, 2002, M1.

3. See Donald C. Richter, *Chemical Soldiers: British Gas Warfare in World War I* (Lawrence: University Press of Kansas, 1992).

4. See Hans Zinsser, *Rats, Lice and History* (Boston: Atlantic Monthly, 1950).

5. Laurie Garrett, "The Next Pandemic?" *Foreign Affairs* 84 (July/August 2005): 6.

6. John M. Barry, *The Great Influenza: The Epic Story of the Deadliest Plague in History* (New York: Viking Press, 2004).

7. Laurie Garrett, *The Coming Plague: Newly Emerging Diseases in a World Out of Balance* (New York: Penguin Books, 1994), 157.

8. See Timothy V. McCarthy and Jonathan B. Tucker, "Saddam's Toxic Arsenal: Chemical and Biological Weapons in the Gulf Wars," in *Planning the Unthinkable: How New Powers Will Use Nuclear, Biological, and Chemical Weapons,* ed. Peter R. Lavoy, Scott D. Sagan, and James J. Wirtz (Ithaca, N.Y.: Cornell University Press, 2000), 47–78.

9. Richard K. Betts, "The New Threat of Mass Destruction," *Foreign Affairs* 77 (January/February 1998): 26.

10. U.S. Congress, Office of Technology Assessment, *Proliferation of Weapons of Mass Destruction: Assessing the Risks* (Washington, D.C.: Government Printing Office, 1993).

11. Thomas L. McNaugher, "Ballistic Missiles and Chemical Weapons: The Legacy of the Iran-Iraq War," *International Security* 15 (Fall 1990): 5–34.

12. Richard A. Falkenrath, Robert D. Newman, and Bradley A. Thayer, *America's Achilles Heel: Nuclear, Biological, and Chemical Terrorism and Covert Attack* (Cambridge, Mass.: MIT Press, 1998), 226–27.

13. This account is based primarily on Jessica Stern, *The Ultimate Terrorists* (Cambridge, Mass.: Harvard University Press, 1999), 60–68.

14. Garrett, *The Coming Plague,* 237–40.

15. Elizabeth A. Fenn, *Pox Americana: The Great Smallpox Epidemic of 1775–82* (New York: Hill and Wang, 2001), 88–91.

16. See Ken Alibeck, *Biohazard* (New York: Random House, 1999).

17. Joseph Cirincione, with Jon B. Wolfstahl and Miriam Rajkumar, *Deadly Arsenals: Tracking Weapons of Mass Destruction* (Washington, D.C.: Carnegie Endowment for International Peace, 2002).

18. See Falkenrath, Newman, and Thayer, *America's Achilles Heel,* 167–215.

19. Quoted in Falkenrath, Newman, and Thayer, *America's Achilles Heel,* 168.

CHAPTER 5: THE PROLIFERATION OF WEAPONS OF MASS DESTRUCTION

1. Kenneth M. Pollack, *The Threatening Storm: The Case for Invading Iraq* (New York: Random House, 2002), 76–77.

2. Memo from Ayman al-Zawahiri to Muhammad Atef, April 15, 1999, quoted by Alan Cullison, "Inside Al Qaeda's Hard Drive," *Atlantic Monthly* 294 (September 2004): 62.

3. "Plutonium Con Artists Sentenced in Russian Closed City of Sarov," *NIS Export Control Observer,* no. 11 (Monterey, Calif.: Center for Nonproliferation Studies, Monterey Institute of International Studies, November 2003).

4. Matthew Bunn, Anthony Wier, and John P. Holdren, *Controlling Nuclear Warheads and Materials: A Report Card and Action Plan* (Cambridge, Mass.: Nuclear Threat Initiative and the Project on Managing the Atom, Harvard University, March 2003).

5. Richard Betts, "The New Threat of Mass Destruction," *Foreign Affairs* 77 (January/February 1998): 26–41.

6. John F. Kennedy, quoted by Glenn Seaborg, *Kennedy, Khrushchev, and the Test Ban* (Berkeley: University of California Press, 1981), 198–99.

7. For the text of the treaty and a listing of the current signatories, see www.state.gov/www/global/arms/treaties.npt1.html.

8. *Final Report of the National Commission on Terrorist Attacks upon the United States,* Authorized Edition [hereafter *9/11 Commission Report*] (New York: W. W. Norton, 2004), 367.

9. Daniel Benjamin and Steven Simon, *The Age of Sacred Terror* (New York: Random House, 2002), 146.

10. Dafna Linzer, "U.S. Shifts Stance on Nuclear Treaty," *Washington Post,* July 31, 2004, A1; *9/11 Commission Report,* 368.

11. David Albright and Holly Higgins, "A Bomb for the Ummah," *Bulletin of the Atomic Scientists* 59 (March/April 2003): 53–54.

12. "Interview with Bin Laden: 'World's Most Wanted Terrorist,'" ABC News.com.

13. Matthew Bunn and Anthony Wier, *Securing the Bomb: An Agenda for Action* (Cambridge, Mass.: Nuclear Threat Initiative and the Project on Managing the Atom, Harvard University, May 2004), 5.

14. Bunn and Wier, *Securing the Bomb,* 36.

15. Jeffrey Fleishman, "Sting Unravels Stunning Mafia Plot," *Philadelphia Inquirer,* January 12, 1999.

16. International Atomic Energy Agency, "Calculating the New Global Nuclear Terrorist Threat" (Vienna: November 2001).

17. Quoted in *Arms Control and Disarmament Agreements: Texts and Histories of the Negotiations* (Washington, D.C.: U.S. Arms Control and Disarmament Agency, 1990), 131.

18. Rodney J. McElroy, "The Geneva Protocol of 1925," in *The Politics of Arms Control Treaty Ratification,* ed. Michael Krepon and Dan Caldwell (New York: St. Martin's, 1991), 125–66.

19. U.S. Senate, Committee on Foreign Relations, "Statement of John Holum, Director, U.S. Arms Control and Disarmament Agency," March 22, 1994.

20. For the text of the Chemical Weapons Convention and a listing of the current signatories, see www.opcw.org.

21. James B. Petro and David A. Relman, "Understanding Threats to Scientific Openness," *Science* 302 (December 12, 2003): 1989.

22. Joseph Cirincione, *Deadly Arsenals: Tracking Weapons of Mass Destruction* (Washington, D.C.: Carnegie Endowment for International Peace, 2002), 49.

23. Leon V. Sigal, *Disarming Strangers: Nuclear Diplomacy with North Korea* (Princeton, N.J.: Princeton University Press, 1998).

24. Cirincione, *Deadly Arsenals,* 246–49.

25. See President George W. Bush's commencement address at West Point and the *National Security Strategy of the United States 2002* (Washington, D.C.: White House, September 2002), available at www.whitehouse.gov.

26. Bob Woodward, *Plan of Attack* (New York: Simon and Schuster, 2004).

27. President George W. Bush, "State of the Union Address," *New York Times,* January 29, 2003.

28. Robert S. Norris and William M. Arkin, "NRDC Nuclear Notebook: Global Nuclear Stockpiles, 1945–2000," *Bulletin of the Atomic Scientists* 56 (March/April 2000): 79.

29. Robert S. Norris and Hans M. Kristensen, "Nuclear Notebook: Russian Nuclear Forces, 2003," *Bulletin of the Atomic Scientists* 59 (July/August 2003): 70–72.

30. Graham Allison, Ashton B. Carter, Steven E. Miller, and Philip Zelikow, *Cooperative Denuclearization: From Pledges to Deeds* (Cambridge, Mass.: Center for Science and International Affairs, John F. Kennedy School of Government, Harvard University, 1993).

31. George Perkovich, Joseph Cirincione, Rose Gottemoeller, Jon B. Wolfsthal, and Jessica T. Mathews, *Universal Compliance: A Strategy for Nuclear Security,* draft report (Washington, D.C.: Carnegie Endowment for International Peace, June 2004), 90.

32. Howard Baker and Lloyd Cutler, "A Report Card on the Department of Energy's Nonproliferation Programs with Russia" (Washington, D.C.: Department of Energy, January 10, 2001), iii.

33. Database on Nuclear Smuggling, Theft and Orphan Radiation Sources, Center for International Security and Cooperation, Stanford University, 2002. Also see the databases produced by the Center for Nonproliferation Studies at the Monterey Institute of International Studies, available at www.nti.org.

34. Bunn et al., *Securing Nuclear Weapons and Materials,* 10.

35. Chaim Braun, Friedrich Steinhauler, and Lyudmila Zaitseva, "International Terrorists Threat to Nuclear Facilities," *Austrian Military Periodical,* Special Edition on Nuclear Material Protection, 2003, 19.

36. George J. Tenet, "The Worldwide Threat 2004: Challenges in a Changing Global Context," Testimony to the U.S. Senate, Select Committee on Intelligence, February 24, 2004.

37. Matthew Bunn and Anthony Wier, "Preventing a Nuclear 9/11," *Washington Post,* September 17, 2004, B7.

38. See Perkovich et al., *Universal Compliance,* 45, table 5.1: Stocks of Weapons—Usable Plutonium (in Metric Tons).

39. Bunn et al., *Securing Nuclear Weapons and Materials,* vi.

40. Perkovich et al., *Universal Compliance,* 44 (italics original).

41. Bunn and Wier, *Securing the Bomb,* 3.

42. Secretary of Energy Spencer Abraham, "Remarks to the Second Moscow International Nonproliferation Conference," quoted by Bunn and Wier, *Securing the Bomb,* 43.

43. Bunn and Wier, *Securing the Bomb,* 3.

44. Bunn and Wier, *Securing the Bomb,* 79.

45. Perkovich et al., *Universal Compliance,* 90.

46. Linzer, "U.S. Shifts Stance on Nuclear Treaty, A1.

47. Quoted in "Arms Control Efforts Say Ban on Production of Key Nuclear Materials for Weapons Should Be Universal and Verifiable," Media Advisory, Arms Control Association, July 30, 2004.

48. See *National Security Strategy of the United States,* 2002.

CHAPTER 6: DISEASE

1. Thucydides, *History of the Peloponnesian War,* trans. Rex Warner (London and New York: Penguin, 1954).

2. William McNeil, *Plagues and Peoples* (New York: Anchor Books, 1976), 212–13.

3. Robert S. Gottfried, *The Black Death* (New York: Free Press, 1985), 77.

4. McNeil, *Plagues and Peoples,* 120–21; Jared Diamond, *Guns, Germs, and Steel: The Fates of Human Societies* (New York: W. W. Norton, 1997), 210.

5. FX Cable Television Channel, *Smallpox,* broadcast originally in January 2005.

6. Jordan S. Kassalow, *Why Health Is Important to U.S. Foreign Policy* (New York: Council on Foreign Relations and Milbank Memorial Fund, 2001), 6.

7. Comment of Laurie Garrett at the Program on "Health and Security: Why It Should Top the Agenda," Council on Foreign Relations, December 13, 2004, transcript, 2, available at www.cfr.org.

8. National Intelligence Council, *The Global Infectious Disease Threat and Its Implications for the United States,* National Intelligence Estimate, NIE-99-17D (Washington, D.C.: January 2000), 14.

9. International Bank for Reconstruction and Development, *World Bank Atlas,* 35th ed. (Washington, D.C.: World Bank, 2003), 24.

10. Council on Foreign Relations and Milbank Memorial Fund, *Addressing the HIV/AIDS Pandemic: A U.S. Global AIDS Strategy for the Long Term* (New York: Milbank Memorial Fund, 2004), 13.

11. Roll Back Malaria Campaign, World Health Organization, available at www.rbm.who .int.

12. Jeffrey Sachs, quoted by Maggie Farley, "Ending Extreme Poverty Is Realistic, Economist Tells U.N.," *Los Angeles Times,* January 18, 2005, A3.

13. Laurie Garrett, *The Coming Plague: Newly Emerging Diseases in a World Out of Balance* (New York: Penguin Books, 1995), 104.

14. P. E. Olson et al., "The Thucydides Syndrome: Ebola Déjà Vu (or Ebola Reemergent?)" *Emerging Infectious Diseases* 2 (April–June 1996): 155–56.

15. Garrett, *The Coming Plague*, 53–55.

16. Laurie Garrett, "The Next Pandemic?" *Foreign Affairs* 84 (July/August 2005): 12.

17. Stefan Lovgren, "Is Asian Bird Flu the Next Pandemic?" *National Geographic News*, December 7, 2004, available at news.nationalgeographic.com; also see "Bird Flu May Have Spread from Person to Person, Study Says," Bloomberg, January 24, 2005, available at www.bloomberg.com/apps/news/.

18. Laurie Garrett, "The Return of Infectious Disease," *Foreign Affairs* 75, no. 1 (January/February 1996): 66.

19. Nicolo Barquet and Pere Domingo, "Smallpox: The Triumph over the Most Terrible of the Ministers of Death," *Annals of Internal Medicine,* October 15, 1997, 636–38, quoted by Robert O. Keohane and Joseph S. Nye, Jr., "Introduction," in *Governance in a Globalizing World,* ed. Joseph S. Nye, Jr., and John D. Donahue (Washington, D.C.: Brookings Institution Press, 2000), 3.

20. Joshua Lederberg, quoted by Michael S. Gottlieb, "The Future of an Epidemic," *New York Times,* June 5, 2001, 23.

21. *World Bank Atlas*, 24.

22. Holly Burkhalter, "The Politics of AIDS," *Foreign Affairs* 83, no. 1 (January/February 2004): 8.

23. David Gordon, Briefing at the United States Institute of Peace, Washington, D.C., May 8, 2001, quoted by International Crisis Group, *HIV/AIDS as a Security Issue,* ICG Report (Washington, D.C., and Brussels: 19 June 2001), 1.

24. *World Bank Atlas,* 24.

25. U.S. National Intelligence Council, *Mapping the Global Future,* Report of the 2020 Project (Washington, D.C.: Government Printing Office, December 2004), 37.

26. Council on Foreign Relations and Milbank Memorial Fund, *Addressing the HIV/AIDS Pandemic,* 5.

27. *World Bank Atlas,* 26.

28. See, for example, the recruitment announcement in the *Journal of the American Medical Association (JAMA)* 292, no. 23 (December 15, 2004): 2930.

29. President George W. Bush, Address to the United Nations General Assembly, September 21, 2004, available at www.whitehouse.gov.

30. Council on Foreign Relations and Milbank Memorial Fund, *Addressing the HIV/AIDS Pandemic,* 22.

31. James Wolfensohn, "Impact of AIDS on Peace and Security in Africa," speech delivered to the UN Security Council Special Session, January 10, 2000, available at www.un.org; quoted by P. W. Singer, "AIDS and International Security," *Survival* 44 (Spring 2002): 145.

32. Singer, "AIDS and International Security," 145–58.

33. UN Programme on HIV/AIDS, "AIDS and the Military," May 1998, available at www.unaids.org.

34. Singer, "AIDS and International Security," 154–55.

35. International Crisis Group, *HIV/AIDS as a Security Issue.*

36. International Crisis Group, *HIV/AIDS as a Security Issue,* 4.

37. International Crisis Group, *HIV/AIDS as a Security Issue,* 9.

38. *World Bank Atlas,* 24.

39. World Bank estimate, quoted by International Crisis Group, *HIV/AIDS as a Security Issue*, 12.

40. British House of Commons, Select Committee on International Development, "HIV/AIDS: The Impact on Social and Economic Development," March 29, 2001; cited by International Crisis Group, *HIV/AIDS as a Security Issue*, 15.

41. George W. Bush, "President's Emergency Plan for AIDS Relief," available at www.whitehouse.gov.

42. President William Jefferson Clinton, State of the Union Address, January 2000; cited by Daniel Benjamin and Steven Simon, *The Age of Sacred Terror* (New York: Random House, 2002), 165.

43. Anthony Lake, *6 Nightmares: Real Threats in a Dangerous World and How America Can Meet Them* (Boston: Little, Brown, 2000).

44. Laurie Garrett, "The Nightmare of Bioterrorism," *Foreign Affairs* 80 (January/February 2001): 76; Joseph Cirincione, *Deadly Arsenals: Tracking Weapons of Mass Destruction* (Washington, D.C.: Carnegie Endowment for International Peace, 2002), 49.

45. Richard K. Betts, "The New Threat of Mass Destruction," *Foreign Affairs* 77 (January/February 1998): 36–37.

46. U.S. National Intelligence Council, *Mapping the Global Future*, 16.

47. Donald R. Hopkins, *The Greatest Killer: Smallpox in History* (Chicago: University of Chicago Press, 2002).

48. Sam Howe Verhovek, "Philanthropy Inc.," *Los Angeles Times*, January 27, 2005, A18.

49. World Health Organization, "Malaria and HIV/AIDS Interactions and Implications: Conclusions of a Technical Consultation," June 23–25, 2004.

50. Council on Foreign Relations and Milbank Memorial Fund, *Addressing the HIV/AIDS Pandemic*, 11.

51. Council on Foreign Relations, "Focus on Women Policy Symposium," November 30, 2004, transcript available at www.cfr.org.

52. *World Bank Atlas*, 26.

53. *World Bank Atlas*, 18.

54. U.S. National Intelligence Council, *Mapping the Global Future*, 39.

55. Walter Gibbs, "Nobel Peace Laureate Seeks to Explain Remarks about AIDS," *New York Times*, December 10, 2004, 21.

56. Christine Soares, "Polio Postponed," *Scientific American* (January 2005): 18.

57. Garrett, "The Nightmare of Bioterrorism," 78.

58. U.S. National Intelligence Council, *Mapping the Global Future*, 30.

CHAPTER 7: CYBER-THREATS

1. Government of Canada, Office of Critical Infrastructure Protection and Emergency Preparedness, "Al Qaeda Cyber Capability," Report TA01-001, December 20, 2001, available at falcon.jmu.edu/~ramseyil/baldwin.htm#C.

2. Available at nytimes.com/2002/11/01/international/asia/01STAN.html.

3. Dan Verton, "Exclusive: Bin Laden Associate Warns of Cyberattacks," *Computerworld*, November 18, 2002, available at www.computerworld.com/securitytopics/security/story/0,10801,76000,00.htm.

4. Francis Bacon, *Religious Meditations,* quoted in *The Oxford Dictionary of Quotations,* 3rd ed. (New York: Oxford University Press, 1980), 28.

5. Walter B. Wriston, *The Twilight of Sovereignty: How the Information Revolution Is Transforming Our World* (New York: Charles Scribner's Sons, 1992), xii.

6. Quoted by Roger C. Molander, Andrew S. Biddle, and Peter A. Wilson, *Strategic Information Warfare: A New Face of War* (Santa Monica, Calif.: RAND, 1996), xi.

7. Sun Tzu, *The Art of War* (New York: Delacorte, 1983), 77.

8. Example taken from John Arquilla, "The Strategic Implications of Information Dominance," *Strategic Review* 22 (Summer 1994): 25.

9. See John Arquilla and David Ronfeldt, "Cyberwar Is Coming!" *Comparative Strategy* 12 (Summer 1993): 141–65.

10. F. W. Winterbotham, *The Ultra Secret* (New York: Dell, 1994); Ronald W. Clark, *The Man Who Broke Purple* (London: Weidenfeld and Nicholson, 1977).

11. Alvin Toffler, *Powershift: Knowledge, Wealth, and Violence at the Edge of the 21st Century* (New York: Bantam Books, 1990), 270.

12. George P. Shultz, *Turmoil and Triumph: My Years as Secretary of State* (New York: Charles Scribner's Sons, 1993), 44.

13. Quoted by Wriston, *The Twilight of Sovereignty,* 103.

14. U.S. National Intelligence Council, *Mapping the Global Future,* Report on the 2020 Project (Washington, D.C.: Government Printing Office, December 2004), 75.

15. U.S. General Accounting Office, *Information Security: Computer Attacks at Department of Defense Pose Increasing Risks,* GAO/AIMD-96-84 (Washington, D.C.: Government Printing Office, May 1996), 10.

16. Martin C. Libicki, "What Is Information Warfare?" *Strategic Forum,* no. 28 (Washington, D.C.: Institute for National Strategic Studies, National Defense University, May 1995).

17. George J. Tenet, "Global Realities of Our National Security," Statement before the Senate Foreign Relations Committee on the Worldwide Threat in 2000, March 21, 2000.

18. U.S. National Intelligence Council, *Mapping the Global Future,* 95.

19. For definitions of these techniques, see Dorothy E. Denning, *Information Warfare and Security* (Reading, Mass.: Addison-Wesley, 1999), 269.

20. Gabriel Weimann, "Cyberterrorism: How Real Is the Threat?" *Special Report* 119 (Washington, D.C.: U.S. Institute of Peace, May 2004), 2.

21. David Ronfeldt, John Arquilla, Graham E. Fuller, and Melissa Fuller, *The Zapatista Social Netwar in Mexico* (Santa Monica, Calif.: RAND, 1998).

22. For the latest figures, see www.cert.org.

23. See www.messagelabs.com.

24. Cassell Bryan-Low, "Growing Number of Hackers Attack Web Sites for Cash," *Wall Street Journal,* November 11, 2004, 1.

25. Quoted by Weimann, "Cyberterrorism," 2.

26. "Testimony of Federal Bureau of Investigation Director Louis Freeh," Senate Select Committee on Intelligence, May 10, 2001, available at fbi.gov/congress/congress01/freeh051001.htm.

27. Dan Verton, *Black Ice: The Invisible Threat of Cyberterrorism* (New York: McGraw-Hill Osborne Media, 2003).

28. *National Strategy to Secure Cyber Space,* February 2003, available at www.globalsecurity.org.

29. Council on Foreign Relations, available at www.terrorismanswers.com/groups/alqaeda3.html.

30. Dennis Lormel, "Testimony before the Senate Judiciary Subcommittee on Technology, Terrorism and Government Information," July 9, 2002, available at www.fbi.gov/congress.congress02/idtheft.htm.

31. David Bank, "Tighter Cyber Protection Is Urged by Computer-Security Industry," *Wall Street Journal,* December 7, 2002, A3.

32. John Arquilla, "Preparing for Cyberterrorism—Badly," *The New Republic,* May 1, 2000, 16.

33. Gina Kolata, "Veiled Messages of Terror May Lurk in Cyberspace," *New York Times,* October 30, 2001, F1.

34. Lt. Col. Gregory J. Rattray, USAF, *Strategic Warfare in Cyberspace* (Cambridge, Mass.: MIT Press, 2001), 8.

CHAPTER 8: DRUGS AND THUGS

1. See "Deadly Waves Explained," *The Boston Globe,* December 28, 2004, A15.

2. Tim Johnson, "Aftermath of a Disaster: Tsunami Death Toll Escalates in Indonesia," *Houston Chronicle,* January 13, 2005, A12.

3. "Now Comes the Hard Part," *South China Morning Post,* January 15, 2005, 17.

4. Doctors Without Borders, "Make a Donation," available at www.doctorswithout borders-usa.org/donate/.

5. David Pallister, "Tsunami Disaster: Urgent Donations on Target, UN Says," *Guardian* (London), January 12, 2005, 15.

6. Thomas L. Friedman, *The Lexus and the Olive Tree* (New York: Farrar, Straus and Giroux, 1999), 39–58.

7. Terry Terriff, Stuart Croft, Lucy James, and Patrick M. Morgan, *Security Studies Today* (Cambridge: Polity, 1999), 150–51.

8. Roy Godson and Phil Williams, "Strengthening Cooperation against Transsovereign Crime: A New Security Imperative," in *Beyond Sovereignty: Issues for a Global Agenda,* ed. Maryann K. Cusimano (New York: Bedford/St. Martin's, 2000), 111.

9. Amy O'Neill Richard, *International Trafficking in Women to the United States: A Contemporary Manifestation of Slavery and Organized Crime,* An Intelligence Monograph (Washington, D.C.: Center for the Study of Intelligence, Central Intelligence Agency, November 1999).

10. *Trafficking in Persons Report 2004* (Washington, D.C.: U.S. Department of State, June 2004), 6. The United Nations has put the number at four million persons trafficked each year. See Amnesty International, *Broken Bodies, Shattered Minds: Torture and Ill-Treatment of Women* (London: Amnesty International Publications, 2001), 16.

11. David Masci, "Human Trafficking and Slavery," *CQ Researcher* 14 (March 26, 2004): 275.

12. *Trafficking in Persons Report 2004,* 15.

13. Masci, "Human Trafficking and Slavery," 275.

14. *Trafficking in Persons Report 2004,* 14. Here, as elsewhere, the U.S. State Department's estimate is lower than that provided by some NGOs and UN agencies, which use twelve billion dollars as an estimate. See Masci, "Human Trafficking and Slavery," 275.

15. Masci, "Human Trafficking and Slavery," 277.

16. *Country Reports on Human Rights Practices, 2003* (Washington, D.C.: U.S. Department of State, February 25, 2004), India, available at www.state.gov/g/drl/rls/hrrpt/2003/27947.htm.

17. See Jane Perlez and Evelyn Rusli, "Uncounted Costs: Legions of Orphans and Broken Hearts," *New York Times,* January 7, 2005, A3; John Carvel, "Agencies Warn on Adopting Orphans," *Guardian* (London), January 7, 2005, 6.

18. "Trafficking in Women and Children: A Market Perspective," in *Illegal Immigration and Commercial Sex: The New Slave Trade,* ed. Phil Williams (Portland, Ore.: Frank Cass, 1999), 146.

19. Fred Halliday, *The World at 2000* (New York: Palgrave Macmillan, 2001), 104–105.

20. Office of National Drug Control Policy, "Drug Facts: Marijuana," January 12, 2005, available at www.whitehousedrugpolicy.gov/drugfact/marijuana/index.html.

21. See Steve Coll, *Ghost Wars: The Secret History of the CIA, Afghanistan, and Bin Laden, from the Soviet Invasion to September 10, 2001* (New York: Penguin, 2004), 485.

22. Office of National Drug Control Policy, "Fact Sheet: Drug Data Summary," March 2003, available at www.whitehousedrugpolicy.gov/publications/factsht/drugdata/index.html.

23. "Crisis Facing Colombians Is Called Worst in Hemisphere," *New York Times,* May 11, 2004, A8.

24. United Nations Office on Drugs and Crime, *Afghanistan Opium Survey, 2004,* November 2004, available at www.unodc.org/pdf/afg/afghanistan_opium_survey_2004.pdf.

25. Stockholm International Peace Research Institute, "Government and Industry Data on National Arms Exports," available at www.sipri.org/contents/armstrad/at_gov_ind_data.html.

26. Richard F. Grimmett, "Conventional Arms Transfers to Developing Nations, 1994–2001," Congressional Research Service, August 6, 2002, CRS-3.

27. *Small Arms Survey 2002: Counting the Human Cost* (New York: Oxford University Press, 2002), 156–57.

28. Grimmett, "Conventional Arms Transfers to Developing Nations, 1994–2001," CRS-3.

29. Coll, *Ghost Wars,* 337.

30. Coll, *Ghost Wars,* 337–40.

31. Douglas Jehl and David E. Sanger, "U.S. Expands List of Lost Missiles," *New York Times,* November 6, 2004, 1.

32. Greg Krikorian, "LAX Guards against Portable Missile Attacks," *Los Angeles Times,* December 14, 2004, B1.

33. See Edward J. Laurance, *Light Weapons and Intrastate Conflict: Early Warning Factors and Preventive Action,* A Report to the Carnegie Commission on Preventing Deadly Conflict, July 1998, 13–19; and Jeffrey Boutwell and Michael T. Klare, eds., *Light Weapons and Civil Conflict: Controlling the Tools of Violence* (Lanham, Md.: Rowman & Littlefield for the Carnegie Commission on Preventing Deadly Conflict, 1999), 1–5.

CHAPTER 9: THE STATE OF THE STATE

1. Steve Mufson, "U.S. Urged to Target Nations That Aid Terrorism; N.Y., Pentagon Attacks Are Called Acts of War," *Washington Post,* September 12, 2001, A12.

2. Richard A. Clarke, *Against All Enemies: Inside America's War on Terror* (New York: Free Press, 2004), 32. Later, according to Clarke (232), Wolfowitz argued that Osama bin Laden "could not do all these things like the 1993 attack on New York, not without a state sponsor." President Bush disputed the details but not the substance of Clarke's account of the conversation on September 12. See *Final Report of the National Commission on Terrorist Attacks upon the United States*, Authorized Edition [hereafter *9/11 Commission Report*] (New York: W. W. Norton, 2004), 334.

3. Secretary Colin L. Powell, "Remarks to the United Nations Security Council," New York City, February 5, 2003, available at www.state.gov/secretary/rm/2003/17300.htm.

4. Stephen M. Walt, "The Renaissance of Security Studies," *International Studies Quarterly* 35 (1991): 212.

5. A noteworthy exception to this rule is the Human Security Network, a loose affiliation of states organized by Canada and Norway in 1999 in order to focus attention on the security (defined as freedom from fear and freedom from want) of individuals. Of course, attention to human security supplements rather than displaces the normal focus on national security. See the website of the Human Security Network at www.humansecuritynetwork .org/.

6. Common Article 1 of the International Covenant on Civil and Political Rights and the International Covenant on Economic, Social, and Cultural Rights states that "all peoples have the right of self-determination."

7. In addition to the fifty-five autonomous states extant in 1900, there were seventy-five colonial dependencies and protectorates. Freedom House, *Democracy's Century: A Survey of Global Political Change in the 20th Century*, available at www.freedomhouse.org/reports/ century.pdf. There are more than 191 states in the world today, but exactly how many more depends on who does the counting. Recognizing (and therefore counting) states is a highly political matter that requires determining, for instance, whether the Republic of China (Taiwan) is autonomous, contrary to the claims of the People's Republic of China, or whether the Holy See is truly a state or a political/religious entity that is sui generis.

8. See R. J. Rummel, *Statistics of Democide: Genocide and Mass Murder since 1900* (New Brunswick, N.J.: Transaction, 1997); and *Death by Government* (New Brunswick, N.J.: Transaction, 1994).

9. See, for summary data, Union of International Associations, "Number of international organizations in this addition by type (2004/2005)," available at www.uia.org/statistics/ organizations/types-oldstyle_2003.pdf.

10. A. LeRoy Bennett and James K. Oliver, *International Organizations: Principles and Issues*, 7th ed. (Upper Saddle River, N.J.: Prentice Hall, 2002), 81–82.

11. See the data provided by the Stockholm International Peace Research Institute (SIPRI) at www.sipri.org (free registration required). According to SIPRI figures, U.S. military expenditures for 2004 accounted for 47 percent of the world total of $1,035,000,000,000 (current dollars).

12. *CIA World Factbook*, available at www.cia.gov/cia/publications/factbook, "Rank order— GDP—per capita," www.cia.gov/cia/publications/factbook/rankorder/2004rank.html.

13. *CIA World Factbook*, "Tuvalu."

14. Freedom House, *Democracy's Century*.

15. Freedom House, *Democracy's Century*.

16. Samuel P. Huntington, *The Third Wave: Democratization in the Late Twentieth Century* (Norman: University of Oklahoma Press, 1991), 15.

17. United Nations, *Human Development Report 1999* (New York: Oxford University Press, 1999), 238–41.

18. Andrew Reynolds, "Women in the Legislatures and Executives of the World: Knocking at the Highest Glass Ceiling," *World Politics* 51 (July 1999): 557, 561.

19. Robin Wright, "Mongolian Women Typify a New Global Activism," *Los Angeles Times,* February 22, 2000, A8.

20. Francis Fukuyama, "Women and the Evolution of World Politics," *Foreign Affairs* 77 (September/October 1998): 33–36.

21. Robert D. Kaplan, *An Empire Wilderness: Travels into America's Future* (New York: Random House, 1998), 3–20. Part I of this book is entitled "The Last Redoubt of the Nation-State."

22. Richard N. Rosecrance, *The Rise of the Virtual State: Wealth and Power in the Coming Century* (New York: Basic Books, 1999).

23. Barry Buzan, *People, States and Fear: An Agenda for International Security Studies in the Post–Cold War Era,* 2nd ed. (Boulder, Colo.: Lynne Rienner, 1991), 90–96.

24. See Inis L. Claude, Jr., "Myths about the State," in *States and the Global System: Politics, Law and Organization* (New York: St. Martin's, 1988), 13–27.

25. Mohammed Ayoob, "Defining Security: A Subaltern Realist Perspective," in *Critical Security Studies: Concepts and Cases,* ed. Keith Krause and Michael C. Williams (Minneapolis: University of Minnesota Press, 1997), 121.

26. Michael Howard, *The Lessons of History* (New Haven, Conn.: Yale University Press, 1991), 4.

27. Thomas Hobbes, *Leviathan,* ed. C. B. Macpherson (New York: Penguin Books, 1968), chap. 13.

28. UN High Commissioner for Refugees, "Basic Facts," available at www.unhcr.org/.

29. See Michael Mandelbaum, "Foreign Policy as Social Work," *Foreign Affairs* 75 (January/February 1996): 16–32.

30. Francis Fukuyama, *The End of History and the Last Man* (New York: Avon Books, 1993); Robert D. Kaplan, *The Coming Anarchy: Shattering the Dreams of the Post–Cold War* (New York: Vintage Books, 2000).

31. Kaplan, *The Coming Anarchy,* 7–8.

32. Robert I. Rotberg, "Failed States in a World of Terror," *Foreign Affairs* 81 (July/August 2002): 127–40.

33. Clarke, *Against All Enemies,* 84–89.

34. Barry Bearak, "Taliban Plead for Mercy to the Miserable in a Land of Nothing," *New York Times,* September 13, 2001, A18.

35. Quoted in Thomas L. Friedman, *The Lexus and the Olive Tree: Understanding Globalization,* rev. and exp. ed. (New York: Anchor Books, 2000), 403.

36. Thomas E. Ricks, "Shift from Traditional War Seen at Pentagon," *Washington Post,* September 3, 2004, A1.

37. *9/11 Commission Report,* 361–62.

CHAPTER 10: ETHNIC CONFLICT AND SECURITY

1. Charles King, *Ending Civil Wars,* Adelphi Paper 308 (London: International Institute for Strategic Studies, March 1997), 15.

2. The World Bank, *World Bank Atlas* (Washington, D.C.: World Bank, 2003), 46.

3. International Institute for Strategic Studies, *The 2004 Chart of Armed Conflict* (London: International Institute for Strategic Studies, 2004).

4. "Remarks by the Honorable Kofi Annan," Conference on Preventing Deadly Conflict among Nations in the 21st Century, University of California at Los Angeles, April 22, 1998.

5. *World Bank Atlas,* 46.

6. John M. Goshko, "Regional Conflicts Threaten 42 Million around World, U.S. Study Finds," *Washington Post,* April 5, 1996, 13–14.

7. Michael E. Brown, ed., *The International Dimensions of Internal Conflict* (Cambridge, Mass.: MIT Press, 1996), 575.

8. Jack Snyder, "Nationalism and the Crisis of the Post-Soviet State," *Survival* 35, no. 1 (Spring 1993): 5.

9. Snyder, "Nationalism and the Crisis of the Post-Soviet State," 5.

10. David A. Lake and Donald Rothchild, *Ethnic Fears and Global Engagement: The International Spread and Management of Ethnic Conflict,* Policy Paper 20 (San Diego: Institute on Global Conflict and Cooperation, University of California, January 1996), 8.

11. Seyom Brown, *New Forces, Old Forces and the Future of World Politics,* Post–Cold War Edition (New York: HarperCollins, 1995), 162.

12. Ted Robert Gurr, *Minorities at Risk: A Global View of Ethnopolitical Conflict* (Washington, D.C.: U.S. Institute of Peace Press, 1993).

13. David Welsh, "Domestic Politics and Ethnic Conflict," *Survival* 35, no. 1 (Spring 1993): 65.

14. Carnegie Commission on Preventing Deadly Conflict, *Preventing Deadly Conflict: Final Report* (Washington, D.C.: Carnegie Corporation of New York, 1997), 151.

15. UN Department of Public Information, "General Assembly Adopts $3.2 Billion 2005–2006 Peacekeeping Budget," Press Release GA/10356, June 22, 2005, available at www.un.org/News/Press/docs/2005/ga10356.doc.htm.

16. Kenneth Allard, *Somalia Operations: Lessons Learned* (Washington, D.C.: National Defense University Press, 1995), 15.

17. *Yugoslavia: Death of a Nation,* Part I: "The Cracks Appear," Discovery Channel, video. This excellent series contains video footage of Milosevic's visit to Kosovo, a chilling video record of conflict in the making.

18. Cathal J. Nolan, *The Longman Guide to World Affairs* (White Plains, N.Y.: Longman, 1995), 110.

19. Stephen Engelberg and Tim Weiner, "Srebrenica: The Days of Slaughter," *New York Times,* October 29, 1995, 1.

20. U.S. Central Intelligence Agency, *World Factbook 1994,* CD-ROM version (Grand Rapids, Mich.: Wayzata Technology, 1994), "Rwanda."

21. UN Security Council, *Second Progress Report of the Secretary-General of the United Nations Assistance Mission for Rwanda,* S/1994/360 (New York: March 30, 1994), para. 27.

22. J. Matthew Vaccaro, "The Politics of Genocide: Peacekeeping and Disaster Relief in Rwanda," in *U.N. Peacekeeping, American Politics, and the Uncivil Wars of the 1990s,* ed. William J. Durch (New York: St. Martin's, 1996), 367.

23. Carnegie Commission, *Preventing Deadly Conflict,* 3.

24. Scott R. Feil, *Preventing Genocide: How the Early Use of Force Might Have Succeeded in Rwanda* (Washington, D.C.: Carnegie Commission on Preventing Deadly Conflict, April 1998), 5.

25. Romeo A. Dallaire, *Shake Hands with the Devil: The Failure of Humanity in Rwanda* (New York: Carroll and Graf, 2004).

26. Andrew Kohut and Robert C. Toth, "Arms and the People," *Foreign Affairs* 73, no. 6 (November/December 1994): 47–61.

27. Chester A. Crocker, "The Lessons of Somalia," *Foreign Affairs* 74, no. 3 (May/June 1995): 7.

28. Richard Holbrooke, *To End a War* (New York: Modern Library, 1998).

29. U.S. Department of State, "Background Note: Sudan," available at www.state.gov/r/pa/co/bgn/5424.htm.

30. Scott Anderson, "How Did Darfur Happen?" *New York Times Magazine,* October 17, 2004, 56.

31. U.S. Department of State, Bureau of Democracy, Human Rights and Labor, "Sudan: International Religious Freedom Report 2004," available at www.state.gov/g/drl/rls/irf/2004/35384.htm.

32. Anthony Lake and John Pendergast, "Stopping Sudan's Slow-Motion Genocide," *Boston Globe,* May 20, 2004, A19.

33. Quoted by Eric Reeves, "Darfur: Ongoing Genocide," *Dissent* (Fall 2004): 20.

34. See, for example, Kevin M. Cahill, ed., *Preventive Diplomacy: Stopping Wars before They Start* (New York: Center for International Health and Cooperation/Basic Books, 1995).

35. Carnegie Commission, *Preventing Deadly Conflict,* 35.

36. Carnegie Commission, *Preventing Deadly Conflict,* 37.

CHAPTER 11: THE ROOT OF ALL EVIL?

1. I Timothy 6:10.

2. Alvin Toffler, *Powershift: Knowledge, Wealth, and Violence at the Edge of the 21st Century* (New York: Bantam Books, 1990), 313.

3. *Final Report of the National Commission on Terrorist Attacks upon the United States,* Authorized Edition [hereafter *9/11 Commission Report*] (New York: W. W. Norton, 2004), 378.

4. *National Security Strategy of the United States* (Washington, D.C.: White House, September 2002), available at www.whitehouse.gov.

5. Jacob Viner and Albert O. Hirschman, *National Power and the Structure of International Trade* (Berkeley: University of California Press, 1980); Klaus Knorr, *Power and Wealth* (New York: Basic Books, 1973); Klaus Knorr and Frank Trager, eds., *Economic Issues and National Security* (Lawrence: University Press of Kansas, 1977).

6. Maggie Farley, "Development Curbed by AIDS, U.N. Says," *Los Angeles Times,* July 16, 2004, A3.

7. Jacob Viner, "Power versus Plenty as Objectives of Foreign Policy in the Seventeenth and Eighteenth Centuries," *World Politics* 1 (1948–49): 59.

8. Arthur Herman, *To Rule the Waves: How the British Navy Shaped the Modern World* (New York: HarperCollins, 2004).

9. Quoted by William Grimes, "The Rise of the British Empire from Its Navy's Point of View," *New York Times,* December 15, 2004, B11.

10. Richard N. Haass, *Economic Sanctions: Too Much of a Bad Thing,* Policy Brief 34 (Washington, D.C.: Brookings Institution, June 1998), available at www.brookings.edu/comm/policybriefs/pb34.htm.

11. Haass, *Economic Sanctions*.

12. Gary Clyde Hufbauer, Jeffrey J. Schott, and Kimberly Ann Elliott, *Economic Sanctions Reconsidered: History and Current Policy*, 2nd ed., 2 vols. (Washington, D.C.: Institute for International Economics, 1990).

13. James C. Ngobi, "The United Nations Experience with Sanctions," in *Economic Sanctions: Panacea or Peacebuilding in a Post–Cold War World?* ed. David Cortright and George A. Lopez (Boulder, Colo.: Westview, 1995), 17–18.

14. Meghan L. O'Sullivan, *Shrewd Sanctions: Statecraft and State Sponsors of Terrorism* (Washington, D.C.: Brookings Institution, 2003), 35–44.

15. Robert A. Pape, "Why Economic Sanctions Do Not Work," *International Security* 22, no. 2 (Fall 1997): 90–136.

16. *National Security Strategy of the Unites States*, 2002.

17. John J. Hamre and Gordon R. Sullivan, "Toward Postconflict Reconstruction," *Washington Quarterly* 25, no. 4 (Autumn 2002), 85.

18. O'Sullivan, *Shrewd Sanctions*, 3.

19. Sir Michael Howard, "'9/11' and After: A British View," *Naval War College Review* 55, no. 4 (Autumn 2002), 18.

20. "UN Envoy Considering Taliban Meeting," CNN.com, October 30, 2001.

21. Lisa D. Cook, "The Next Battleground in the Terror War," *Hoover Digest*, no. 1 (2004): 71.

22. *9/11 Commission Report*, 367.

23. Joseph S. Nye, Jr., "Terrorism," in *Power in the Global Information Age* (New York: Routledge, 2004), 212.

24. See John T. Rourke and Mark A. Boyer, *International Politics on the World Stage*, 5th ed. (Boston: McGraw-Hill, 2004), 339, fig. 12.2, "Economic Aid as a Percentage of Donor GNP, 2002."

25. Nye, "Terrorism," 213.

26. Susan Strange, "What Is Economic Power and Who Has It?" *International Journal* 30, no. 2 (Spring 1975): 218.

27. Charles P. Kindleberger, *The World in Depression* (Berkeley: University of California Press, 1973).

28. Stephen Flynn, *America the Vulnerable: How Our Government Is Failing to Protect Us from Terrorism* (New York: HarperCollins, 2004).

CHAPTER 12: ECOLOGICAL DISASTERS AND RESOURCE WARS

1. Robert D. Kaplan, *The Coming Anarchy: Shattering the Dreams of the Post–Cold War* (New York: Random House, 2000), 19–20. The essay, entitled "The Coming Anarchy," first appeared in *The Atlantic Monthly*, February 1994, 44–76.

2. Matilda Lee, "State of the Planet," *Ecologist* 32, no. 7 (September 2002): 6.

3. Edward O. Wilson, *The Diversity of Life* (New York: W. W. Norton, 1999), 215–80.

4. Rainforest Action Network, "Species Extinction," available at www.ran.org/info_center/factsheets/03b.html.

5. George M. Woodwell, "Fiddling While the World Burns," Woods Hole Research Center, available at www.whrc.org/resources/online_publications/essays/2001-FiddlingAmicus.html.

6. Arctic Climate Impact Assessment, *Impacts of a Warming Arctic* (Cambridge: Cambridge University Press, 2004), 2.

7. United Nations Environment Programme, "Land Degradation: Africa," africa.unep .net/land-Degradation/content2.asp.

8. Donald Smith, "When Green Earth Turns into Sand," *National Geographic News,* December 19, 2000, available at news.nationalgeographic.com/news/2000/12/1219_tanzania .html.

9. Jacqueline Vaughn Switzer, with Bary Bryner, *Environmental Politics: Domestic and Global Dimensions,* 2nd ed. (New York: St. Martin's, 1998), 12.

10. Eric Nagourney, "A Turning Point in Smog History," *International Herald Tribune,* August 14, 2003, 9. See also Peter Brimblecombe, *The Big Smoke: A History of Air Pollution in London since Medieval Times* (London: Methuen, 1987).

11. Among the early arguments for the view that environmental issues raise significant national security concerns, see Lester R. Brown, *Redefining National Security,* Worldwatch Paper 14, October 1977 (Washington, D.C.: Worldwatch Institute, 1977); Jessica Tuchman Mathews, "Redefining Security," *Foreign Affairs* 68 (Spring 1989): 162–77; and Thomas F. Homer-Dixon, "On the Threshold: Environmental Changes as Causes of Acute Conflict," *International Security* 16 (Fall 1991): 76–116.

12. Peter H. Gleick, "Water, War and Peace in the Middle East," *Environment* 36 (April 1994): 11. The biblical account is found in Exodus 14.

13. Gleick, "Water, War and Peace in the Middle East," 11.

14. Roger D. Masters, *Fortune Is a River: Leonardo Da Vinci and Niccolo Machiavelli's Magnificent Dream to Change the Course of Florentine History* (New York: Diane, 1998).

15. John Childs, "A Short History of the Military Use of Land in Peacetime," *War in History* 4 (1997): 87.

16. Robert M. Gum and Maurice H. Weeks, "Smoke and Obscurants," *Military Review* 76 (September/October 1996): 84–90.

17. Matthew L. Wald, "Amid Ceremony and Ingenuity, Kuwait's Oil Well Fires Are Declared Out," *New York Times,* November 7, 1991, A3; Frederick Warner, "The Environmental Consequences of the Gulf War," *Environment* 33 (June 1991): 6–9, 25–26.

18. Ian Fisher, "In Congo War's Wake, a Massacre of Wildlife," *New York Times,* July 28, 1999, A10.

19. "Air Force Resumes Use of Depleted Uranium," *Boston Globe,* April 6, 2002, A2.

20. Jonathan Schell, *The Fate of the Earth* (New York: Alfred A. Knopf, 1982).

21. See Carl Sagan, "Nuclear War and Climatic Catastrophe: Some Policy Implications," *Foreign Affairs* 62 (Winter 1983/84): 257–92; Starley L. Thompson and Stephen H. Schneider, "Nuclear Winter Reappraised," *Foreign Affairs* 64 (Summer 1986): 981–1005.

22. Jennifer Nyman, "The Dirtiness of the Cold War: Russia's Nuclear Waste in the Arctic," *Environmental Policy and Law* 32 (2002): 47–52.

23. Sophia Kishkovsky, "In 15 Hours, Submarine *Kursk* Is Raised from Sea Floor," *New York Times,* October 9, 2001, A7.

24. Anahad O'Connor, "Adding Weight to Suspicion, Sonar Is Linked to Whale Deaths," *New York Times,* October 9, 2003, A23.

25. "Whaling Commission's Science Panel Says Marine Mammals Threatened by Man-Made Noise," Press Release, Natural Resources Defense Council, available at www.nrdc.org/ media/pressreleases/040720.asp.

26. Thomas F. Homer-Dixon, *Environment, Scarcity, and Violence* (Princeton, N.J.: Princeton University Press, 1999), 12.

27. Peter H. Gleick, "Water and Conflict: Fresh Water Resources and International Security," *International Security* 18 (Summer 1993): 79–112.

28. Bill McKibben, "A Special Moment in History," *Atlantic Monthly* 281 (May 2001): 56–57.

29. Daniel Yergin tells this story well, and in considerable detail, in *The Prize: The Epic Quest for Oil, Money and Power* (New York: Simon and Schuster, 1992), 305–27.

30. Michael T. Klare, *Blood and Oil: The Dangers and Consequences of America's Growing Dependency on Imported Petroleum* (New York: Metropolitan Books, 2004), 7.

31. "Top World Oil Net Exporters, 2003," Energy Information Administration, Department of Energy [hereafter EIA], available at www.eia.doe.gov/emeu/cabs/topworldtables1_2 .html.

32. "Freedom in the World, 2005: Civic Power and Electoral Politics," Freedom House, available at www.freedomhouse.org/research/survey2005.html.

33. "Country Analysis Briefs: Caspian Sea Region," EIA, December 2004, available at www.eia.doe.gov/emeu/cabs/caspian.html.

34. "Country Analysis Briefs: World Oil Transit Chokepoints," EIA, April 2004, available at www.eia.doe.gov/emeu/cabs/choke.html.

35. U.S. Department of Energy, *Annual Energy Outlook 2005* (Washington, D.C.: Energy Information Administration, 2005), table 16, 41.

36. Klare, *Blood and Oil,* 17.

37. *Annual Energy Outlook 2005,* table 34, 115.

38. "Petroleum Products Consumption," EIA, March 2003, available at www.eia.doe .gov/neic/infosheets/petroleumproductsconsumption.html.

39. *Mapping the Global Future: Report of the National Intelligence Council's 2020 Project* (Washington, D.C.: National Intelligence Council, December 2004), 62.

40. Jeremy Rifkin, *The Hydrogen Economy* (New York: Jeremy P. Tarcher/Putnam, 2002), 22.

41. David Goodstein, *Out of Gas: The End of the Age of Oil* (New York: W. W. Norton, 2004), 17.

42. See James A. Baker III, with Thomas M. DeFrank, *The Politics of Diplomacy: Revolution, War and Peace, 1989–1992* (New York: G. P. Putnam's Sons, 1995), 336–37.

43. Jimmy Carter, "State of the Union Address 1980," January 23, 1980, Jimmy Carter Library and Museum, available at www.jimmycarterlibrary.org/documents/speeches/ su80jec.phtml.

44. Klare, *Blood and Oil,* 46–47.

45. "U.S. Policy toward the Iran-Iraq War," National Security Decision Directive 114, November 26, 1983, available via the National Security Archive, George Washington University, www2.gwu.edu/~nsarchiv/NSAEBB/NSAEBB82/iraq26.pdf.

46. *Final Report of the National Commission on Terrorist Attacks upon the United States,* Authorized Edition [hereafter *9/11 Commission Report*] (New York: W. W. Norton, 2004), 55–56.

47. The White House, *A National Security Strategy for a New Century* (Washington, D.C.: December 1999), 42.

48. McKibben, "A Special Moment in History," 64.

49. Dennis Clark Pirages and Theresa Manley DeGeest, *Ecological Security: An Evolutionary Perspective on Globalization* (Lanham, Md.: Rowman & Littlefield, 2004), 70.

50. U.S. Environmental Protection Agency, "Global Warming: Climate," available at yosemite.epa.gov/oar/globalwarming.nsf/content/climate.html.

51. Timothy E. Wirth, C. Boyden Gray, and John D. Podesta, "The Future of Energy Policy," *Foreign Affairs* 82 (July/August 2003): 138–39.

52. This discussion of uncertainty in climate prediction is drawn from David G. Victor, *Climate Change: Debating America's Policy Options* (New York: Council on Foreign Relations, 2004), 12–16.

53. The "Yoda" comment was made by Pentagon spokesman Lt. Cdr. Dan Hetladge, quoted in Keay Davidson, "Pentagon-Sponsored Climate Report Sparks Hullabaloo in Europe," *San Francisco Chronicle,* February 25, 2004, A2. Marshall's work at RAND on counterforce targeting is discussed in Gregg Herken, *Counsels of War* (New York: Alfred A. Knopf, 1985), 79–81. For the origins of OSD/NA and Marshall's role in it, see Khurram Husain, "Neocons: The Men behind the Curtain," *Bulletin of the Atomic Scientists* 59 (November/December 2003): 68–70.

54. Peter Schwartz and Doug Randall, *An Abrupt Climate Change Scenario and Its Implications for United States National Security* (Washington, D.C.: Department of Defense, Office of Net Assessment, October 2003).

55. Schwartz and Randall, *An Abrupt Climate Change Scenario,* 14.

56. *Mapping the Global Future,* 76.

57. Klare, *Blood and Oil,* 180–202.

58. Rifkin, *The Hydrogen Economy,* 125.

59. Schwartz and Randall, *An Abrupt Climate Change Scenario,* 19.

CHAPTER 13: LIVING IN THE SHADOW OF THE WORLD TRADE CENTER

1. Quoted by Fred Kaplan, *Wizards of Armageddon* (New York: Simon and Schuster, 1983), 9–10.

2. Quoted by Bob Woodward, *Plan of Attack* (New York: Simon and Schuster, 2004), 24.

3. Former head of the Soviet navy, Admiral Sergei Gorshkov was focused—some would say obsessed—by the Japanese attack; he mentioned it in almost every one of his public speeches and articles.

4. Ian Lesser et al., *Countering the New Terrorism* (Santa Monica, Calif.: RAND, 1999).

5. Brian Jenkins quoted by Jonathan R. White, *Terrorism: An Introduction* (Pacific Grove, Calif.: Brooks/Cole, 1991), 5.

6. Walter Laqueur, *The Age of Terrorism* (Boston: Little, Brown, 1987), 72.

7. Jessica Stern, *The Ultimate Terrorists* (Cambridge, Mass.: Harvard University Press, 2000), 11.

8. United States Code, Title 22, Section 2656f(d).

9. Bruce Hoffman, "The American Perspective," *Survival* 42, no. 2 (Summer 2000): 166.

10. Richard A. Falkenrath, "Confronting Nuclear, Biological and Chemical Terrorism," *Survival* 40, no. 3 (Autumn 1998): 52.

11. Bruce Hoffman in Lesser et al., *Countering the New Terrorism,* 11.

12. See "The Killing Fields," *Economist,* September 15, 2001, 18.

13. *Los Angeles Times,* September 15, 2001, A16.

14. Warren Christopher, *Chances of a Lifetime* (New York: Charles Scribner's Sons, 2001), 230.

15. There are many analyses of deterrence; two of the best are Patrick M. Morgan, *Deterrence Now* (Cambridge: Cambridge University Press, 2003) and Alexander L. George and Richard Smoke, *Deterrence in American Foreign Policy: Theory and Practice* (New York: Columbia University Press, 1974).

16. John Lewis Gaddis, "The Long Peace: Elements of Stability in the Postwar International System," *International Security* 10 (Spring 1986): 99–142.

17. James A. Baker III, with Thomas M. DeFrank, *The Politics of Diplomacy: Revolution, War and Peace, 1989–1992* (New York: G. P. Putnam's Sons, 1995), 359.

18. John D. Steinbruner, *Principles of Global Security* (Washington, D.C.: Brookings Institution, 2000), 35.

19. Steinbruner, *Principles of Global Security,* 36.

20. *National Security Strategy of the United States* (Washington, D.C.: White House, September 2002), available at www.whitehouse.gov.

21. *The National Security Strategy of the United States,* 2002.

22. Peter Navarro and Aron Spencer, "September 11, 2001: Assessing the Costs of Terrorism," *Milken Institute Review* (Fourth Quarter 2001): 16–31.

23. Steve Kosiak's estimates are quoted by Gregg Easterbrook, "In an Age of Terror, Safety Is Relative," *New York Times,* June 27, 2004, sec. 4, 1.

24. Charles Kupchan, "The Rise of Europe, America's Changing Internationalism, and the End of U.S. Primacy," in *American Hegemony,* ed. Demetrios James Caraley (New York: American Academy of Political Science, 2004), 123.

25. George W. Bush, "West Point Commencement Speech," in James F. Hoge, Jr., ed., *Foreign Affairs, America and the World: Debating the New Shape of International Politics* (New York: W. W. Norton, 2002), 364–71.

26. *The National Security Strategy of the United States,* 2002.

27. John Lewis Gaddis, *Surprise, Security, and the American Experience* (Cambridge, Mass.: Harvard University Press, 2004).

28. Robert Jervis, "Understanding the Bush Doctrine," in *American Hegemony,* ed. Caraley, 3.

29. Michael Walzer, *Arguing about War* (New Haven, Conn.: Yale University Press, 2004), 146.

30. Larry Diamond, *Squandered Victory: The American Occupation and the Bungled Effort to Bring Democracy to Iraq* (New York: Times Books, 2005); David L. Phillips, *Losing Iraq: Inside the Postwar Reconstruction Fiasco* (Boulder, Colo.: Westview, 2005).

31. The report is available on the Department of State website, available at www.state.gov.

32. The originally released version of the report indicated that terrorism was at a twenty-year low, but this conclusion was based on erroneous calculations and statistics that were later corrected; see Steven R. Weisman, "State Department Report Shows Increase in Terrorism," *New York Times,* June 23, 2004, A12.

33. Jared Diamond, *Guns, Germs, and Steel: The Fates of Human Societies* (New York: W. W. Norton, 1997).

34. Joel Kotkin and Fred Siegel, "Attacks Threaten Future of Cities," *Los Angeles Times,* October 14, 2001, M6.

35. For the principal works that outline the major elements of the cooperative security approach, see Ashton B. Carter, William J. Perry, and John D. Steinbruner, *A New Concept of*

Cooperative Security, Brookings Occasional Paper (Washington, D.C.: Brookings Institution, 1992); Janne Nolan, ed., *Global Engagement: Cooperation and Security in the 21st Century* (Washington, D.C.: Brookings Institution, 1994); Ashton B. Carter and William J. Perry, *Preventive Defense: A New Security Strategy for America* (Washington, D.C.: Brookings Institution, 1999); and John D. Steinbruner, *Principles of Global Security* (Washington, D.C.: Brookings Institution, 2000).

36. Carter, Perry, and Steinbruner, *A New Concept of Cooperative Security,* 6.

37. Several of these elements are described by Nolan, *Global Engagement,* 10, 574.

38. Carter and Perry place great emphasis on this, describing the Clinton administration's efforts to denuclearize the former USSR in *Preventive Defense;* see also Graham Allison, *Nuclear Terrorism: The Ultimate Preventable Catastrophe* (New York: Times Books, 2004). Dan Caldwell first proposed this in "Permissive Action Links: A Description and Proposal," *Survival* (May/June 1987), 224–36.

39. Walzer, *Arguing about War,* 9.

40. Steinbruner, *Principles of Global Security,* 227.

41. Steinbruner, *Principles of Global Security,* 22.

CHAPTER 14: SEEKING SECURITY IN AN INSECURE WORLD

1. Max Singer and Aaron Wildavsky, *The Real World Order: Zones of Peace, Zones of Turmoil* (Chatham, N.J.: Chatham House, 1993).

2. Charles Krauthammer, "The Unipolar Moment," *Foreign Affairs* 70 (America and the World 1990/91): 23–33.

3. Kenneth N. Waltz, *Theory of International Politics* (Reading, Mass.: Addison-Wesley, 1979), 112.

4. *Final Report of the National Commission on Terrorist Attacks upon the United States,* Authorized Edition [hereafter *9/11 Commission Report*] (New York: W. W. Norton, 2004), 361.

5. President William J. Clinton, "Remarks by the President at the U.S. Coast Guard Academy's 119th Commencement," U.S. Coast Guard Academy, New London, Connecticut, May 17, 2000, available at www.clintonfoundation.org/legacy/051700-speech-by-president-at-us-coast-guard-academy.htm.

6. John Muir, *My First Summer in the Sierra* (Boston: Houghton Mifflin, 1911), 110.

7. James D. Wolfensohn, "Fight Terrorism by Ending Poverty," *New Perspectives Quarterly* 19 (Spring 2002): 42.

8. *National Security Strategy of the United States of America* (Washington, D.C.: White House, September 2002), v.

9. For a provocative discussion of the problem that popularized the use of the term "blowback," see Chalmers Johnson, *Blowback: The Costs and Consequences of American Empire* (New York: Metropolitan Books, 2000).

10. Richard Norton-Taylor, "Thinktank: Invasion Aided al-Qaida," *Guardian* (London), October 20, 2004, available at www.guardian.co.uk/Iraq/Story/0,2763,1331362,00.html.

11. Douglas Frantz et al., "The New Face of Al Qaeda," *Los Angeles Times,* September 26, 2004, A1.

12. *The World Factbook 2004* (Washington, D.C.: Central Intelligence Agency, 2004), available at www.cia.gov/cia/publications/factbook/.

13. Princeton N. Lyman and J. Stephen Morrison, "The Terrorist Threat in Africa," *Foreign Affairs* 83 (January/February 2004): 83.

14. Council on Foreign Relations and Milbank Memorial Fund, *Addressing the HIV/AIDS Pandemic: A U.S. Global AIDS Strategy for the Long Term* (New York: Milbank Memorial Fund, 2004), 5.

15. U.S. National Intelligence Council, *Mapping the Global Future*, Report of the 2020 Project (Washington, D.C.: Government Printing Office, December 2004), 9.

16. UN Department of Public Information, "Secretary-General Salutes International Workshop on Human Security in Mongolia," Press Release SG/SM/7382, May 8, 2000, available at www.un.org/News/Press/docs/2000/20000508.sgsm7382.doc.html.

17. Ken Booth, *Strategy and Ethnocentrism* (New York: Holmes and Meier, 1979).

18. Joseph S. Nye, Jr., and Sean M. Lynn-Jones, "International Security Studies: A Report of a Conference on the State of the Field," *International Security* 12 (Spring 1988): 10–11.

19. For a useful overview of feminist perspectives on security, see J. Ann Tickner, *Gendering World Politics: Issues and Approaches in the Post–Cold War Era* (New York: Columbia University Press, 2001), 36–64.

20. Although her concern relates more to the nature of the state and to issues of jurisprudence, this is essentially the point made by Catharine A. MacKinnon in *Toward a Feminist Theory of the State* (Cambridge, Mass.: Harvard University Press, 1989).

21. Mohammed Ayoob, "Defining Security: A Subaltern Realist Perspective," in *Critical Security Studies: Concepts and Cases,* ed. Keith Krause and Michael C. Williams (Minneapolis: University of Minnesota Press, 1997), 121.

Selected Bibliography

Allison, Graham. *Nuclear Terrorism: The Ultimate Preventable Catastrophe.* New York: Times Books, 2004.

Arquilla, John, and David Ronfeldt, eds. *In Athena's Camp: Preparing for Conflict in the Information Age.* Santa Monica, Calif.: RAND, 1997.

Art, Robert J., and Kenneth N. Waltz, eds. *The Use of Force: Military Power and International Politics,* 5th ed. Lanham, Md.: Rowman & Littlefield, 1999.

Bacevich, Andrew J. *The New American Militarism: How Americans Are Seduced by War.* New York: Oxford University Press, 2005.

Baldwin, David. "The Concept of Security." *Review of International Studies* 23, no. 1 (January 1997): 5–26.

Beckman, Peter R., Paul W. Crumlish, Michael N. Dobkowski, and Steven P. Lee. *The Nuclear Predicament: Nuclear Weapons in the Twenty-first Century.* 3rd ed. Upper Saddle River, N.J.: Prentice Hall, 2000.

Benjamin, Daniel, and Steven Simon. *The Age of Sacred Terror.* New York: Random House, 2002.

Betts, Richard. "Should Strategic Studies Survive?" *World Politics* 50, no. 1 (October 1997): 7–33.

———. "The New Threat of Mass Destruction." *Foreign Affairs* 77, no. 1 (January/February 1998): 26–41.

Blacker, Coit D., and Gloria Duffy, eds. *International Arms Control: Issues and Agreements.* 2nd ed. Stanford, Calif.: Stanford University Press, 1984.

Booth, Ken. "Security and Emancipation." *Review of International Studies* 17 (1991): 313–26.

———. "Human Wrongs and International Relations." *International Affairs* 71 (January 1995): 103–26.

———. "Security and Self: Reflections of a Fallen Realist." In *Critical Security Studies: Concepts and Cases,* edited by Keith Krause and Michael C. Williams, 83–119. Minneapolis: University of Minnesota Press, 1997.

Booth, Ken, and Moorhead Wright. *American Thinking about War and Peace.* New York: Barnes and Noble, 1978.

Brodie, Bernard, ed. *The Absolute Weapon: Atomic Power and World Order.* New York: Harcourt, Brace, 1946.

———. *Strategy in the Missile Age.* Princeton, N.J.: Princeton University Press, 1959.

———. *War and Politics.* New York: Macmillan, 1973.

Brown, Michael E., ed. *Ethnic Conflict and International Security.* Princeton, N.J.: Princeton University Press, 1993.

————. *Grave New World: Security Challenges in the 21st Century.* Washington, D.C.: Georgetown University Press, 2003.

Brown, Michael E., and Richard N. Rosecrance, eds. *The Costs of Conflict: Prevention and Cure in the Global Arena.* Lanham, Md.: Rowman & Littlefield, 1999.

Brown, Seyom. *The Causes and Prevention of War.* New York: St. Martin's, 1987.

Bull, Hedley. *The Anarchical Society: A Study of Order in World Politics.* New York: Columbia University Press, 1977.

————. *The Control of the Arms Race.* 2nd ed. New York: Frederick A. Praeger, 1965.

Buzan, Barry, and Eric Herring. *The Arms Dynamic in World Politics.* Boulder, Colo.: Lynne Rienner, 1998.

Buzan, Barry, and Gerald Segal. "Rethinking East Asian Security." *Survival* 36, no. 2 (Summer 1994): 3–21.

Buzan, Barry, and Ole Waever. *Regions and Powers: The Structure of International Security.* Cambridge: Cambridge University Press, 2003.

Buzan, Barry, Ole Waever, and Jaap de Wilde. *Security: A New Framework for Analysis.* Boulder, Colo.: Lynne Rienner, 1998.

Caldwell, Dan. *American-Soviet Relations: From 1947 to the Nixon-Kissinger Grand Design.* Westport, Conn.: Greenwood, 1981.

————. *The Dynamics of Domestic Politics and Arms Control.* Columbia: University of South Carolina Press, 1991.

Cameron, Maxwell A., Robert J. Lawson, and Brian W. Tomlin, eds. *To Walk without Fear: The Global Movement to Ban Landmines.* New York: Oxford University Press, 1999.

Carnegie Commission on Preventing Deadly Conflict. *Preventing Deadly Conflict: Final Report.* Washington, D.C.: Carnegie Commission on Preventing Deadly Conflict, 1997.

Carnesale, Albert, and Richard N. Haass, eds. *Superpower Arms Control: Setting the Record Straight.* Cambridge, Mass.: Ballinger, 1987.

Carter, Ashton B., and William J. Perry. *Preventive Defense: A New Security Strategy for America.* Washington, D.C.: Brookings Institution, 1999.

Cerny, Philip G. "The New Security Dilemma: Divisibility, Defection and Disorder in the Global Era." *Review of International Studies* 26 (2000): 623–46.

Cha, Victor D. "Globalization and the Study of International Security." *Journal of Peace Research* 37, no. 3 (2000): 391–403.

Chipman, John. "The Future of Strategic Studies: Beyond Grand Strategy." *Survival* 34, no. 1 (Spring 1992): 109–31.

Clausewitz, Carl von. *On War.* Edited and translated by Michael Howard, Peter Paret, and Bernard Brodie. Princeton, N.J.: Princeton University Press, 1976.

Cohen, Eliot. "A Revolution in Warfare," *Foreign Affairs* 75, no. 2 (March/April 1996): 37–54.

Cote, Owen R., Jr., Sean Lynn-Jones, and Steven E. Miller, eds. *New Global Dangers: Changing Dimensions of International Security.* Cambridge, Mass.: MIT Press, 2004.

Croft, Stuart, and Terry Teriff, eds. *Critical Reflections on Security and change.* Portland, Ore.: Frank Cass, 2000.

Del Rosso, Steven J., Jr. "The Insecure State: Reflections on 'The State' and 'Security' in a Changing World." *Daedalus* 124, no. 2 (Spring 1995): 175–207.

Diamond, Jared. *Guns, Germs, and Steel: The Fates of Human Societies.* New York: W. W. Norton, 1997.

————. *Collapse: How Societies Choose to Fail or Succeed.* New York: Viking, 2005.

Drell, Sidney, and James E. Goodby. *The Gravest Danger: Nuclear Weapons*. Stanford, Calif.: Hoover Institution, 2003.

Dyson, Freeman. *Weapons and Hope*. New York: Harper and Row, 1984.

Eberstadt, Nicholas. "Population Change and National Security." *Foreign Affairs* 70, no. 3 (Summer 1991): 115–31.

Erickson, Johan. *Threat Politics: New Perspectives on Security, Risk and Crisis Management*. Burlington, Vt.: Ashgate, 2001.

Evans, Gareth. "Cooperative Security and Intrastate Conflict." *Foreign Policy* 96 (Fall 1994): 3–20.

Flynn, Stephen. *America the Vulnerable: How Our Government Is Failing to Protect Us from Terrorism*. New York: HarperCollins, 2004.

Freedman, Lawrence. *Evolution of Nuclear Strategy*. New York: Macmillan, 1989.

———. "International Security: Changing Targets." *Foreign Policy* 110 (Spring 1998): 48–64.

———. *The Revolution in Strategic Affairs*. Adelphi Paper 318. London: Oxford University Press for the International Institute for Strategic Studies, April 1998.

George, Alexander L., and William Simons. *The Limits of Coercive Diplomacy*. 2nd ed. Boulder, Colo.: Westview, 1994.

George, Alexander, and Richard Smoke. *Deterrence in American Foreign Policy: Theory and Practice*. New York: Columbia University Press, 1974.

Gray, Colin. "New Directions for Strategic Studies: How Can Theory Help Practice?" *Security Studies* 1, no. 4 (Summer 1992): 610–35.

———. *Villains, Victims and Sheriffs: Strategic Studies and Security for an Inter-War Period*. Hull: University of Hull Press, 1994.

Gurr, Ted Robert. "Peoples against States: Ethnopolitical Conflict and the Changing World System." *International Studies Quarterly* 38, no. 3 (September 1994): 347–78.

Gurr, Ted Robert, and Barbara Harff. *Ethnic Conflict in World Politics*. Boulder, Colo.: Westview, 1994.

Haftendorn, Helga. "The Security Puzzle: Theory-Building and Discipline Building in International Security." *International Studies Quarterly* 35, no. 1 (March 1991): 2–17.

Herz, John. "Idealist Internationalism and the Security Dilemma." *World Politics* 2, no. 2 (1950): 157–80.

———. *International Politics in the Atomic Age*. New York: Columbia University Press, 1959.

Jervis, Robert. *Perception and Misperception in International Politics*. Princeton, N.J.: Princeton University Press, 1976.

———. "Was the Cold War a Security Dilemma?" *Journal of Cold War History* 3 (Winter 2001): 36–60.

Job, Brian, ed. *The Insecurity Dilemma*. Boulder, Colo.: Lynne Rienner, 1992.

Katzenstein, Peter J. *The Culture of National Security: Norms and Identity in World Politics*. New York: Columbia University Press, 1996.

Keohane, Robert, and Joseph S. Nye, Jr. "States and the Information Revolution." *Foreign Affairs* 77, no. 5 (September/October 1998): 81–94.

Khalilzad, Zalmay M., and John P. White, eds. *The Changing Role of Information in Warfare*. Santa Monica, Calif.: RAND, 1999.

Klare, Michael. *Resource Wars: The New Landscape of Global Conflict*. New York: Henry Holt, 2001.

Knorr, Klaus. *The Power of Nations: The Political Economy of International Relations*. New York: Basic Books, 1975.

Knorr, Klaus, ed. *Historical Dimensions of National Security*. Lawrence: University Press of Kansas, 1976.

Knorr, Klaus, and Frank N. Trager, eds. *Economic Issues and National Security*. Lawrence: University Press of Kansas, 1976.

Kolodziej, Edward A. "What Is Security and Security Studies? Lessons from the Cold War." *Arms Control* 13, no. 1 (April 1992): 1–32.

———. "Renaissance in Security Studies? Caveat Lector!" *International Studies Quarterly* 36, no. 4 (December 1992): 421–38.

———. *Security and International Relations*. New York: Cambridge University Press, 2005.

Krause, Keith, and Michael Williams. "Broadening the Agenda of Security Studies." *Mershon International Studies Review* 40 (October 1996).

Krause, Keith, and Michael Williams, eds. *Critical Security Studies: Concepts and Cases*. Minneapolis: University of Minnesota Press, 1997.

Lake, Anthony. *6 Nightmares: Real Threats in a Dangerous World and How America Can Meet Them*. Boston: Little, Brown, 2000.

Lake, David A., and Donald Rothchild, eds. *The International Spread of Ethnic Conflict: Fear, Diffusion, and Escalation*. Princeton, N.J.: Princeton University Press, 1998.

Lott, Anthony D. *Creating Security: Realism, Constructivism, and U.S. Security Policy*. Burlington, Vt.: Ashgate, 2004.

Mandel, Robert. "What Are We Protecting?" *Armed Forces and Society* 22, no. 3 (Spring 1996): 335–55.

———. *Deadly Transfers and the Global Playground: Transnational Security Threats in a Disorderly World*. Westport, Conn.: Greenwood, 1999.

———. *Security, Strategy and the Quest for Bloodless War*. Boulder, Colo.: Lynne Rienner, 2004.

Mandelbaum, Michael. *The Fate of Nations: The Search for National Security in the Nineteenth and Twentieth Centuries*. New York: Cambridge University Press, 1981.

———. *The Nuclear Revolution: International Politics before and after Hiroshima*. New York: Cambridge University Press, 1981.

Mathews, Jessica Tuchman. "Redefining Security." *Foreign Affairs* 68, no. 2 (Spring 1989): 162–77.

Moran, Theodore H. "International Economics and Security." *Foreign Affairs* 69, no. 5 (Winter 1990/91): 74–90.

———. *American Economic Policy and National Security*. New York: Council on Foreign Relations, 1993.

Morgan, Patrick M. *Deterrence Now*. Cambridge: Cambridge University Press, 2003.

Mueller, John. *Retreat from Doomsday: The Obsolescence of Major War*. New York: Basic Books, 1989.

Newhouse, John. *War and Peace in the Nuclear Age*. New York: Alfred A. Knopf, 1989.

Nye, Joseph S., Jr. "Arms Control after the Cold War." *Foreign Affairs* 68, no. 5 (Winter 1989/90): 42–64.

Nye, Joseph S., Jr., and Sean M. Lynn-Jones. "International Security Studies: A Report of a Conference on the State of the Field." *International Security* 12, no. 4 (Spring 1988): 5–27.

Nye, Joseph S., Jr., and William Owens. "America's Information Edge." *Foreign Affairs* 75, no. 2 (March/April 1996): 20–36.

Paris, Roland. "Human Security: Paradigm Shift or Hot Air?" *International Security* 26, no. 2 (Fall 2001): 87–102.

Paul, T. V., Richard J. Harknett, and James J. Wirtz, eds. *The Absolute Weapon Revisited: Nuclear Arms and the Emerging International Order*. Ann Arbor: University of Michigan Press, 1998.

Ralph, Jason G. *Beyond the Security Dilemma: Ending America's Cold War*. Burlington, Vt.: Ashgate, 2001.

Rothschild, Emma. "What Is Security?" *Daedalus* 124, no. 3 (Summer): 53–98.

Schelling, Thomas C. *The Strategy of Conflict*. New York: Oxford University Press, 1960.

———. "The Role of Deterrence in Total Disarmament." *Foreign Affairs* 40 (April 1962): 392–406.

———. *Arms and Influence*. New Haven, Conn.: Yale University Press, 1966.

Sheehan, Michael. *International Security: An Analytical Survey*. Boulder, Colo.: Lynne Rienner, 2004.

Sheehan, Michael, ed. *National and International Security*. Burlington, Vt.: Ashgate, 2000.

Sigal, Leon V. *Hang Separately: Cooperative Security between the United States and Russia, 1985–1994*. New York: Century Foundation, 2000.

Singer, J. David. *Deterrence, Arms Control and Disarmament: Toward a Synthesis in National Security Policy*. Columbus: Ohio State University Press, 1962.

Singer, P. W. *Corporate Warriors: The Rise of the Privatized Military Industry*. Ithaca, N.Y.: Cornell University Press, 2003.

Smoke, Richard. *Paths to Peace: Exploring the Feasibility of Sustainable Peace*. Boulder, Colo.: Westview, 1987.

———. *National Security and the Nuclear Dilemma: An Introduction to the American Experience in the Cold War*. 3rd ed. New York: McGraw-Hill, 1993.

Steinbruner, John D. *Principles of Global Security*. Washington, D.C.: Brookings Institution, 2000.

Stern, Jessica. *The Ultimate Terrorists*. Cambridge, Mass.: Harvard University Press, 1999.

Suhrke, Astri. "Human Security and the Interest of States." *Security Dialogue* 30, no. 3 (September 1999): 265–76.

Terriff, Terry, Stuart Croft, Lucy James, and Patrick M. Morgan. *Security Studies Today*. Cambridge: Polity, 1999.

Toffler, Alvin, and Heidi Toffler. *War and Anti-War: Survival at the Dawn of the 21st Century*. Boston: Little, Brown, 1993.

Ullman, Richard. "Redefining Security." *International Security* 8, no. 1 (Summer 1983): 129–53.

United States. National Intelligence Council. *The 2015 Project Report*. Washington, D.C.: Government Printing Office, 2000.

———. The White House. *National Security Strategy of the United States 2002*. Available at www.whitehouse.gov.

———. *Mapping the Global Future*. Report on the 2020 Project. Washington, D.C.: Government Printing Office, 2004.

———. The 9/11 Commission. *Final Report of the National Commission on Terrorist Attacks upon the United States*. New York: W. W. Norton, 2004.

Waever, Ole, Barry Buzan, Morton Kelstrup, and Pierre Lamaitre. *Identity, Migration and the New Security Agenda in Europe*. London: Pinter, 1993.

Walt, Stephen M. "The Renaissance of Security Studies." *International Studies Quarterly* 35, no. 2 (June 1991): 211–40.

Wriston, Walter B. *The Twilight of Sovereignty: How the Information Revolution Is Transforming Our World*. New York: Charles Scribner's Sons, 1992.

———. "Bits, Bytes, and Diplomacy." *Foreign Affairs* 76, no. 5 (September/October 1997): 172–82.

Index

About the Authors

Dan Caldwell, Distinguished Professor of Political Science at Pepperdine University, is the author of three previous books and editor of four others. He has published widely in the areas of arms control and U.S. foreign policy.

Robert E. Williams Jr. is associate professor of political science at Pepperdine. His research focuses on human rights, international security, and the intersection of the two.